THE ROBBER WITH A WITCH'S HEAD

THE ROBBER WITH A WITCH'S HEAD

MORE STORIES FROM THE GREAT TREASURY OF SICILIAN FOLK AND FAIRY TALES COLLECTED BY LAURA GONZENBACH

TRANSLATED AND EDITED

BY JACK ZIPES

ILLUSTRATIONS BY JOELLYN ROCK

ROUTLEDGE
NEW YORK AND LONDON

Published in 2004 by
Routledge
270 Madison Avenue
New York, NY 10016
www.routledge-ny.com

Published in Great Britain by
Routledge
2 Park Square
Milton Park, Abingdon,
Oxon OX14 4RN
www.routledge.co.uk

Routledge is an imprint of the Taylor & Francis Group.

10 9 8 7 6 5 4 3 2 1

Library of Congress Cataloging-in-Publication Data

Sicilianische märchen. English. Selections.
  The robber with a witch's head : more stories from the great treasury of Sicilian folk and fairy tales / collected by Laura Gonzenbach ; translated and edited by Jack Zipes ; illustrations by Joellyn Rock.
      p. cm.
  Includes bibliographical references.
  ISBN 0-415-97069-5 (alk. paper)
  1. Folklore--Italy--Sicily. 2. Folklore--Italy--Sicily--Classification. I. Gonzenbach, Laura, 1842-1878. II. Zipes, Jack David. III. Title.
  GR177.S5G63 2004
  398.2'09458--dc22   2004013106

To Luisa Rubini
With Gratitude and Admiration

Contents

Contents

Contents

LAURA GONZENBACH'S
BURIED TREASURE*
JACK ZIPES

It may be misleading to call Laura Gonzenbach's collection of Sicilian fairy tales a buried treasure. After all, her book, *Sicilianische Märchen* (1870), received favorable reviews from Italian and German scholars when it appeared in Germany. In addition, her stories played a prominent role in the American folklorist Thomas F. Crane's book *Italian Popular Tales* (1885). However, ever since then her work has been more or less forgotten if not indeed buried. Indeed, why pay attention to a book of Sicilian fairy tales published not in Sicilian or Italian, but in German by a Swiss woman born in Messina with no academic or literary standing? In the twentieth century, Gonzenbach was dismissed by most of the leading Sicilian and Italian folklorists, partly because she had stolen their fire and published "their" precious native tales in a foreign language before they did in their own. Only in 1964 did her granddaughter, Renata La Racine, try to recall the significance of her grandmother's undertaking by publishing the first Italian translation of a selection of the Sicilian tales with her publication of *Tradizione popolare nelle fiabe siciliane di Laura von Gonzenbach*, but to no avail. Not long after, in 1979, the German folklorist Rudolf Schenda endeavored repeatedly to point out the great value of her collection in two important

---

* This introduction was first printed in *Beautiful Angiola: The Great Treasury of Sicilian Folk and Fairy Tales* (2004), which contains fifty tales from Gonzenbach's collection. It has been slightly revised for this edition to include references to the tales in both *Beautiful Angiola* and *The Robber with a Witch's Head*.

essays.* Some ten years later, in 1989, a truncated version of *Sicilianische Märchen* without introduction or notes was published by Greno in Nördlingen. Though it, too, sought to restore the fame of the collection, it was largely ignored. Finally, in 1999, the gifted Italian folklorist Luisa Rubini published the first complete Italian translation, *Fiabe siciliane*, with an insightful introduction and comprehensive notes. Yet even this superb book has drawn little notice by the general public in Europe. What will it take, I have asked myself, to honor the Gonzenbach collection of tales as perhaps the most important collection of fairy tales, legends, and anecdotes in the nineteenth century, more important have than the Brothers Grimm? Why is it really so pertinent today for understanding folklore and popular culture?

It may seem an exaggeration to assert that Gonzenbach's book is much more interesting and important than the *Children's and Household Tales* (1812–1815) of the Brothers Grimm or to privilege the Gonzenbach work over other fine and useful nineteenth-century European collections, but I am not exaggerating. Gonzenbach's collection is uniquely authentic and fascinating: though published in high German, the tales were literally written down from the mouths of Sicilian peasants and lower-middle class women. They represent more genuinely and more candidly the female if not feminist perspective on life, reveal social conditions from the point of view of an oppressed lower class, and do so with gusto, bitterness, and even hope. Such a partisan viewpoint is not evident in most collections of the nineteenth century with the exception of the dialect tales collected by the great Sicilian folklorist, Giuseppe Pitrè. In this regard, Gonzenbach's narratives are in stark contrast to the highly stylized and censored tales of the Brothers Grimm that were constantly changed and edited by Wilhelm. Unlike him, Laura Gonzenbach did not intermediate as censor, philologist, and German nationalist. She may have edited the tales somewhat to bring out her own progressive views about women. We do not know this for sure. Certainly she did *not* purge the tales of their sexual inferences, brutality, violence, and frankness the way other Sicilian and mainstream European collectors did. She was not as prudish as many of the male folklorists in the nineteenth century. Unfortunately, we know little about Laura Gonzenbach's editorial work and personal life because

---

* See Rudolf Schenda, "Laura Gonzenbach und die Sicilianischen Märchen: Bemerkungen zu den deutsch italienischen Volksliteratur-Beziehungen im Risorgimento," *Fabula* 20 (1979): 205–216, and Rudolf and Susanna Schenda, "La donna e il lavoro nelle fiabe siciliane raccolte da Laura Gonzenbach e Giuseppe Pitrè," in Rudolf Schenda, *Folklore e letteratura popolare: Italia—Germania—Francia*, trans. Maria Chiara Figliozzi e Ingeborg Walter (Rome: Istituto della Enciclopedia Italiana, 1986), pp. 279–287.

most of the family papers were destroyed in the Messina earthquake of 1908. Yet what we do know is definitely worth recalling before I deal in greater detail with the significance of her collection.

Laura Gonzenbach was born in Messina, a city of approximately 90,000 inhabitants, on the island of Sicily on December 26, 1842,* the day after Christmas. Her father, Peter Viktor Gonzenbach (1808–1885), was a commercial agent from St. Gallen, Switzerland, and her mother, Julie Aders (1806–1847), was originally from a respectable middle-class family in Elberfeld, Germany. Gonzenbach moved to Messina in his adolescence about 1823 and quickly made a successful career for himself working for Swiss and German textile firms. After he met his wife in the late 1820s, they married on June 24, 1830, in Malta and had seven daughters and one son: Magdalena (1831), Ludwig David (1833), Emilie (1834), Anna (1836), Gertha Elisabeth (1839), Clara Victoria (1840), Laura (1842), and Elisa (1846). Three of the girls died at a very young age, and the son passed away at twenty-one.

An ambitious and gifted individual, Peter Viktor Gonzenbach, known as Don Vittorio, began developing his own mercantile business during the 1830s and also served as the Swiss consul in Messina, which was a thriving port city with a small elite class of German, Swiss, and French merchants. Laura profited, as did her sisters, from the family's privileged position in this society and received an excellent education at home and in a small private school attached to the German-Swiss community in Messina. The person most responsible for Laura's education was her sister Magdalena because their mother had died in 1847, when Laura was only five. Magdalena was an extraordinary young woman. Cosmopolitan, trained in all the arts, classical literature, and the sciences, she took charge of the household and the family salon after her mother's death, and her father, a liberal democrat, gave her free rein. A woman ahead of her times, she supported suffragette causes and later had close connections to women's journals in Italy. In 1870 she translated into German the important feminist Fanny Lewald's book, *Für und Wider die Frauen* (*For and Against Women*) and later founded a school for girls in Messina, the first of its kind.

---

* For the most comprehensive study of Laura Gonzenbach and her work, see the excellent book by Luisa Rubini, *Fiabe e mercanti in Sicilia: La raccolta di Laura Gonzenbach. La comunità tedesca a Messina nell'Ottocento* (Florence: Leo S. Olschki, 1998). See also Rudolf Schenda, "Laura Gonzenbach e la sua raccolta di fiabe siciliane. Considerazioni sugli scambi italo-tedeschi in tema di letteratura popolare all'epoca del Risorgimento," in *Folklore e letteratura popolare: Italia—Germania—Francia* (Rome: Istituto della Enciclopedia Italiana, 1986), 265–278.

Her influence on her younger sister Laura, with whom she was very close, cannot be underestimated. By the time she was a teenager, Laura could speak four languages (German, French, Italian, and Sicilian) fluently, play musical instruments, and was well versed in literature and the arts. Because she could not attend a university (it was not customary to provide a higher education for young women at that time) she participated in the cultural activities at her father's house and in other salons in Messina and was esteemed as an exceptional storyteller. At the age of twenty-seven, she married the Italian colonel François Laurent La Racine (1818–1906), originally from Savoy, and had five children with him. Soon after her marriage she moved with her husband to Naples. Nothing is known about her life with La Racine or the conditions under which she died on July 16, 1878, in Messina. There is, however, a tombstone in Messina marking her young death at age thirty-six.

The Gonzenbachs were Protestants, and there were two small German Protestant communities in Messina and Palermo. When the position of minister became vacant in Messina in 1860, Peter Viktor Gonzenbach, head of the community, recruited Dr. Otto Hartwig (1830–1903), a theologian and historian, who had recently completed his studies in Marburg, to fill the position. Hartwig was obligated to hold services on Sundays for the German and Swiss community and to attend to their religious needs for a period of five years. His duties also included participating in soirées at different homes, joining a bowling club, attending concerts, and, in general, taking part in the cultural life of the community. His primary contacts were with the European merchants, doctors, and teachers, very little with the Sicilians, but he did undertake research for a book about Sicilian history and took various trips on the island. Among his acquaintances was Laura Gonzenbach, whom he regarded as a formidable teller of fairy tales. After he fulfilled his contract and left Sicily, he called upon her to help him collect tales for one of his books, for he had decided to include some in an appendix to demonstrate the special character of Sicilian culture. As he explained to Laura in a letter, he wanted just a few tales for the second volume of his history of Sicily, *Aus Sizilien: Kultur- und Geschichtsbilder* (1867–1869).

Unlike Hartwig, who never mastered the Sicilian dialect, Gonzenbach had grown up on the island with a thorough knowledge of Sicilian, and she had met numerous Sicilian peasant women in Messina and Catania and in the small villages near Mt. Etna, where she spent summer vacations. Because these women were generally reticent about talking to outsiders, especially men, Gonzenbach had a unique opportunity to form acquaintances with them and win their trust. Most of the tales she collected for Hartwig were told to her by peasant women with the names of Lucia, Cicca Crialesi, Nunzia Giuffridi, and Bastiana, but she also wrote down stories told to her by lower middle-class informants such as Antonia Centorrino and probably young single women such as Elisabetta and Concetta Martinotti, Francesca Rusullo, Peppina Guglielmo, and Caterina Certo. In addition there was at least one male storyteller, a peasant named Alessandro Grasso, who shared tales he had learned from his mother. Assisted by her older sister, Magdalena, Gonzenbach endeavored to write the tales down just as she had heard them. In a letter to Hartwig, she stated:

> Now I'd like to tell you that I've done my best to write down the tales exactly as they were told to me. However, I've not been able to recapture the genuine charm of these tales that lies in the manner and way the tales are told by these Sicilian women. Most of them tell the tales in a lively fashion by acting out the entire plot with their hands making very expressive gestures. While talking, they even stand up and walk around the room when it's appropriate. They never use "he says" because they change the people's voices always through intonation.*

Familiar with the folk tradition of storytelling, Gonzenbach also knew German literary tales, probably the tales of the Brothers Grimm, perhaps even French tales. This background enabled her—even though she never lived in Germany or Switzerland for any length of time—to find a suitable literary voice for her translation of the dialect tales. In practice, Gonzenbach translated these tales immediately into German and had to find an adequate style of narration. One cannot say that her tales are "authentic" folk tales, especially because she made some stylistic changes as did Hartwig and Reinhold Köhler (1830–1892), who eventually provided the notes to her edition.† Nevertheless, they are probably as close as one can come to the Sicilian oral tradition, with the exception of the dialect collections of Sicilian tales and legends published by Giuseppe Pitrè.‡ Their "naiveté," their use of direct

---

* Laura Gonzenbach, *Sicilianische Märchen*, ed. Otto Hartwig. Notes by Reinhold Köhler, 2 vols. (Leipzig: W. Engelmann, 1870), p. ix.

† See Köhler's notes in the original edition, Laura Gonzenbach, *Sicilianische Märchen. Aus dem Volksmund gesammelt* (1870).

‡ See Giuseppe Pitrè, *Otto Fiabe e Novelle popolari siciliane* (Bologna: Tipografia Fava e Garagnani, 1873); *Fiabe, novelle e racconti popolari siciliani*, 4 vols. (Palermo: Pedone Lauriel, 1875), Vols. 4–7 of *Biblioteca delle tradizioni popolari siciliane*; *Fiabe e Leggende popolari siciliane* (Palermo: Pedone Lauriel, 1888).

expressions, proverbs, quick transitions, sudden breaks, and lack of long explications indicate clearly that the tales are more stamped by oral modes of narration than literary. Moreover, Gonzenbach remained faithful to the ideological perspective of women from the lower class whose struggle against oppression is a major theme in the tales.

Through Hartwig, Gonzenbach was well aware, even though she was twenty-eight with no formal academic training, that there was a strong scholarly interest in collections of Italian folk tales, songs, and stories in Germany. Therefore, after he wrote her in 1868 and she agreed to help him show German readers how fascinating Sicilian folklore was, she eagerly sought to provide him with as many tales as she could. At first she sent him about ten, and then, to his surprise, another eighty-two tales in 1868. To his credit, Hartwig realized how extraordinary they were and decided to publish them separately as a book, not as an appendix, but the collaboration on this project could not be completed in 1868. Although a brilliant scholar, Hartwig was primarily a historian, and, indeed, wrote an important essay on the history of the Sicilian language and its relationship to the growth of nationalism to introduce Gonzenbach's collection. Yet he knew little about folklore and therefore recruited Reinhold Köhler, at the time Germany's foremost scholar on international folklore, to write the significant notes for each one of the tales. This was a great boon for the edition, which was finally published by Wilhelm Engelmann in Leipzig at Christmas in 1869, but with the publication date of 1870.

What distinguishes Gonzenbach's collection from most others of the nineteenth century is the variety of the tales, their proximity to the oriental and occidental storytelling traditions, the dominance of female informants, and the abundant references to Sicilian peasant customs and beliefs. There are explicit details of ferocious familial conflicts, arbitrary violence, sadistic punishment, and immoral love—in short, an acknowledgment of aspects of life generally censored in most nineteenth-century collections. Moreover, as I have emphasized, the tales have a distinct feminine if not "feminist" lower-class perspective. All the more reason they are so significant: they explicitly and implicitly reveal the desires and complaints of women whose voices are difficult to hear in the nineteenth-century collections assembled by male scholars. But it is not only this female perspective that makes them so interesting—and I shall address this aspect shortly—it is the manner in which the tales are framed without happy endings, for the Sicilian tales make a clear distinction about who can be happy and who will not be happy until social conditions are changed. It is the candor of these tales that is so striking, and I want to say a few words about this social candor before turning to a discussion of the unusual representation of women and lower-class figures in Gonzenbach's collection. It is truly astonishing that Laura Gonzenbach could accomplish what she did in her twenties, that is, to capture the tone and atmosphere of Sicilian oral tales in a foreign "high" language, namely *Hochdeutsch*, with a literary bent that retains a fresh if not sassy outlook on life.

In his book, *Customs and Habits of the Sicilian Peasants*, Salvatore Salomone-Marino, a contemporary of Laura Gonzenbach who collaborated with Giuseppe Pitrè to preserve the folklore of Sicily at the end of the nineteenth century, depicts many instances in the daily lives of the peasants when they entertained themselves with songs, poems, and all sorts of stories. At one point he remarks:

> On winter evenings the streets are dark, cold, silent: the whole life of the rustic family is concentrated around the hearth, where great firebrands burst out. These are not the meetings in the company of the neighborhood; now every family stays by itself. The womenfolk spin or reel; grandma or the mother keeps the children's mouths hanging open with her skill, mimicry, and incredible emotion:
> "... they relate of ancient times
> Tales of sorcerers and Queens."
> The boys who request these stories and want to learn are the pretext; the narrator is quite willing and addresses her words even to the adults, who are known always to be pleased to listen at length for the thousandth time as she tells of the fantastic and strange supernatural beings, those men of valor and peerless bravery—to ineffable delight and the fantasies they excite.*

Although Salomone-Marino at times romanticizes the life of the peasants, he is for the most part an accurate observer of their customs and traditions. He reports that there were specific occasions like sowing and harvesting when men would also tell the stories. Within the family, however, the prominent storytellers were women, which is why women also figure predominantly as the narrators in the dialect collections of Pitrè and Salomone-Marino and in Gonzenbach's book. Most importantly, the tales preserved by these women reveal a great deal about the central historical role played by storytelling in Sicily to maintain customs and belief systems; they demonstrate fascinating interconnections with tales from other cultures; and they provide a candid perspective on the hard lives led by the Sicilian peasants.

---

* Salvatore Salomone-Marino, *Customs and Habits of the Sicilian Peasants*, ed. and trans. Rosalie N. Norris (Rutherford, N.J.: Fairleigh Dickinson Press, 1981): 6–7.

Given the long history of various conquests of the island and colonization by the Greeks, Italians, Arabs, Normans, Spaniards, French, Austrians, and English throughout the past twenty centuries or more, the stories that entered the oral tradition of storytelling in Sicily evince an astonishing cross-fertilization and are clearly international in nature. At the same time, the tales were constantly altered to reflect the changing conditions on the island so that they became closely tied to Sicilian customs and practices. Tales told in Sicilian evolved during the late Middle Ages. A Sicilian dialect did not really begin to flourish until the time of the Norman invasions of the eleventh and twelfth centuries when numerous Italians also emigrated to Sicily, and gradually different forms of a Sicilian dialect became the lingua franca of the country. There was never one standard form of dialect, just as customs varied from region to region on the island. The Sicilian peasants did, however, share other things in their daily lives up through the twentieth century— exploitation, deprivation, and suffering. The invasions and wars fought on Sicilian soil were constant, and often entire cities and villages were wiped out and destroyed, not just by foreign soldiers but by rival communities. There were famines and plagues that almost every generation of Sicilians experienced from the Middle Ages to the twentieth century. The forests and fertile land were gradually devastated and exploited by the nineteenth century; roads were not built; irrigation was limited; and the peasants were always obliged to work for landlords who took most of their produce. The homes of the peasants consisted generally of a large room with partitions, and some of the animals, vital for their survival, slept in this room as well. The peasants ate very little meat, and they generally divided the labor, with the men working cooperatively in the fields or woods, and the women weaving, spinning, taking care of the children, and performing most of the domestic chores.

Although we cannot claim to know fully what the tales they told meant to the Sicilian peasants, they clearly used them to comment on their lives and on how they wished to change them. What is striking is the stark realistic perspective of the storytellers in the Gonzenbach collection. Almost all the tales begin with a lack or grave catastrophe: a king and queen cannot have children, and when they do, they give birth to a snake, beast, or a child who is cursed; children are abandoned or kidnapped by clouds, ogres, and sorcerers who abuse them; young girls and boys are beaten or threatened by a teacher or another authority figure; a family is so poor that the children decide to leave home or are sent away to find their fortune; women encounter men who often prey on them or want to humiliate them; jealous sisters and brothers plot to bring about the downfall of their more fortunate sibling; daughters or stepdaughters face mothers and stepmothers who want to kill them; young men and women must fulfill impossible tasks, otherwise they will be eaten.

Almost all the tales end with similar formulaic refrains such as:

- And then they all lived happily and content, but we were left without a cent.
- She remained happy and content, but we still can't pay the rent.
- And they remained rich and consoled, and we just sit here and are getting old.
- They continued to live happy and content, but we were left empty-handed.
- The king and Maruzza lived for a long time still, rich and consoled, and we have nothing as we get old.
- Indeed, they all celebrated a splendid wedding and remained happy and content, but we just sit here and gaze at each other, and our day is spent.

Perhaps the latent reality of the peasants' oppression and their hatred for their situation explain the often brutal punishment of the evildoers at the end of the tales: a nasty and ugly daughter has her head chopped off and pieces of her body are served as salted tuna fish to her wicked mother; another sinister mother is boiled in oil; a traitor has his head chopped off; a stupid king burns himself to death; an evil queen is cooked in oil and thrown to the dogs to be devoured; a lascivious priest is burned at the stake and has his ashes strewn to the wind.

Yet such fantasies of violent retribution that might usher in a more just world never quite make it to the surface of the tales. The tellers remain dispassionate and choose a style that emphasizes distance: whatever has happened—good or bad—did not happen to them. At most they were witnesses. More often than not their stories belong to another time. As storytellers their main task is to make the extraordinary seem ordinary, to integrate the miraculous into their listeners' lives and so to insist on the possibility of sudden radical change in spite of seemingly insuperable odds. They make clear, however, that if someone happened to become rich or fortunate, the storyteller and her family did not share in the good fortune. They are always left behind, poor, without a cent, getting older.

Are these what we call fairy tales?

Well, not all the stories in the Gonzenbach collection are fairy tales. There are legends, fables, and folk anecdotes. The majority are indeed fairy tales, and despite the realistic concise telling of tales that are often lurid and terrifying, they are also filled with hope and intended to make listeners yearn for better days. There are also lessons to be learned, and many are wish-fulfillments that exhibit a profound belief in magic and the miraculous. Most of the Sicilian peasants had to live by their wits and do severe manual labor, and if they fell upon hard times, they called upon miraculous intervention. It is therefore interesting to see how the narrators did not disguise the injustices they suffered and the viciousness of class conflict in their tales because miracles rarely did occur. The peasants had to take fate into their own hands.

Peasants are indeed the protagonists in tales such as "Ferrazzanu," "Sciauranciovi," "The Shepherd Who Made the Princess Laugh," and "Peasant Truthful," to name but a few. The lower-class figures are clearly smarter than their lords and masters, and they inevitably find ways to embarrass them, avoid punishment, and even kill them. For instance, Sciauranciovi has no qualms about deceiving a nobleman three different times and finally leading him to his death. He deals with the upper class just as the aristocrats dealt with him and his friends. For instance, the intriguing queen in "Prince Scursini" and "The Pig Queen" have no scruples in lying to the parents of artisans and feeding their daughters to their ruthless bestial sons, who murder them. No wonder the peasants respond in kind and perhaps with more justification by taking brutal revenge.

Lies and deceit abound in all the tales, and if there is one major theme that unites them, it concerns the *Word*—giving one's word, not a written word. One's word is one's life. Words can literally determine one's fortune and fate. For instance, there are several tales in which a prince leaves a woman, his true bride, after she has liberated him, to go to his parents' castle and to fetch garments for her that will make her look more respectable and beautiful for the people at the court. She warns him that if he is kissed by his mother or anyone at the castle, he will forget about her. The prince gives her his word that he will remain true to her and tells her not to worry. However, he is always unavoidably kissed and always forgets his true bride until she finds a way to break the spell cast on him through her own words, which recall his pledge. Curses can only be broken by words that count in one's life.

Certainly, this is one of the reasons why the narrators kept these tales alive, for the words have a relevance not only within the plot and narrative strategy of the tale, but they bring out the pertinence of the stories in such a way that the hearers will remember to tell what has a meaning for their lives. The words of the tale touch them emotionally and are absorbed by them, for they are weapons of the weak. They bear messages for survival. They bare some naked truths and demand that we pay attention to why we use words the way we do, and how we can use words to resolve discomforting social conditions. Words are given in trust. Words form the curses, spells, and vows that determine the action of all the protagonists.

One prime example is the legendary scoundrel, Giufà, a folk figure, whose antics were first recorded in Arabic tales during the late Middle Ages but were readily adapted and spread in Sicily and southern Italy. Indeed, Giufà is related to many other bumpkins and rascals in the European tradition in tales about Hans (German), Pietro (Italian), Pierre (French), and Jack (British and American). Giufà takes words literally, and consequently he has a limited sense of the world, for he cannot grasp how words are used metaphorically and idiomatically to articulate commands, wishes, instructions, and so forth, which don't mean what they bespeak or express. He rarely catches the inferences and implications of words; he is apt to make foolish mistakes and kill people or animals without thinking that he has committed a mistake. He even kills his baby sister and a shepherd without much remorse. Some of his own words are fortunate because he coincidentally discovers things with malapropisms that most people do not notice. His mother, a wise peasant woman, is the only one who can more or less control and save him because she understands the duplicity and ambiguity of words, and that her son lives by the literal word. Giufà is really not a dunce. He is someone who believes in the literal meaning of words and does not know how to communicate with a world that uses words and clothes to veil the meanings of its actions. This is why he ridicules his relatives when they are not hospitable because he does not wear the proper garments. This is why he exposes a greedy bishop and tricks some robbers.

Giufà's actions are related to those of the peasant son in "Clever Peppe," who virtually tortures a robber captain for breaking his word to him. Once again it is the country bumpkin who insists on the virtue of words, and he takes his revenge because he and his mother would have become poverty-stricken and hungry if he had not used his brains to regain the food that he had been sent to procure. But Peppe goes to an extreme to punish the robber captain. The violation of words leads to violence because the peasant s do not see a just or peaceful way to remedy their situation. For the most part, only the upper classes maintain trust in written contracts, pacts, and treaties, even though they are constantly broken.

The fairy tales in the Gonzenbach collection—and not only in her collection—keep words alive in narrative form that otherwise might have disappeared. The narrators want us to recall events and situations that should never be forgotten, for they mark what is still lacking in our lives—trust in words, social justice, and human compassion. Many of the tales have a religious aspect due to the influence of the Catholic religion in Sicily. However, the use of such figures as Saint Joseph, Jesus, and Mary has very little to do with religious orthodoxy. For instance, Saint Joseph is more like a wizard or sorcerer than a pious man, and he is consequently more fascinating because he is also more human. He is a favorite in many of the tales because he brings work and food to the poor and helps offset injustices. The faith that the characters demonstrate in God is always repaid because the Lord does not break his word. Miracles occur if one keeps the faith, and one's goose will be cooked if one presumes too much or questions the order of the world as is the case of "The Rooster Who Wanted to Become Pope" and "The Hermit." Humility is necessary for salvation, but not always. It is generally the theme of the legends and religious fairy tales. It is also generally reserved for women as in "The Humiliated Princess," but it is a contested topic, and throughout Gonzenbach's collection there are a number of stories that inform us about an insurrection in the making, a longed-for change in the relations between men and women, or about the need to discard humility and to defend oneself against abuse.

In fact, the metaphorical struggles in the tales do not only pit peasants against their aristocratic masters and so project class conflict, they also speak to gender conflicts and expose men as oppressive masters. Here again it is worth quoting some passages from Salomone-Marino's *Customs and Habits of the Sicilian Peasants*:

> Husband and wife do not caress openly; they outwardly treat each other with a certain gravity, the more pronounced in him, but not because their feelings are less strong. She keeps the best for him, the most useful, the finest things.
>
> But things do not always go so smoothly and sweetly. On some days the husband is in a bad humor, whether because household matters go badly, or various other reasons supercharge him with electricity, awaiting only a light for him to go off violently. Woe to the wife who, in such moments, does not do her work well, breaks a household utensil, dares to make a remark to her man, or is lacking in the least regard and obedience due him as a master! He suddenly loses the light of reason and his traditional calm, and the wife must submit in holy peace, often undeservedly, to the nastiest insults, bestial punches, kicks, beatings, or blows given with the first object the furious man grabs hold of. She bears bruises, swellings, sometimes wounds and fractures, but still she does not let out a cry; she puts up no resistance, doesn't weep at all for fear of worse, nor does she spread in public the woes and hell she endures in her family.
>
> And the husband is truly an absolute master. After such mistreatment and blows, he claims that the woman is humbled (which she is willingly)

to accord her peace; and he jeers at her into the bargain, trying to justify his bestial behavior; a dozen sound beatings (he always says) are as necessary as bread; if nothing else, it is handy way to stretch your skin, so you will eat more and get fat!*

If the situation of Sicilian peasant women was more or less the way Salomone-Marino describes it—and we have no reason to doubt him—it becomes more clear why the female narrators depict many young women in their tales who seek to break away from home and determine their own fates. This is not to say that the storytellers intentionally changed tales to project the possibility of liberation for women. However, when compared to many of the tales in the Grimms' collection and other nineteenth-century books of folk tales, there is clearly a preponderance of audacious, smart, independent, and resourceful female protagonists in the Gonzenbach collection.

Sorfarina serves as the model of the "emancipated woman" among the tales recorded by Laura Gonzenbach, one of the reasons that I placed her story first in the collection *Beautiful Angiola*. She is an unusual figure in the European folk-tale tradition. An educated woman, beautiful and smart, she marries a belligerent and revengeful prince, who behaves like a stubborn brute. Why Sorfarina loves him and does not abandon him is an open question. Perhaps it is because she never finished educating him while they were in school together. Perhaps she sees something in him that others cannot see. She tolerates him while sitting in a well and seduces him as a prostitute in different cities. Then she uses her magic powers, her art, to form the type of life she desires. However, toward the end of the tale, she cannot trust the prince who tries to kill her, and when he thinks he has done the foul deed, he tries to commit suicide. Their reconciliation at the very end is bittersweet. Sorfarina is in control of the situation, but she must forever be on her guard, for here is a man who relentlessly wants to prove he is the absolute master of his household and will stop at nothing—even though his wife has borne him three children—to establish his manhood.

Sorfarina refuses to be humiliated, and there are numerous tales in *Beautiful Angiola* and *The Robber with a Witch's Head* such as "The Green Bird," "The Snake Who Bore Witness for a Maiden," "Betta Pilusa," "Beautiful Cardia," "The Daughter of the Sun," "The Clever Maiden,"

---

* Salvatore Salomone-Marino, *Customs and Habits of the Sicilian Peasants*, ed. & trans. Rosalie N. Norris (Rutherford, N.J.: Fairleigh Dickinson University Press, 1981), pp. 42–43.

"Maruzzedda" and others in which the female protagonist is audacious and uses her wits to gain what she wants. The threat of violation and exploitation remains constant, but the experience gained by the young woman in fending for herself is a kind of guarantee that she will not tolerate abuse in the future.

In contrast to what was allowed in Sicilian society, whether a woman came from the lower or upper class, many of the heroines in these tales travel or wander by themselves. As a rule, Sicilian women were actually prevented from leaving their homes unless they married. In the tales, however, many leave their homes for different reasons and are often glad to do so: some run away from jealous sisters or mothers and find work in a castle; some are orphans and must seek work as a secretary or maid; some are forced to work as nurses in dangerous situations. They all seek their own fortune that will generally be of their own making. Yet they are invariably threatened by predators who try to violate them. In "The Story of Oh My" and "The Robber with a Witch's Head," young women leave home only to be confronted by sadistic killers who murder females because they do not act like slaves. Such brutality may very well be a representation of how badly women were treated during this period in Sicily. Whatever the case may be, the tales are liberating alternatives to the actual conditions suffered by the women, perhaps even by the storytellers themselves.

Just how unique and different, that is, emancipatory the Gonzenbach tales are in contrast to the classical Grimm tales can be demonstrated easily by comparing some of the same tale types such as "Beautiful Angiola" with "Rapunzel," "Lignu di Scupa" with "Rumpelstiltskin," "Betta Pilusa" with "All Fur," or others. In the Grimms' final version of 1857, Rapunzel is essentially a passive victim, unable to break away from the witch, and, consequently, she is severely punished for wanting to escape her prison. In Gonzenbach's tale, Angiola defies the witch and escapes with the prince. She continually outwits her mother/witch, and though she is cursed, she uses an intermediary, the dog, to gain the happiness that she desires. The ending is particularly interesting because the witch shows her defiant daughter compassion. This ending may have something to do with a woman's more considerate perspective on a tale that traditionally makes women appear hapless and hopeless.

Of course, it would be a grave mistake to characterize the Gonzenbach collection as feminist or politically subversive. Like the best of the dialect collections, although they were not recorded in dialect, the tales do not mince words, and because they were not heavily edited or adapted to make them appropriate reading for children and bourgeois families, they are startling in the frank and brusque manner in which they portray internecine strife and class struggles. They may be startling for us, but they were accepted and appreciated by the listeners to the tales, which included children of all ages. Then, as now, children are exposed to all kinds of stories, whether we approve of the narratives or not; and then, more than now, these stories along with songs, dance, and music were their major form of entertainment and means of learning about their lives and ways to change them.

Because Laura Gonzenbach and the two men who assisted her, Hartwig and Köhler, did not alter the tales very much, that is, they did not sweeten them or tone down the violent conflicts and the depiction of feisty women, her collection never became the proper bedtime reading or school reading for German children who were weaned on tales by the Grimms, Ludwig Bechstein, and Hans Christian Andersen. Luisa Rubini refers to Gonzenbach's narratives as "Buchmärchen" or book fairy tales, similar to the designation that some scholars have applied to the Grimms' texts. This is generally a term that tries to define the difference between "authentic" oral tales (*Volksmärchen*) and literary fairy tales (*Kunstmärchen*), to distinguish the peculiarity of tales that stem from the oral tradition but are recorded in high German and stylized according to the artistic gifts of the collector. Certainly this is the correct term for the Grimms' tales, for the brothers made vast changes in tales they wrote down from their informants, combined different versions, censored them, and took many of their texts from literature. This is not exactly how Rubini uses this term when discussing the tales of Laura Gonzenbach. She is more concerned with distinguishing them from modern methods of collecting through the use of tape recorders and cameras that do not pay attention to general rules of punctuation and grammar. The modern recordings on paper have different marks to indicate changes, movements, and breaks, and all the pauses, mistakes, and repetitions of the storyteller are noted. In contrast, Gonzenbach's book tales were intended to make the reading flow more smoothly for the reader without adding other versions and constantly rewriting the original texts. At the same time, she did her best, as she frankly wrote, to recapture the authenticity of the tales as she heard them.

This is impossible, and she even admits it. And because we do not know exactly how she went about her collecting, we are left with many intriguing questions that can never be answered but are worthwhile posing. Did Gonzenbach sit there with pen in hand and immediately translate the dialect tales she heard into high German? Did she just listen and then return home and write them down from memory? How much did Magdalena help her, for we know that she spent the summer vacation with Gonzenbach while she was collecting the tales? How intimate was her relationship to the peasant women? To the slightly more affluent storytellers? Who told her which tale, for she did not write down the name of the informant for each tale? What went on in her mind as she heard these tales? Did she discuss them with her sister Magdalena? Which were her favorites? Did she make some slight changes to make the tales more emancipatory, or were most of the tales truly recorded as they were told? Did she delete details of a scatological or erotic nature? To what extent did Hartwig and Köhler edit the tales? Hartwig insists that he made very few changes. Is there really a great difference between the manner and content of tales told by women and those by men?

We can make some important comparisons with the dialect tales in the resplendent collections of Giuseppe Pitrè. We might also compare here one of Gonzenbach's stories with another in Sicilian dialect.

The dialect text of one story called "The Story of the Three Sisters," recorded by Salvatore Morganti, ends this way:

> "I remember everything," he responded, "and I fall to your feet and ask you to pardon me for all the suffering that I've caused you. I have changed, and I shall be your loyal and tender lover until death. Pardon me, my love."
>
> They made peace and went to sit down at the table to eat, but as he approached her to throw himself into the arms of his lover, the maiden quickly took out a dagger and stabbed him in his heart.
>
> "I'm dying," he said as he fell, "by the hands of a traitor."
>
> The maiden grabbed him by his hair and dragged him down to the foot of the stairs where she buried this lover. The three sisters became owners of this rich palace, but they were not happy because the price of blood is always bitter.

The Gonzenbach tale "The Courageous Maiden" in *Beautiful Angiola* ends somewhat differently:

> So the nobleman went upstairs. When he saw her two sisters, he asked who they were.
>
> "My chambermaids," she answered, and she kept the nobleman there through her polite conversation until it became evening.
>
> "Can I also have the honor of dining with you tonight?" she said, and the nobleman stayed. During the meal, however, she handed him the bottle with the sleeping potion. As soon as he drank a little of it, he sank into a deep sleep. Then she took a little knife and slit his throat so that he died for his sins without confession or absolution. Afterward the maiden called her sisters, and all three dragged him to a deep well and threw him into it. At midnight the door opened once again, and the dark figure

entered and said to the youngest sister, "You have saved me through your courage, and now all these treasures belong to you. Live well. Tonight I have come for the last time because now I have found peace."

Upon saying this, she disappeared and never returned. Meanwhile, the three sisters remained in the magnificent castle, and each one of them married a fine gentleman. Indeed, they remained happy and content, and we were left without a cent.

What are we to conclude when we compare the different styles and endings? The version by Morganti is more succinct in its style and appears to capture the vindictiveness of the dead woman, whose murder is avenged by a maiden who shows no mercy to the repentant murderer. The story by Gonzenbach is more elaborate and explanatory. There is a sense that the young women, who were very poor, will be happy. Morganti's text cannot envision happiness smeared by blood. His text presents the woman as first subjecting herself completely. She apparently embraced her subservient position to her lover. Gonzenbach's tale does without such a scene of abject submission. Moreover, she shows a kind of sisterhood with the ghostly woman, and her protagonist seems to emphasize the need and reward for women's communal action against oppressive masters. Instead her ending suggests peace and contentment—at least for the tale's protagonist and her sisters as immediate beneficiaries.

But both tales are bloody, and both are more similar in tone and style than different. Gonzenbach does not minimize the brutal crime suffered by the dead lady; she does not really soften the way the youngest sister kills the nobleman and has his body discarded. Both tales are about ruthless revenge and the reward reaped by three hard-working sisters. The versions by male and female storytellers do not contradict each other. In fact, it may be that the Gonzenbach tale was also told by a male. We cannot be sure, but we can say that while the tales are not exactly feminist, they are not book tales, and they are candid about the humiliation and oppression that women did not want to suffer. Morganti's tale resembles a great deal of the popular broadsides and colportage of the time and has a strong moral conclusion, as if to protect the reputation of Sicilian folklore. The Gonzenbach version envisions a happier end brought about by women who have solidarity with one another. This is, indeed, quite a difference.

As Laura Gonzenbach herself stated, it is difficult on the printed page to capture the flavor and the gesticulations that a storyteller imparts when she tells a tale. We cannot imagine the emphases, shifts of voice, movements of the body, the eye contact, articulated meanings, or the interruptions by the listeners. Nor can we envision the context. Was it the hearth or dinner table? Whose home? Who was there? Nevertheless, the tales that she collected are riveting because she gave them a voice that will continue to resonate today. Her tales, recorded on a tiny island that was the crossroad between oriental and occidental worlds for hundreds of years, recall how cruelty and viciousness have always marred our daily lives, and how words can hold us spellbound for magical moments and alleviate our suffering if we take them seriously and search for the fortunate alternatives they propose.

A Note on the Translation and Acknowledgments

We do not know how Laura Gonzenbach would have ordered the tales when she sent them to Otto Hartwig, but we do know that Reinhold Köhler determined the organization and the placement of the narratives according to tale types. Such categorization is certainly helpful to the scholar, but most other readers will probably find the artificial repetition of plots and motifs in the two-volume German publication of *Sicilianische Märchen* boring. The tales were not told to Laura Gonzenbach to bore her or other listeners. Therefore, I have taken the liberty of mixing the tales according to my taste. I chose the first three tales in *Beautiful Angiola* because I believe that they emphasize the central role women play in many of the narratives and enable readers to grasp how strongly the female narrators were invested in their tales. I have also brought to the front, so to speak, many of the tales that one finds in the classical collections of Charles Perrault, Mme d'Aulnoy, the Brothers Grimm, and Ludwig Bechstein, so that readers familiar with the literary fairy-tale tradition, may readily compare the so-called classics with the "deviant," if not devious, Sicilian analogues. Otherwise, my ordering is arbitrary. That is, I mixed most of the tales without a conceptual purpose except to present more of a kaleidoscope of stories than an orderly progression.

The translation itself did not present major problems because Gonzenbach's style is not complicated, and her command of German was excellent as well as her knowledge of standard phrases, motifs, and topoi. Nevertheless, her translation of Sicilian dialect tales into high

German raises some issues, which is why Sicilian folklorists like Giuseppe Pitrè, Salvatore Salmone-Marino, and Giuseppe Cocchiara, to name but a few, were reluctant to acknowledge Gonzenbach's achievement. Certainly, in their eyes, her translation was a kind of betrayal if not an illegitimate expropriation of what belonged to the Sicilian people.

But there is always a struggle for appropriation, adaptation, and authenticity whenever tales are translated, and printed. This is what makes them so interesting, especially if we admit to their conflicting nature.

In his brilliant foreword to Zora Neale Hurston's *Every Tongue Got to Confess: Negro Folk-tales from the Gulf States,* John Edgar Wideman remarked: "How speech is represented in writing raises more than questions of aesthetics. An ongoing struggle for authority and domination is present in any speech situation interfacing former slaves with former masters, minority with major culture, spoken with written. Such interfaces bristle with extralinguistic tensions that condition and usually diminish mutual intelligibility" (p. xv). As much as a translation may seek to recuperate words, language, customs, and proverbs of a particular dialect used by an oppressed people to form bonds and understanding, it also destroys, omits, and obfuscates the historical conditions and context in which the oral tales were told and appreciated. Authentic or definitive renderings of oral folk tales in written languages are virtually impossible, even if the collector takes down the story in the vernacular with signs denoting tone and gesticulation. The contextual moment cannot be recaptured. The relevance cannot be completely discerned. Sometimes, one must ask oneself, why collect? Why translate and transliterate? Why trespass? Dialects and so-called minor languages are dying, and they are doing so rapidly. The early folklorists—many of them amateurs or philologists—began recognizing this during the latter part of the nineteenth century and so helped bring into being folklore as a profession. As much as they could, they wanted to preserve languages, customs, belief systems, and artifacts in the original to document the everyday life of communities. The people or common folk could speak for themselves, but they had not been educated to write and organize things for themselves. Therefore, educated scholars, no matter how colonialist or condescending their attitude toward the common folk, committed themselves to inscribing into history those narratives that might have otherwise died or undergone such momentous changes that they would be rendered unrecognizable.

To collect, transcribe, and translate folklore is to recognize the values of common people and to esteem their position in the world even if one does not comprehend fully what the words of these people represent in the web of relations of power and authority. When Laura Gonzenbach went to the peasant women in the region of Catania and Messina, she did so as an authority figure of the upper class who had, at best, a dim understanding of what it meant to lead the life of a peasant or common laborer. Nevertheless, she inspired trust among her informants, who provided her with more tales than she had ever imagined she would receive, and they would have told her even more if she had so desired. Perhaps they trusted her because she showed them respect, gave them money, and demonstrated that she cared for them despite all differences of rank and experience. We don't know. Perhaps she even shared some of their attitudes and beliefs and felt a bond with them as women. Perhaps she had a deep affection for sounds of the first tongue she encountered and used before she learned German, for most of the European children in privileged homes learned Sicilian first from nurses, nannies, and servants before they were introduced to the "cultivated" language of their parents. We have no concrete information on any of that, but we may wonder what Laura Gonzenbach felt and thought as she heard these marvelous tales—tales she may have even heard when she was very young—and then wrote them down in German.

There is not one trace of dialect in Gonzenbach's German translation. The language she uses is literary German. As she recorded the tales on paper and sought the appropriate German words and expressions, she more than likely thought about what an educated German might expect as he or she read folk tales. Her primary and intended reader was such a man, Otto Hartwig, the German theologian turned historian. She had to find the forms and words that he would approve, and she probably also censored herself, unless the peasant women already censored themselves by omitting curse words, sexual inferences, and other speech that had no place in the literature of this era's polite classes. Traces of Gonzenbach's desire to capture the language of her informants, however, survive in her many footnotes and explanations of Sicilian terms. Because I am familiar with many of the extant Sicilian dialect versions of the tales Gonzenbach collected, I know how different they are from her high German renderings. At the same time, I have been surprised at how closely Gonzenbach held to the plots and the terse and abrupt manner in which the tales were obviously told. The dialect tales give a good indication of the tone and color of the tales, and, fortunately, her German equivalents do not embellish or improve the tales with smooth transitions and clearer motivation. Gonzenbach respected the "authorial" and ideological perspective of the narrators, and I have tried to follow her example, for the value of the translated narratives lies in the manner in which they retain the viewpoint of the lower-class perspective and style. There is no clear uniform ideology in the tales, but Gonzenbach's translation keeps alive the anger, disappointment, hope, and hardiness of the storytellers, who view life from the bottom and do not mask their sentiments.

It is foolish to generalize about translation, for each text brings its own demands and difficulties. For an educated woman such as Gonzenbach, translating tales told by lower-class informants, mainly women, into an upper-class language was not only a very particular process of retention, but it also meant to confront how discontented people thought and spoke and contended, or wished to contend, with oppression. Despite the different languages, Sicilian and high German, Gonzenbach managed to convey the spirit of insurrection and provocation with which the tellers imbued their tales. I sincerely hope I have managed to retain this spirit from Gonzenbach's words in this English translation.

My work on this project would not have been possible if I had not been guided and assisted by the very gracious Luisa Rubini, who has paved the way for scholars seriously interested in Gonzenbach and Sicilian folklore. As usual, Bill Germano, a superb editor and friend, has been closely involved in this project. I have also benefited from the advice and suggestions of Nancy Canepa, Carol Dines, Carmelo Lettere, Patrizia McBride and Joseph Russo. Last but not least, I want to thank Robert Sims for overseeing the production of this book.

Jack Zipes
Rome, June 7, 2003

1

THE CLEVER MAIDEN

Once upon a time there were two brothers. One had seven sons, and the other had seven daughters. Whenever the father with the seven sons met his brother, he would greet him by saying, "Oh brother, you with your seven flower pots, and me with my seven swords! How's it going?"*

These words aggravated the brother enormously, and when he came home, he was always in a bad mood and irritable. His youngest daughter, however, was marvelously beautiful and also very clever. One day, when she saw that her father was once more in a bad mood, she asked him what was wrong.

"Oh, my child," he responded, "it's because of my brother. He always mocks me for having only seven daughters and no sons. And he does this whenever he sees me. 'Oh brother, you with your seven flower pots, and me with my seven swords! How's it going?'"

"You know what, father," the clever maiden said, "when your brother says something like that next time, you're to respond that your daughters are much smarter than his sons and you want to make a bet: Tell him he's to send out his youngest son, and you'll send out your youngest daughter, and whoever's first to rob the prince's crown will win the bet."

"All right, I'll do that," the father said, and the next time he met his brother, who began teasing him, he said, "You know what, brother, my

---

* O ssu frate, vui cu setti grasti, e ju cu setti spadi.

I

daughters are much smarter than your sons, and to show you that I'm right — I'd like to make a bet with you. Send out your youngest son, and I'll send out my youngest daughter, and we'll see which of the two can steal the prince's crown first."

The brother agreed, and the maiden and the young man set out. After they had traveled for a while, they came to a little river* with a great deal of flowing water. The maiden took off her shoes, lifted her skirt, and waded cheerfully through the water. But the young man thought, "Why should I get my feet wet? I'll wait until all the water has all flown by and the bed is empty." So he sat down, and in order to help the water flow faster and disappear, he took a nutshell and used it to bail water from the stream onto the bank and into the sand. In the meantime his cousin kept going until she met a farmer boy. "Oh, what a handsome young man!" she said, "Give me your clothes, and I'll give you mine in exchange."

The boy agreed, and the maiden took his clothes and put them on. Then she continued on her way until she came to the city in which the prince lived. As soon as she found the royal palace, she began walking up and down in front of it. The prince stood on the balcony, and when he saw the handsome young man, he called out and asked him what his name was.

"My name's Giovanni, and I'm a stranger here," she answered. "I'm looking for a job and was wondering whether I could enter your service."

"Do you want to be my secretary?" the prince asked.

She agreed, and the prince took her into his service. Soon he became fonder and fonder of her with each passing day. When he looked at her beautiful white hands, he kept thinking: "Those are not the hands of a man. Giovanni is certainly a maiden!" So he went to his mother and told her what he thought, but she answered, "I can't believe this. Why should Giovanni be a maiden!"

"No mother," the prince said. "I'm certain that Giovanni is not a man. Just look at his fine white hands.

> Giovanni walks to the writing stand
> and writes with a fine, exquisite hand.
> He's got a woman's style and way
> and makes me lovesick the entire day.†

---

* Fiumara.

† Giuvanni scrivi
  Cu manu suttili
  Modu di donna
  Ca mi fa muriri.

"Well, my son," the queen said, "if you want to be certain about all of this, take him into the garden. If he picks a pink carnation, then he's a maiden. But if he picks a rose, he's definitely a man."

The prince did exactly what his mother told him to do. He called his faithful servant and said, "Let's take a little walk in the garden."

"Of course, your majesty," the clever maiden answered, and they went into the garden, but she kept herself from looking at the tulips. Instead, she picked a rose and put it in her lapel.

"Just look at the beautiful pink carnations!" the prince exclaimed.

But the maiden answered, "Why should we care about pink carnations? After all, we're not girls!"*

Now the prince went to his mother, who said, "You see, I told you so!"

"No, mother," he answered. "I won't let you talk me out of this, for

Giovanni walks to the writing stand
and writes with a fine, exquisite hand.
He's got a woman's style and way
and makes me lovesick the entire day.

"You know what," the queen said. "Why don't you propose that you go swimming in the sea together? If he accepts, then you shall know for certain whether he is a man or woman."

Then the prince called his secretary to him and said, "Giovanni, it's so warm today. Let's go swimming in the sea."

"Why not?" the clever maiden answered. "Let's go right now, your majesty."

When they reached the beach, however, the maiden said all of a sudden, "Oh, your majesty, I forgot to bring towels with us. Wait here a moment while I return to the castle and fetch them."

So she ran back into the castle, went to the queen, and said, "The prince wants his gold crown right away and has asked that you give it to me without delay."

The queen gave her the gold crown, and the clever maiden wrote on a piece of paper:

---

* The girl prefers pink carnations because, even though they do not stand out, they have a wonderful aroma, while the boy is more concerned with beauty. Moreover, the carnation is a symbol of happy love. The girl throws a carnation to her lover when she accepts his proposal.

I came as a virgin
I go as a virgin.
The prince's been tricked
with cunning and wit.*

She fastened the sheet of paper on the gate, mounted a horse, and rode away with the crown. When she came to the little stream, her cousin was still sitting there and bailing water with his nutshell. She showed him the gold crown and laughed at him.

"Wasn't my father, right?" she said. "We are indeed smarter than you are!"

Upon saying this, she rode through the stream and returned home in good spirits. In the meantime, the prince was still waiting for his secretary, and when he finally lost his patience and went home, he saw the sheet of paper on the gate from a distance. After he read it, he ran to his mother and was stricken with grief.

"Didn't I tell you," he said, "that Giovanni was a maiden? Now she's gone, and I wanted to have her for my wife."

He ordered his horse to be saddled and set out on his way to search for the beautiful maiden. He rode straight ahead for a long time, and whenever he met some people, he asked them whether they had seen a handsome young man come riding by, but nobody could give him any information. Finally he came to the little river where the son of the other brother was still bailing water with the nutshell.

"Hey, my handsome lad," he called out, "did you by chance see a young man with a gold crown come riding by here?"

"That was my cousin," the fellow answered. "She's certainly home by now."

"Well then, lead me to her," the prince said, and they went to the maiden's home together. In the meantime, she had put on women's clothes and looked even more beautiful. When the prince caught sight of her, he rushed to her and said, "You are to become my wife!"

Then he took her to his castle, and she invited her father and sisters to come. Indeed, they all celebrated a splendid wedding and remained happy and content, but we just sit here and gaze at each other the whole day long.

---

* Schetta vinni
  Schetta mi nni vaju,
  E lu figghiu ddu rè
  Gabbatu l'aju.

2

THE ROBBER WITH A WITCH'S HEAD

Once upon a time there was a king who had three beautiful daughters, but the youngest was the most beautiful and the smartest among them. One day the king called her and said, "Come, my child, and clean the lice from my head."

The youngest daughter did this and found a louse. The king put the louse in a large jar with fat and kept it there for many years. Then one day he had the jar split open. The louse had grown into such a monster that everyone was terrified, and the king had it killed. Afterward he ordered the monster to be skinned and had the skin nailed to the door and said, "Whoever can guess the animal from which this skin came can have my oldest daughter as his bride."

Princes and noblemen came from far and wide and sought to court the beautiful princess, but nobody could solve the riddle, and so they all had to die a miserable death.

Now there was also a robber who lived alone in a wild region. He had a witch's head* that he kept in a small basket, and he always obtained good advice from the head whenever he wanted to undertake anything. He had heard how many princes and noblemen had lost their lives because they could not solve the difficult riddle, so he went to the

---

* Testa di mavara.

5

witch's head and asked, "Tell me, head, which animal's skin did the king have nailed over the door?"

"A louse," the head answered.

Now the robber was in good spirits and set out for the city. Along the way people asked him where he was going.

"I'm going to the city and want to woo the king's oldest daughter," he answered.

"Well, you're heading toward certain death," the people told him.

When he arrived in the city, he had the servants announce to the king that he wished to try to solve the riddle. The king had him enter, showed him the skin, and asked, "Can you tell me which animal's skin this is?"

"A rabbit?" said the robber.

"Wrong!"

"Perhaps, it's from a dog?"

"Wrong!"

"Is the skin perhaps the skin of a louse?"

Since the robber did indeed solve the riddle, the king gave him his oldest daughter as his wife. When the wedding ceremony was over, the robber said to the king, "I want now to return home with my wife."

The princess embraced her father and her sisters and departed with her husband. After they had roamed a long time, they came to a wild, desolate region, and the princess said, "Oh, where are you leading me?! It's so ugly here!"

"Just follow me!" the robber answered.

Finally they arrived at this house, which was so dark and unattractive that the princess said again, "Do you really live here? Oh, how unfriendly it is!"

"Just come inside," the robber answered.

Now the poor princess had to live in this house and work hard. On the second day the robber said, "I've got to go and look after some business. You take care of the house."

Then he turned to the witch's head and spoke softly, "Pay attention to what she says about me."

As soon as the robber was away, the princess could no longer keep everything within herself and began to curse her husband because she had not really wanted to marry him and could not stand him at all.

"This villain!" she said. "I wish he would break his neck! I hope he has bad luck for the rest of his life!" And she went on and on.

But the witch's head heard everything and told the robber when he returned home. Then the robber grabbed the princess, cut off her head, and threw her into a little room in which there were other corpses of young women whom he had murdered in the same way. The next day he

set out for the king's court, and when he arrived, the king asked him, "How is my daughter doing?"

"My wife is in very good health and happy," the robber answered, "but she is somewhat bored and would like to have her middle sister keep her company."

So the king gave him the second daughter, and he took her into that wild region.

"Oh, brother-in-law," the princess said, "how spooky this region is! Where are you taking me?"

"Just follow me!" the robber answered.

When they arrived at the robber's house, the princess asked again, "Oh, brother-in-law, is this your house? This ugly house?"

"Just come inside," the robber said.

"Where is my sister?" she asked.

"You don't have to worry about your sister. Just do the work I tell you to do."

So the princess had to work hard, and her heart became filled more and more with rage and hate against her brother-in-law. One day he said to her, "I must go and look after my business and won't be home until this evening."

Then he went to the witch's head and said, "Pay attention to what she says about me."

Now the princess gave vent to her hatred and began cursing the robber. She called him a villain and wished him nothing but bad luck. However, when the robber returned home, the witch's head told him everything, and the poor princess was not treated any better than her sister.

Now the robber journeyed to the court once more, and the king asked him how things were going with his two daughters.

"Oh, very well," the robber replied. "But they would love to have their youngest sister with them so they could all be together."

So the king also gave him his youngest daughter, who was, however, very smart, and when they went into the wilderness, she said. "Oh no, brother-in-law, how beautiful this region is! Do you really live here?"

And when they came to the house, she said again, "Oh my, how beautiful this house is!"

When they went inside, she took care not to ask about her sisters. Instead she began cheerfully doing her work. Then the robber went to look after his business once more and the witch's head had to pay attention to everything the princess might say. When she completed her work, she kneeled down and prayed loudly for the robber and wished him all the best. In her heart, however, she wished that he would be struck by bad luck. In the evening the robber returned and asked the witch's head right away, "Well, what did she say about me?"

"Oh, we've never had a maiden like her here before!" the head said. "She prayed for you the entire day and had nothing but pious wishes for you!"

The robber was very happy and said to the princess, "Because you have been more intelligent than your sisters, you will have it good here, and I'll also show you where your sisters are."

So, he led her into the little room and showed her the dead sisters.

"You did the right thing, brother-in-law, in killing them if they did not honor and respect you," the clever princess said.

Now things went well for her with the robber, and she was the mistress in the house. But one day when the robber had gone away for several days, she went into his room, looked around, and noticed the witch's head. It was in its basket nailed above the window. Since she was so smart, she called to the head, "What are you doing up there? Why don't you come down to me. It will be better for you."

"No," the head answered. "I feel much better up here and have no desire to come down there."

But the princess flattered the witch's head so much that the head was fooled and finally let itself be brought down.

"My, you have such tangled hair!" the princess said. "Come with me and I'll comb it so that it is fine."

So the witch's head followed her into the kitchen, and the princess took a comb and began combing the head. She had just heated up the oven to make some bread, and while she was combing the head's hair, she carefully wound the long braid around her arm and all at once flung the head into oven. Then she shut the door and calmly let the head burn.

Now the robber's life was tied to the life of the head, and while it burned, the robber felt his health and his life weaken, and he died. In the meantime the princess climbed up to the window where the basket had been hanging and had served as the head's dwelling place. There she found a small jar with an ointment, and when she took it and rubbed it on her sisters, they returned to life. Then she revived all the other young women, who took as much of the robber's treasures as they could carry and returned to their parents. As for the three sisters, they went back to their father and lived with him happily and content until they married three handsome princes.

3

THE CLEVER FARMER'S DAUGHTER

Once upon a time there was a young king who went hunting. When it gradually turned dark, he realized that he had become separated from his entourage, and only his messenger was still with him. By nightfall they could no longer find their way home out of the dense forest, so they wandered about for many hours until they finally noticed a light in the distance. When they approached it, they saw that it was a cottage, and the king sent his messenger to wake the people inside. He knocked at the door, and soon a farmer appeared and asked from inside, "Who's knocking so late at night?"

"His majesty, the king, is standing outside," the messenger responded. "He cannot find the way back to his castle. Would you please give him food and a place to stay?"

The farmer quickly opened the door, woke his wife and daughter, and told them to slaughter a chicken and broil it. When the meal was ready, they asked the king to make do with the little they could offer him. The king took the chicken and divided it. He gave the father the head; the mother the breast, and the daughter the wings; he kept the thighs for himself and gave the feet to the messenger. Afterward they all went to bed.

The mother, however, said to her daughter, "Why did the king divide the chicken in such an unusual way?"

"It's quite clear," she answered. "He gave the head to father because he is the head of the family. He gave you the breast because you nurture us as our dear old mother.* He gave me the wings because I'll fly away from here one day. He kept the thighs because he is a rider, and he gave his messenger the feet so that he can run much faster."

The next morning they prepared breakfast for the king and showed him the right path home. When the king arrived at his castle, he took a beautiful roasted chicken, a large cake, a little barrel of wine, and twelve thalers. Then he called his messenger and ordered him to take everything to the farmer with the assurance that he would always be in the monarch's good graces.

It was a long way to the farmer's cottage, and the messenger became tired and hungry. Finally, he could no longer resist his appetite, and cut off half the chicken and devoured it. After a while he became thirsty and drank half the wine. When he traveled a bit farther and looked at the cake, he thought, "It's surely good!" and he also ate half the cake. Now he thought: "If I'm going to take half of everything, I might as well be fair and go all the way," and so he took six of the twelve thalers.

Eventually he reached the farmer's cottage and delivered half the chicken, half the cake, half a barrel of wine, and half of the thalers. The farmer and his family were extremely pleased by the honor the king showed them, and they asked the messenger to express their gratitude to him. However, when the daughter saw that everything was half of what it should have been, she told the messenger she would like him to give a special message to the king that he was to repeat word for word.

"First you must say to the king: Why is it, my God, that he who sings in the night sings only halfway? Can you remember this?"†

"Oh, yes!" the messenger answered.

"Then you also have to say to him: It is half moon. But why, my God, half the moon? Can you remember this?"

"Certainly," the messenger answered.

"Then you must also say to him: It was closed on top and closed on the bottom. But why, my God, only half? You won't forget that, will you?"

"Certainly not," the messenger said.

---

* Pirchí siti vecchiaredda.

† Chiddu chi a notti canta
  O Diu, menzu pirchí?
  La luna a quinta decima,
  O Diu, menza pirchí?
  Stuppatu susu e jusu
  O Diu, menza pirchí?
  Li dudici misi did l'annu
  O Diu, sei pirchí?

"Finally, you must say to him: The year has twelve months. Then, why God, just six?"

The messenger promised to say everything exactly as she told him and set out on his way. Just to make sure he would remember everything, he kept repeating it along the way. When he arrived at the castle, the king asked him, "Well, did you deliver everything as I told you?"

"Yes, your majesty," the messenger answered. "But I'm also supposed to deliver a message to you from the farmer's daughter. First, she said: 'Why is it, my God, that he who sings in the night sings only halfway?'"

"What!" cried the king. "You ate half the chicken?"

"Please, your majesty," the messenger said, "first hear my entire message. Then she said: 'It is half moon. But why, my God, half the moon?'"

"What?" yelled the king. "You also ate half the cake?"

"Please, your majesty," the messenger replied. "Let me finish. The third thing she said was: 'It was closed on top and closed on the bottom. But why, my God, only half?'"

"What?" the king yelled again. "You also drunk half the barrel of wine?"

"Please, your majesty," the messenger said. "Let me finish my message. Finally she said: 'It is half moon. But why, my God, half the moon?'"

"Well, you also stole half the thalers, didn't you?" the king cried.

Then the messenger fell to his knees and asked for the king's forgiveness. Indeed, the king was so pleased by the maiden's cleverness that he forgave the messenger. As for the maiden, the king sent a magnificent coach with beautiful clothes, and he took her for his wife.

They remained happy and content
But we can't even pay the rent.

4

THE COUNT AND HIS SISTER

Once upon a time there was a count who had a very beautiful sister, more beautiful than the sun. In fact, the count refused to let her marry because he thought that no man would ever be good enough for her. So when he himself married, he kept his sister in his house, and whenever he gave his wife a beautiful dress as a present, he gave his sister the same one.

Now the king lived across from the count's house, and one evening the count's beautiful sister said to her lamp:

My golden lamp,
Silver wick so fine,
Send me a sign
to find the king.
Tell me just what he wants to make.
Is he asleep? Is he awake?*

---

* Lampa mia d'oru,
 Micciu miu d'argentu,
 Chi fa lu re? Dormi o vigghia?

Since the lamp was a magic lamp, it answered,

Step softly, mistress, step softly,
the king is sleeping soundly.*

So the beautiful young lady rushed across the street and went into
the king's chamber. When the sun began to rise, she rushed back to her
house, and nobody knew where she had gone. She did the same thing
the next evening, and the king fell into great despair because he could
not learn who the beautiful lady was who had slept with him two nights
in a row. He told this to the count, who advised him to do the following: "When the beautiful lady discards her dress tonight, hide it. This
way we'll be able to learn who she is."

The king did what he said, and when the beautiful young lady came
into his room again and took off her dress, he took it away and hid it,
and when she wanted to flee at sunrise, she could not find her dress and
had to leave without it. The king showed the dress to the count, who was
shocked and thought, "This was the dress that I recently gave to my wife
and my sister. Could it be one of them?"

His wife showed him her dress right away, and then he went to his
sister and asked her to show him her dress.

"I'll fetch it right away," she answered. "I've been keeping it in a
closet."

However, she went quickly to her brother's wife and said to her,
"Dear sister-in-law, please lend me your dress for a moment," and then
she brought it back to her brother. Since the dresses were exactly alike,
the count was completely fooled. But now the beautiful lady no longer
went to the king.

Soon the count's sister noticed that she was going to have a child, so
she hid herself from her brother, and when her time came, she gave birth
to a lovely boy. She placed him in a basket and covered him with the
most beautiful, sweet smelling flowers and sent him to the king. When
the king took off the flowers and caught sight of the gorgeous child, he
thought for sure it was his son and summoned the count.

"Some unknown woman has sent this child to me," he said. "I'm sure
it was the beautiful lady who came to me. I wish I knew how to find her."

"Your majesty," the count answered, "why don't you organize a big
party and invite all the ladies of the city to attend. Then have your

---

* Ntrasti, Signura,
  Chi lu re dormi a st'ura.

14

servants build a huge fire and bring out the child. Once he is there, pretend that you want to throw the baby into the fire, and you'll see that the mother of this child will reveal herself."

So the king threw a large party. All the ladies of the city came together, and among them was the count's sister. In the middle of the party, the king had his servants bring out a huge basin with burning fire. Then he pointed to the baby in the basket and said, "Do you all see this lovely child? An unknown woman has recently sent this babe to me. What should I do with the child? I think I want to burn it."

All at once there was a voice that cried out in lament, "Oh, my son, my son!"

The count's sister rushed to the baby. When the count heard her cry, he pulled out his sword and wanted to murder his sister, but the king grabbed him by the arm and declared:

Stop, oh count, forget the shame. Don't take her life.
Your sister will soon become the king's own wife.*

Soon thereafter a beautiful wedding was celebrated, and the count's sister became queen. Then they lived happy and content, and we are left without a cent.

---

* Fermati Conti, vergogna non è!
  Soru di Conti e mugghièri di re!

5

CLEVER PEPPE

Once upon a time there was a poor washerwoman who had an only son named Peppe, and everyone regarded him as dumb. Now one time during Carnival, all the people began cooking macaroni and roasting sausages in their homes, and only the poor washerwoman had nothing to eat but dry bread. So Peppe said, "All the people have good things in their homes today. Why should we alone eat dry bread? Give me your chicken. I want to sell it and buy some macaroni and sausage with the money I get."

"Are you crazy?" his mother replied. "Do you want me to sell my last chicken? Then I'll have nothing at all."

But Peppe kept asking her until she finally relented and gave him the chicken. When he went to the market place, he offered his chicken for sale, and a man came and asked him, "How much do you want for the chicken?"

"Three tari."

"Is it nice and fat?" the man asked and took the chicken in his hands as if he wanted to weigh it. Before Peppe realized what was happening, however, the man disappeared along with the chicken. Just think of how poor Peppe began to moan.

"Oh, now my mother will beat me and kill me! What should I do?"

All of a sudden he saw the thief standing in front of a macaroni shop. He quietly sneaked up behind him and heard the man say, "Put aside twenty pounds of macaroni. Here's the money. Tomorrow I'll send a boy with a white donkey, and you can give him the macaroni."

Now this man was the captain of some robbers and had eleven men under his command. After the robber had bought the macaroni, he went to a sausage shop, and Peppe carefully followed him again.

"Put aside twenty pounds of sausage for me," the captain of the robbers said to the butcher. "Here's the money for it. Tomorrow a boy with a white donkey will come, and you can give him the sausages."

Then the robber went into a cheese shop and also bought twenty pounds of cheese that he left aside to be picked up the next day. Peppe kept sneaking after him and noted everything the robber said and did.

When he returned home, his mother asked right away, "How much did you get for the chicken?"

"Oh mother, listen to what happened to me," and he told her his story.

When the woman heard how he had let the chicken be stolen from him, she took a large stick and gave Peppe a good beating.

"Let me go, mother!" he pleaded. "I'll make sure that the robber pays you back. Just get me a white donkey, and tomorrow I'll give your heart reason to rejoice."

"Oh, what do you want with a white donkey?" the washerman cried. "You numbskull! You're not even capable of selling a chicken!"

But Peppe kept asking until she relented and borrowed a white donkey from a neighbor. The next morning Peppe got up very early and drove the white donkey to the macaroni shop.

"Hey there, good friend, my master has sent me to pick up the twenty pounds of macaroni that he bought here yesterday."

The baker saw the white donkey and thought, "That must be the boy that the customer from yesterday promised to send." So he gave Peppe the macaroni without thinking about it much. Peppe loaded it on to the donkey and drove the animal to the butcher shop.

"Give me the twenty pounds of sausage that my master bought here yesterday" he said, and when the butcher saw the white donkey, he thought it was all right to deliver the sausages to Peppe. Peppe also went to the cheese shop and picked up the twenty pounds of cheese there. Afterward he brought everything to his mother and called out, "Mother, let's eat and drink. Now we've been paid back a fourth of what our chicken was worth."

In the meantime the real boy sent by the captain of the robbers arrived at the macaroni shop with a white donkey and wanted to fetch the macaroni.

"You can't have the macaroni a second time," the baker said. "You were already here once."

"That wasn't me," the boy said.

"Well, I can't help you," the baker responded. "A boy came with a white donkey, and I gave him the macaroni."

The butcher and cheese dealer said the same thing, and the boy had to return to the band of robbers with empty hands, while Peppe and his mother filled themselves with the macaroni and the sausages. The next morning Peppe said, "Mother, the man who stole our chicken has paid us back only one fourth of what it was worth. Fetch me some girl's clothes. I'm going to get him to give me the rest of what he owes us."

When his mother brought him some girl's clothes, he disguised himself as a maiden and went out walking until he came to the house where the twelve robbers lived. Once he was there, he sat down on the threshold and began to weep. Soon after a robber came to the window, looked out, and asked, "Why are you crying, beautiful maiden?"

"Oh, my father told me that I should wait for him here, and now it's almost night and my father still hasn't returned. How can I find my way back home?"

"Now, just calm down," the robber said. "You can stay here, and you'll have a good life with us."

So Peppe went inside, and the twelve robbers gave him food and drink. When it became night, the captain of the robbers said, "This maiden belongs to me, and tonight she will sleep in my room."

"Oh, no," said Peppe. "I can't do that. I would be too ashamed."

"Don't be dumb," the robber said, and he led the supposed maiden into his room, where Peppe saw a great deal of gold and silver lying around, and in a corner was a gallows.

"What is that black thing over there?" Peppe asked.

"That's a gallows," said the captain. "We hang all the people who have insulted us on it."

"How do you do it?" Peppe inquired.

"The person puts his head through the noose," the robber replied, "and then we pull the rope until the person dies."

"Oh, I don't understand how that works. Why don't you show me?"

So the robber stuck his head through the noose, and all of a sudden Peppe jumped over to the gallows and pulled on the rope, but he was not strong enough to strangle the robber. Nevertheless, the robber could barely breathe and could not speak at all. Then Peppe grabbed a large club and beat the robber until he was half dead.

"Oh, you villain, don't you recognize me? I'm the boy whose chicken you stole!" Peppe called out in between beatings. When he finally became tired from hitting the robber, he filled his pockets with gold coins, crept quietly out of the house, and ran back to his mother full of joy.

"Here, mother, take this money. Now half the chicken has been repaid."

The next morning the robbers waited hour after hour for their captain to wake up. When everything remained quiet until noon, they finally broke down the door and found him half strangled and half beaten to death. So they took off the noose and put him to bed, and he could only cough in a low voice, "It was the boy whose chicken I stole."

"Let's get a doctor," the robbers said, and one of them went to the window to see whether a doctor was in the vicinity. All at once he saw a doctor on a donkey riding by. So he called to him and invited him to come inside. However, the doctor was none other than Peppe, who had disguised himself to get back at the robbers one more time.

When the robbers called him, he climbed the stairs slowly and deliberately and was then led to the robber's bed.

"This man is very sick," he said. "I can make him healthy with my medicine, but I shall need some supplies to heal him."

So he sent the robbers out of the house, and each one was to fetch something different, and he remained alone with the sick man.

"Do you recognize me again, you villain?" Peppe asked. "I'm the boy whose chicken you stole."

"Oh, mercy! Don't beat me to death! I'll give you a hundred ounces of gold!"

"I can get that money by myself," Peppe answered. "But you have to repay me for the beating that I received from my mother."

Upon saying this he grabbed a club again and beat the robber until he could no longer continue. Then he filled his pockets with gold coins, left the robber laying in bed half dead, and rode happily back home.

"Here, mother, you see this money. Now we have been repaid three fourths of what the hen was worth."

"Oh, my son, be careful that the robbers don't recognize you."

"What can they do to me?" Peppe said, and the next morning he disguised himself as a street cleaner,* loaded the large waste baskets† on the donkey, and set out on his way to the street where the robbers' house was located.

Meanwhile the robbers were having a discussion among themselves: "What should we do with our captain? Instead of getting better, he's

---

* Munnizzàru.

† Zimmili. These were large sacks that were woven out of coarse raffia or straw, and one loaded them with dung and dirt or vegetables and fruit.

getting worse. Perhaps we should take him to a hospital, but we don't have a way of getting him there."

Just then they looked out the window and saw a street cleaner riding by, and it was Peppe.

"Hey, you handsome fellow," they called, "if you do us a favor, we'll give you an ounce of gold."

"What do you want me to do?"

"We've got a sick man here, and we want to put him in one of your large baskets, and then you can take him to the hospital."

"Good," Peppe answered, and he cleaned out a basket so that the robbers could put their sick captain into it. Then they gave him a gold ounce and tied a money belt around the robber that was filled with gold coins. Peppe pretended now to head for the hospital, but when he was out of the sight of the robbers, he drove the donkey into the mountains on a rocky path.

"Where are you taking me?" the robber asked.

"Just come along, you villain! Don't you recognize me anymore? I'm the boy whose chicken you stole."

"Oh, mercy! Let me live. I'll give you all the money I'm carrying with me."

"I can take that by myself," said Peppe, and he untied the money belt and threw the robber into a ditch and left him lying there.

When he returned home, he gave all the money to his mother and cried out, "So, mother, now the chicken has been paid for. Now we are rich people and can live without any worries."

So from then on, Peppe was no longer regarded by the people as dumb, but as sensible and clever.*

---

* Spertiu. This is from the word spertu, esperto. In German, klug.

6

MARIA, THE EVIL STEPMOTHER, AND THE SEVEN ROBBERS

Once upon a time there was a man whose wife died, and he was left with only a small daughter called Maria.

Maria went to a school where she learned sewing and knitting from a woman. Before she went home each evening, this woman told her time and again, "Make sure you give my warm greetings to your father."

Because she seemed to be so kind, Maria's father thought, "She'd make for a good wife," and so he married her. But when they were married, the woman became quite nasty to poor Maria, for that's the way stepmothers have always been. Finally she could not stand Maria at all, and she said to her husband, "The girl eats too much of our bread. We've got to get rid of her."

But the man said, "I'm not going to kill my own child!"

"Take her with you tomorrow into the fields," the woman said. "Leave her there alone. She won't be able to find her way back home."

The next day the man called his daughter and said to her, "Let's go work in the forest, and we'll take some food with us."

He took a large loaf of bread with him, and they set out on their way. However, Maria was shrewd and had filled her pockets with bran. As she walked behind her father, she threw heaps of bran on the path from time to time. After they had walked for several hours, they came to a steep cliff where the man let the loaf of bread fall over and cried out, "Oh, Maria, the bread fell over the cliff!"

"Don't worry, father," Maria said, "I'll climb down and fetch it."

She went down to the bottom of the cliff and found the bread. But when she returned to the top, her father had disappeared, and Maria was alone. She began to weep, for she was very far from their house and in a strange spot. But then she thought about the heaps of bran and summoned her courage again. Slowly she followed the bran and returned home late at night.

"Oh, father!" she said. "Why did you leave me so alone?"

The man comforted her and talked to her until she calmed down, but the stepmother was angry that Maria had found her way back home. After some time had passed, she told her husband once again to take Maria into the fields and leave her alone in the forest. The next morning the man called his daughter again, and they set out on their way. The father carried a loaf of bread with him once more, but Maria forgot to take bran with her. Once they were deeper in the forest and reached another even steeper cliff, the father let the loaf of bread fall again, and Maria had to climb down to fetch it. When she returned to the top, her father was gone, and she was alone. So she began to weep bitter tears and ran around for a long time looking for the way home, but she only managed to go deeper into the dark forest. Gradually as it turned dark, she suddenly saw a light. She went toward it and came upon a cottage in which she found a table set for dinner and seven beds, but there were no people. Indeed, the house belonged to seven robbers, and therefore Maria hid herself behind the oven. Soon the robbers came home. They ate and drank and then laid down to bed. The next morning they went forth and left their youngest brother there so that he could cook* and clean the house. While they were away, the youngest brother also left to buy a few things†. Then Maria came out from behind the oven and began cleaning the entire house. She finished by sweeping the room and setting the kettle on the fire to cook the beans. Then she hid behind the oven again. When the youngest robber returned, he was astonished to see everything so clean, and when his brothers came home, he told them what had happened. They were all very puzzled and could not imagine how all this had come to pass. The next day the second youngest brother remained behind. He pretended that he had to go away, but he returned right away and saw Maria come out of her hiding place to bring things in order. Maria was terrified when she caught sight of the robber.

---

* Fasola c'à pasta.

† Pi fari a spisa.

"Oh," she pleaded, "please don't kill me. For God's sake!"

Then she told him about her evil stepmother, and how her father had abandoned her in the forest, and how she had hidden herself for two days behind the oven.

"You don't need to be afraid of us," the robber said. "Stay with us. Be our sister and cook, sew, and wash for us."

When the other brothers came home, they, too, were satisfied with Maria, and so Maria remained with the seven robbers, kept house for them, and was always quiet and diligent.

One day as she was sitting at the window and sewing, a poor woman came by and asked for alms.

"Oh!" said Maria. "I don't have much, for I myself am a poor, unfortunate maiden. But I shall be glad to give you whatever I have."

"Why are you so unfortunate?" asked the beggar woman.

Then Maria told her how she had left home and had made her way to the robber's house. The poor woman left and later told the evil stepmother that Maria was still alive. When the stepmother heard this, she was very angry and gave the beggar woman a ring to take to poor Maria. This ring was a magic ring. After a week passed, the beggar woman went to Maria again to ask for alms, and when Maria gave her something, she said, "Look, my child, I have a beautiful ring. Since you have been so kind to me, I want to give it to you as a gift."

Without suspecting anything, Maria took the ring, but when she put it on her finger, she fell down dead. After the robbers returned home and found Maria on the floor, they were very distressed and shed bitter tears. Then they made a beautiful coffin, and after they had adorned her with the most beautiful jewels and placed a great deal of gold inside, they put Maria into the coffin and placed it on a cart drawn by two oxen. When they approached the king's castle, they saw that the door to the stable was wide open and drove the oxen and the cart inside. All this caused the horses to become unsettled, and they began to kick and make noise. When the king heard the racket, he sent a servant to the stable to ask the stable master what had happened. The stable master replied that a cart had come into the stable, but no one was driving it and there was a beautiful coffin on the cart.

The king ordered his men to bring the coffin to him and had them open it. When he glanced at the beautiful dead maiden in the coffin, he began to weep bitter tears and could not bear to leave her. Then he ordered four large wax candles to be set up and lit at the four corners of the coffin. Afterward he sent all the people out of the room, locked the door, fell on his knees next to the coffin, and burst into tears. When it came time for dinner, his mother sent servants to fetch him, but he did not even answer. Instead, he kept weeping even more uncontrollably. So the old queen herself went and knocked on the door and asked him to open up. Still, he did not answer. Then she looked through the keyhole. When she saw her son kneeling next to a corpse, she had her servants break open the door. However, when she saw the beautiful maiden, she herself was very touched and leaned over Maria and took her hand. When she noticed the beautiful ring, she thought it would be a shame to have the ring buried with the girl. So she slipped it off. All of a sudden the dead Maria was alive again, and the young king was extremely pleased and said to his mother. "This maiden is to be my bride!"

"Then it will be as you say!" his mother responded and embraced Maria.

So Maria became the wife of the king and a queen as well, and they lived in glory and happiness until the end of their days.

7

BENSURDATU

Once upon a time there was a king and a queen who had three beautiful daughters, and they loved them more than anything in the world. Indeed, they did everything possible to make them happy and content.

One day the three princesses said, "Dear father, we'd very much like to take a trip into the country today and eat lunch there."

"All right, my dear children, let's do it," the king said and gave the orders right away.

A beautiful lunch was prepared, and the king and the queen and their daughters took a trip into the countryside. After they had eaten, the maidens said, "Dear parents, we'd like to take a walk in the garden for a while. When you're ready to return home, just call us."

No sooner did the maidens go into the garden, however, than a large black cloud came down and carried them off. After some time had passed, the king and queen wanted to return home and called their daughters, who were nowhere to be found. They searched throughout the garden, in the house, and in the fields—all in vain. The three maidens had disappeared, and the situation remained that way. Just think of the grief the king and queen suffered! The poor mother lamented the entire day, while the king issued a proclamation that whoever returned his daughters could have one of them for his wife and become his successor as king.

Now there were two young generals at the court, and they discussed the matter: "Let's set out and search for the princesses. Perhaps this will be our fortune."

So they began their quest, and each one of them had a beautiful horse, a bundle of clothes, and some money. They had to travel for a long, long time, and their money ran out and they had to sell their horses. Finally, they had only the clothes they were wearing on their backs. Since they had become hungry, they went to an inn and ordered something to eat and drink. When they were supposed to pay, they said to the innkeeper, "We don't have any money. The only things we have are the clothes on our backs. Take our clothes as payment, and give us some common garments. We'll stay here and serve you."

The innkeeper agreed, after he brought them some old clothes, the two generals stayed and worked for him.

Meanwhile, the king and queen yearned to see their dear children and kept waiting for them to return. But they did not return, nor did the generals.

Now the king had a poor soldier named Bensurdatu, who had loyally served him for many years. Bensurdatu saw that the king was always sad and said to him one day, "Your majesty, I want to set out and look for your daughters."

"Oh, Bensurdatu, I've lost three daughters and two generals. Do you want me to lose you as well?"

But Bensurdatu said, "Let me depart, your majesty. You'll see. I'll bring back your daughters."

After many conversations the king agreed, and Bensurdatu set out on the same path the generals had taken before him. Eventually he arrived at the same inn and demanded something to eat. The two generals came to serve him. Although they were dressed in poor clothes, he recognized them and was so astonished that he asked what had happened to them. They told him everything, and Bensurdatu called the innkeeper to him and said, "Give them back their clothes. I'll pay you what they owe you."

Once the innkeeper brought back the clothes, the generals got dressed and continued with Bensurdatu on their quest to find the King's beautiful daughters. Again they wandered for a long time and finally came to a desolate, wild region where there was no human dwelling to be seen far and wide. Just as it was getting dark, they noticed a light in the distance, and when they approached it, they found a small cottage and knocked on the door.

"Who's there?" a voice asked.

"Oh, please have mercy, and give us shelter for the night," answered Bensurdatu. "We are tired travelers and have lost our way."

A wise old woman lived in the house, and she opened the door and asked them in.

"Where have you come from, and where are you going?" she asked.

"Oh, my good old woman," Bensurdatu answered, "we've taken on a difficult task. We've set out to search for the king's three daughters."

"Oh, how unfortunate you are! You'll never be able to complete your task. The princesses were abducted by a black cloud, and no one knows where they are now."

Bensurdatu pleaded with the old woman and said, "If you know where they are, then tell us. We want to try our luck."

"Even if I tell you," the old woman said, "you still won't be able to rescue them because you'll have to go down into a deep well. When you reach the bottom, you'll find the princesses, but the two eldest are being guarded by two giants, and the youngest is being held captive by a dragon with seven heads."

When the generals heard all this, they became frightened and did not want to go any farther. But Bensurdatu said, "We've come this far, and now we must finish our work. Tell us where this well is. Early tomorrow morning we shall go there."

The old woman told them and gave them cheese, bread, and wine so that they could strengthen themselves, and after they had eaten, they all laid down to bed. The next morning they thanked the old woman and continued on their journey. They traveled until they came to a well, and one of the generals said, "I'm the eldest and want to go down first."

He tied a rope around himself, took a small bell, and began to descend. No sooner had he gone some distance than he heard such thunder and noise that he became frightened and rang the little bell and let himself be pulled up as fast as he could. Now it was the second general's turn, and things did not go any better for him. When he heard the racket, he became so scared that he rang the little bell and let himself be pulled up in a hurry.

"What brave men you are!" Bensurdatu cried. "Now just let me try."

So he tied the rope around himself and cheerfully began his descent into the well. When he heard the thunder, he thought, "Just make all the noise you want. You can't harm me." As he came to the bottom of the well, he found himself in a very large and beautiful room, and the eldest princess was sitting in the middle. In front of her sat a powerful giant, and she had to clean lice from his hair. As she was doing this, he had fallen asleep. When she saw Bensurdatu, she gesticulated with her hand as if to ask him why he had come. He drew his sword and wanted to approach the giant, but she quickly gave him a signal indicating that he should hide himself. The giant was waking up, and he roared, "I smell human flesh!"

"Oh, where do you think the human flesh could have come from?" the princess answered. "No person could possibly come here. Go back to sleep and rest."

As soon as the giant had fallen asleep again, however, Bensurdatu made a sign to her that she should bend back a little. Then he drew his sword and chopped off the giant's head with one slice so that it flew off into a corner. The princess was extremely happy. She thanked him and gave him a gold crown as a gift.

"Now show me where your sisters are," Bensurdatu said. "I want to rescue them."

So the princess opened a door and led him into a second room where the second princess was sitting with a giant. She, too, had cleaned the lice from his hair until he had fallen asleep. When Bensurdatu and her sister entered the room, she signaled them that they should hide themselves. Indeed, the giant awakened and roared, "I smell human flesh!"

"Where do you think the human flesh could come from?" she answered. "No person could possibly come here. Go back to sleep and rest."

As he was sleeping, however, Bensurdatu came out of his hiding spot and lopped off the giant's head so that it went flying far away. The princess thanked him and rejoiced. She also gave him a gold crown as a gift.

"Now I want to rescue your youngest sister as well," Bensurdatu said, but the princesses responded, "Oh, you'll never succeed in doing that. She's under the power of a dragon with seven heads."

"Take me to her," answered Bensurdatu. "I intend to fight him."

The princesses opened a door for him, and when he entered, he stood in a huge hall where the youngest princess was chained to a wall. In front of her lay the dragon with seven heads. It looked ghastly and stood up ready to swallow poor Bensurdatu, but he did not lose his courage. Instead, he began fighting with the dragon until he had cut off all seven heads. Then he took the chains off the princess, and she embraced him full of joy and gave him a gold crown as a gift.

"Now let's return to the world above," said Bensurdatu.

He led them to the bottom of the well and tied the rope firmly around the eldest daughter, and when he rang the bell, the generals pulled her up. Then they threw the rope back down, and Bensurdatu tied the rope securely around the second princess.

Now only the youngest sister and Bensurdatu were left, and she said, "Dear Bensurdatu, please let yourself be pulled up first. Otherwise, the generals may betray you."

"No, no," answered Bensurdatu, "I won't leave you alone down here. Don't worry. My companions won't betray me."

"All right, if you won't do otherwise," the princess said. "I'll let myself be pulled up first. But you must promise me one thing. You must come to marry me, and if you don't come, I shall never marry anyone else."

Upon hearing this he tied the rope securely around the princess, and the generals pulled her up. However, when they were supposed to throw the rope back down to Bensurdatu, their hearts became filled with envy for the poor soldier, and they betrayed him and left him there. Moreover, they threatened the princesses and forced them to swear that they would tell their parents that the two generals had rescued them.

"And if they ask you about Bensurdatu, you're to say that you never saw him," they said.

So the princesses had to swear, and the two generals took them back to the court. The king and queen were full of joy when they saw their dear children again, and since the generals told them they had rescued their daughters, the king gladly gave them the two eldest daughters as wives.

Let's leave them now and see what happened to poor Bensurdatu.

He waited a long time, but when the rope was not thrown back down, he realized that his companions had betrayed him and thought, "Oh, I'm in trouble! How can I get out of here?" So he went through all the rooms, and in one of them he saw a beautifully covered table. Since he was hungry, he sat down and ate. But he had to remain in the underground for a long time because he could not find a way to climb out of the well. One day, however, as he was going through the rooms, he saw a purse filled with money hanging on a wall. When he took it down, he realized it was a magic purse because it cried out: "What is your command?"

His first wish was to get out of the well, and as soon as he was out, he wished for a large, beautiful ship with a crew and ready to sail. No sooner did he make this wish than a magnificent ship lay before him, and on top of the masthead there was a flag with the inscription: "The King of Three Crowns." So he boarded the ship and sailed to the city where the king lived, and as he entered the harbor, he ordered the canons of the ship to be fired. When the king heard this and saw the beautiful ship, he thought, "What a powerful ruler he must be! He's got three crowns, and I only have one."

Consequently, he got into his coach, went to greet him in the harbor, and invited him to come to his castle. "He would make a nice husband for my youngest daughter!" he thought. His youngest daughter was still not married, and no matter how many men wooed her, she refused to get married.

When the king returned with Bensurdatu, the princess did not recognize him because he was wearing such splendid royal garments. The king said to him, "Noble lord, let us eat and be merry, and if it is possible, it would be an honor for me if you would take my youngest daughter for your wife."

Bensurdatu agreed, and they sat down at the dinner table and ate and were merry. However, the youngest daughter was sad because she thought of Bensurdatu. Then the king said to her, "This noble ruler wants to elevate you and marry you."

"Oh, dear father," she answered, "I have no inclination to marry."

Then Bensurdatu turned to her and said, "What's this, noble maiden? If I were Bensurdatu, you would certainly marry me, wouldn't you?"

And as she looked at him with astonishment, he continued, "Yes, I am Bensurdatu." And he told his story.

When the king and queen heard this, they became extremely happy, and the king said, "Dear Bensurdatu, you are to have my youngest daughter for your wife, and when I die, you shall inherit my throne." Then he turned to the generals sitting at the table and declared, "As for you traitors, you must leave my realm now and never let yourselves be seen again!"

So the two generals had to leave the realm. For three days there were festive celebrations arranged by the king, and Bensurdatu married his youngest daughter. Indeed, they remained happy and content, and we were left without one cent.

8

$\sim$

THE ROOSTER WHO WANTED
TO BECOME POPE

Once upon a time there was a rooster who wanted to go to Rome
and have himself elected Pope. So he set out on his way.
During his journey he found a letter, which he took with him.
At one point he met a hen who asked him, "Mr. Rooster, where are you
going?"

"I'm going to Rome and want to become Pope."

"Will you take me with you?" she asked.

"First I must check my letter to see if you can come," the rooster
said and looked at the letter. "All right, you can come. When I become
Pope, you can become Mrs. Pope."

So Mr. Rooster and Mrs. Hen continued on their way together, until
they met a cat.

"Where are you going, Mr. Rooster and Mrs. Hen?" the cat asked.

"We're going to Rome and want to become the Pope and
Mrs. Pope."

"Will you take me along?"

"Wait until I've checked my letter to see if you can come," the rooster responded. "All right. Come along. You can be our chambermaid."

After a short while they met a weasel,* who asked them, "Where are
you going, Mr. Rooster, Mrs. Hen, and Mrs. Cat?"

---

* Luca, padottola.

32

"We're going to Rome," the Rooster answered. "I want to be the Pope there."

"Will you take me along?"

"Wait until I check my letter," said the Rooster, and after he had looked at it, he continued, "All right. Come along."

So the animals continued traveling on their way to Rome. When it became dark, they came to a little cottage inhabited by a witch, but she had just gone out. So the animals chose a place according to their pleasure. The weasel laid down in the closet, the cat on the warm ashes in the hearth, while the rooster and the hen flew on top of the beams above the door. When the witch came home, she wanted to fetch a candle from the closet, but the weasel hit her in the face with his tail. She wanted to light the candle and went to the fireplace, but she mistook the shining eyes of the cat for glowing coals and tried to light the candle with them. As she stuck the candle into the eyes of the cat, the cat sprang at her face and scratched her terribly. When the rooster heard all the noise, he began to crow very loudly. All at once the witch realized that they were not ghosts but simple animals. So she took a club and chased all four of them out of the house.

The cat and the weasel no longer had any desire to continue the journey, but the Rooster and the Hen continued on their way. When they finally reached Rome, they went into an open church, and the Rooster said to the sacristan, "Let all the bells ring. I'm here to become the Pope."

"All right," said the sacristan. "We can do this. Just come with me."

Then he led Mr. Rooster and Mrs. Hen into the sacristy, where he closed the door and grabbed hold of them. Once he had them in his hands, he twisted their necks and put them into a cooking pot. Then he invited his friends to dinner, and they ate Mr. Rooster and Mrs. Hen with great relish.

9

THE BRAVE PRINCE

Once upon a time there was a king and queen who did not have any children, and they would have very much liked to have had either a son or a daughter. So the king summoned an astrologer, who was to tell him the truth about whether his wife would ever give birth to a child. The astrologer answered: "The queen will give birth to a son, but when he grows up, he will cut your throat."

The king was terrified and ordered a high tower without windows to be built in a desolate region. When the queen gave birth to a son, the king had the baby locked in the tower with a nurse. Now the child lived in the tower and grew by leaps and bounds and became stronger and handsomer with each day. He only knew his nurse and thought that she was his mother.

One day he happened to be eating a piece of goat and found a sharp bone in it. He saved the bone, and later, just for fun, he began to scratch open the wall. Indeed, he was enjoying himself so much that he continued doing this until he had made a small hole through which the sun cast its rays into his room. Astounded by this, he dug further with the bone until the hole was so large that he could stick his head outside. When he now saw the beautiful field with thousands of flowers, the blue sky, and the wide sea, he called his nurse and asked her what all of this was. She told him about the large countries and the marvelous cities that existed, and he felt an irresistible urge to set out into the world and to see all these marvelous things.

"Dear mother," he said, "I can't stand to be in this dark tower anymore. Let's go out and see the world."

"Oh, my son," the nurse said. "Why do you want to go off into the world? We have it good here. I think it's best if we stay where we are."

However, since he begged so fervently and asked her to go with him, and since she loved him so much and could refuse him nothing, she finally relented, tied her things together in a bundle, and set out into the wide world with him.

After they had traveled for a long time, they came to a desolate spot and could not find anything to eat. Just as they were on the brink of starvation, they saw a beautiful castle in the distance and headed straight toward it in order to ask for some food. When they approached the castle, however, they could not see a human being anywhere. They climbed the stairs and walked through all the rooms, but no one was there. However, in one of the rooms there was a table covered with delicious food.

"Mother," the prince said, "there's nobody here. Let's sit down and eat."

So they sat down and ate some of the food. Then they got up and walked through the rooms again looking at all the rich things they contained. All of a sudden the nurse saw a band of robbers approaching.

"Oh, my son," she cried, "they're certainly the men who own this castle. If they find us here, they'll definitely beat us to death."

The prince quickly put on a full armor, took the best sword from the wall, chose the best horse from the stable, and waited for the arrival of the robbers. When they came closer, he began to fight, and since he was so strong, he soon killed every one of them except for their chief.

"Let me live," he cried out to the prince. "If you do, I'll marry your mother, and you'll be my dear son."

So the prince let the chief of the robbers live. The robber chief married the nurse, but he could not forget that the prince had killed all his companions. Since he was afraid of the young man's enormous strength, however, he thought of a scheme that might bring about the prince's downfall. He called his wife and said, "Your son repulses me, and I want to get him out of my sight. Pretend to be sick and tell him you can only be cured if he brings you some lemons. Then I'll send him into a certain garden, and you can be sure he'll never return."

The nurse wept bitter tears and said, "How could I possibly cause my son's death? Let him live. He's done nothing."

But her husband threatened her: "If you don't do this, I'll chop off your head and your son's head."

So she had to obey him and pretended to be sick.

"Dear mother, what's the matter with you?" the prince said. "Tell me what you desire and I'll surely get it for you."

"Oh, my dear son," she answered, "if only I had a few lemons, I'd certainly get well."

"I'll fetch them for you, dear mother!" the young man declared. "Do you know where I can find them?"

"You must go to a certain garden," she replied and told him it was far away in a desolate region and guarded by wild animals.

So the prince set off on his journey. When he came to this region, the animals attacked him and sought to tear him to shreds, but he drew his sword and killed all of them. Then he calmly picked some lemons and returned home in good spirits. When this stepfather saw him approaching, he was terrified and asked him what had happened.

"Oh," the young man answered, "there was a bunch of wild animals in the garden, but I managed to kill them all."

The robber chief was even more frightened and found it even more difficult to tolerate the prince's presence, so he said once more to his wife, "Your son repulses me, and I want him out of my sight. Pretend to be sick and ask him to fetch you some oranges."

"No, no," the nurse spoke. "I'm not going to do this again. Let the poor young man live."

Her husband threatened her until she finally had to obey him, and she pretended to be sick.

"Dear mother, are you sick again?" the prince asked. "I'm sure you want something. Just tell me what it is, and I'll fetch it for you."

"Oh, my son," she answered, "if I only had some oranges to quell my burning thirst!"

"Is that all," he cried, "I'll fetch them for you in no time."

So the stepfather sent him to another garden, which was full of even more wild animals that tried to plunge on top of him and tear him apart. But he drew his sword and killed them all. Then he picked some of the most beautiful oranges and brought them to his mother.

The robber chief was now frightened beyond belief when he saw the prince, who told him how he had killed all the wild animals. Indeed, the robber's fear and hatred grew, and he kept thinking of a way to get rid of him. So he ordered his wife to pretend to be sick again, and she was to tell the prince that nothing could help her get well except for a little bottle of sweat from the sorceress Parcemina. The nurse wept and did not want to do this at all, but her husband threatened her, and she had to obey. So she pretended to be sick, and when the prince came to her, she sighed, "Oh, how sick I am, how sick I am!"

"Mother," the young man said, "isn't there anything that will help you get well? Just tell me. Then I'll travel through the entire world and look for it."

"Oh, my son," the nurse answered, "there is a way. If I had a little bottle of the sweat of the sorceress Parcemina, I would soon recover."

"Mother," he cried, "I'm going to set out and find the way, and if it can be found somewhere in the world, I'll bring it to you."

So he set out, and since he did not know the way, he wandered aimlessly here and there for many days until he came to a dark forest. As soon as he entered it, he became lost, and by evening he could no longer find his way out. All of a sudden he noticed a light in the distance, and as he approached it, he saw a small hut inhabited by a hermit. He knocked at the door and a haggard old man asked him what he desired.

"Oh, father," he answered, "I've lost my way and would like to spend the night here."

"Oh, my son," the old man replied, "what's brought you to this wild region at this time of night?"

"My mother is sick," he said, "and the only thing that can help her get well is a small bottle of the sorceress Parcemina's sweat. That's why I've set out to fetch it."

"Oh, my son," the old man responded, "give up your foolish undertaking. Many princes have tried to obtain the bottle, but none have come back."

But the prince would not let himself be dissuaded, and when dawn arrived, he wanted to continue his quest. The hermit gave him a chestnut and a little bottle and said to him, "I can't advise and help you, but my older brother lives a day's journey farther in the forest. Keep this chestnut in a safe place. It might be of use to you one day. If you succeed in finding the sweat, I'd also like you to bring me a small bottle filled with it."

Then the old man gave him his blessing and let him go. After the prince had traveled an entire day, he noticed light in the distance, and when he approached it, he saw the hut inhabited by the second hermit. He knocked on the door, and the hermit opened it for him. He was even older than his brother. Then the prince told him why he was wandering about the dark forest, and the hermit tried to dissuade him as much as he could from pursuing his quest, but it was all in vain. The next morning the hermit said, "I can't help you, but my brother, who's even much older than I am, lives a day's journey from here deeper in the forest. Perhaps he'll be able to help you. Take this chestnut and put it in a safe place. It will be of use to you one day. If you succeed in obtaining the sorceress Parcemina's sweat, I'd like you to bring me a little bottle full of it."

Upon saying this, the hermit gave him a chestnut, a little bottle, and his blessing, and he let him go. Late that next evening the prince came once again to a hermit who was much older than his brothers and had a long white beard. When this hermit heard about the young man's quest, he also tried to dissuade the prince from continuing his journey, but it was all in vain. The prince did not want to return home without the sweat of the sorceress Parcemina. The next morning, when the hermit let him depart, he gave him a chestnut and a little bottle and showed him the way to his fourth brother who lived a day's journey farther into the forest.

Once more the prince wandered an entire day deeper into the forest, and when it turned dark, he came to the fourth brother. This man did not even live in a hut, but rather in a basket that hung between the branches of a tall tree. He was so ancient that his white beard hung out of the basket and almost reached the ground. He asked the prince what he desired, and the young man told him why he was traveling in the dismal forest.

"Camp out beneath the tree," the hermit said. "Early tomorrow morning I'll tell you what you have to do."

The next morning the hermit woke the prince and said to him: "If you absolutely want to seek your fortune, then go with God. Do you see that steep mountain over there? You must climb it. On top there's a garden with a fountain, and behind it a beautiful castle, whose doors are closed. The keys are lying on the edge of the fountain. Fetch them and open the doors quietly, climb the steps, and walk through all the doors, but make sure that you don't touch a single one of the treasures that are lying about. In the last room you'll find a marvelously beautiful woman lying asleep on the bed. This is the sorceress Parcemina, and the sweat flows down her cheeks. Kneel down next to her, collect the sweat with a sponge, and squeeze the sweat into the bottles. As soon as they are full, flee as fast as you can. Be careful and nimble, and may God be with you."

Upon saying this he blessed him, and the prince set out toward the steep mountain. The higher he climbed, the steeper the mountain became, but he thought about his mother and bravely continued climbing. Finally he reached the top and found everything just as the hermit had predicted. He quickly took the keys from the edge of the fountain, opened the door, climbed the stairs, and walked through the rooms. In the last chamber he found the sorceress Parcemina, who lay on a bed and slept, and the sweat flowed in streams down her face. He kneeled down, took a little sponge, collected the sweat with it, and squeezed it into the little bottles. As soon as they were full, he fled as fast as he could. When he closed the door to the castle, the sorceress Parcemina awoke and began to shriek to wake the other sorceresses. Although they all awoke, they could do nothing against the prince because he had jumped down the mountain with great leaps and bounds. As soon as he entered the forest, he went to the eldest hermit and thanked him for his help.

"Listen, my son," the wise man said, "you're about to return home to your parents, and I'm going to give you this donkey and this sack so you can travel faster. When you see your stepfather, he will burst into a great rage because you succeeded in your quest. Then he'll grab hold of you. Let him do this, and just ask him to put you into the sack after he kills you and to load you on top of the donkey."

So the prince mounted the donkey and rode home. Along the way he stopped at the huts of the other hermits and gave them each a small bottle of the sweat. When he eventually came near his house, he saw his stepfather coming toward him from a distance, and the vicious robber was filled with deadly anger. As he approached the prince, he threatened him and began reproaching him for being so late.

"Father," the prince said, "I realize you can't stand me and want to let out your anger on me. Well, do whatever you want with me, but I have one request. When I'm dead, put me into this sack and tie me tightly onto this donkey so that he can carry me out into the wide world."

Then he surrendered without a fight, and his stepfather kicked and trampled him in his rage until he finally cut off his head and hacked his body into small pieces. When he had satisfied his fury, he thought he might as well fulfill the last wish of the poor prince. So he put all the pieces into the sack and tied it onto the donkey. No sooner did the donkey feel the load he was to carry than he raced straight away with it and ran without stopping until he came to the old hermit who had given the donkey to the prince. The hermit took the pieces from the sack, laid them carefully together, and brought the young man back to life. Then he said to him: "Listen, my son, you cannot return to your parents. At any rate, they're really not your parents, for you are the son of a king, and your father is still ruling in a certain realm. So go there and return to your real parents."

The prince set out and wandered until he came to his father's realm. But before he entered the city, he exchanged his armor for some tattered clothes and wrapped his head in some cloth. Then he said to the people, "I've got some nasty scabs," and they started calling him "scabhead."*

When he finally entered the city he saw that all the houses were ceremoniously decorated, and many people were gathering before the royal castle. He asked a man on the street what was happening.

---

* Tignusu.

"Today is a great holiday," he answered. "In one hour the king will drop a white scarf from the top of the tower, and whoever it falls on will get to marry the king's daughter."

This was the first time that the prince learned that he had a sister, but he did not let anyone notice his surprise. "Well," he remarked, "I want to go there and see if the scarf might fall upon me."

The people laughed at him and cried, "No, no! Just look, scabhead wants to marry the beautiful princess!"

But he did not pay any attention to them. Instead he mixed among the people, and just then, as the king threw the scarf from the top of the tower, it floated down and landed on the dirty scabhead. He was brought before the king, and even though the princess was weeping, she had to take him as her husband. The wedding was to be celebrated that evening. However, the prince went to the priest and said, "Father, you're supposed to wed me tonight to the princess, but I don't want you to say the customary words that will unite us. I must tell you in all due confidence that she's my sister. Don't marry us because it's not time yet to reveal who I really am."

In the evening the wedding was celebrated, but the prince remained in his tattered dirty clothes and did not want to wash or put on clean clothes. When the young married couple was led into the bedroom, he bellowed: "Do you expect me to sleep on a bed like that!? Throw a mattress on the floor over there."

So they did that, and he slept on a corner of the mattress.

Now it so happened one day that a war erupted, and the enemy forces had gathered outside the gates of the city. A great battle was to take place, and the old king was compelled to go to war. That same day the princess went to Scabhead and said, "My mother and I want to view the battle from the walls of the city. Do you want to come?"

"Leave me in peace," he roared. "I really don't care who wins the battle."

But no sooner did they leave him than the prince opened one of the chestnuts given to him by one of the hermits and found a complete suit of armor, the most beautiful in the world, and a horse more royal than any king had ever possessed. Then the prince washed himself, put on the armor, and stormed into the battle where the king's troops had begun to yield. His presence filled the knights with renewed courage, and the enemy was defeated. When the king called for the unknown knight to honor him and thank him for his help, the stranger had disappeared. The prince sat in his corner again and was wearing his dirty tattered clothes.

The next day the enemy forces came with reinforcements, and the king had to enter the battle again. The princess went to the city walls with her mother, and no sooner did they leave than the prince opened his second chestnut and found armor and a horse even more magnificent than the one of the previous day. Now he charged into the battle again, and his presence decided the outcome of the battle once more in favor of the king. After the battle he vanished without a trace, just as he had done on the first day, but he had been wounded in the leg by a lance. That evening the princess noticed that Scabhead had a bandage around his leg and asked him was wrong.

"Nothing," he answered, "I bumped into something."

But she told her parents the next day and said, "Don't you think that he may be the unknown knight who has been so loyal to us?"

However, the king and queen made fun of her. Meanwhile, the king had to do battle with his enemy for a third day. When the prince was left alone, he quickly opened the third chestnut and found armor and a horse that were the most magnificent of all. When he appeared in the midst of the battle, the fortunes of the king shifted, and he defeated the enemy forces so badly that they did not return. Once again the unknown knight disappeared just as quickly as he had on the first day.

That evening there was a great feast in the court to celebrate the glorious victories, and the princess adorned herself for the special event and said to Scabhead, "Here are some royal clothes for you. Don't you want to get dressed up and attend the event?"

"Leave me in peace," he roared. "What should I do at your feasts and celebrations?"

No sooner did she leave, however, than he put on the royal clothes and entered the large hall that was illuminated by candles, and since he was such a handsome young man, everyone stared at him in astonishment. Then he stepped before the king and said, "I'm the dirty scabhead. I'm also the unknown knight who appeared three times in the battle."

The king embraced him and thanked him, but then the prince said, "I'm also your son, my dear father."

The king became terrified and said, "How could you have committed such a sin and have married your sister?"

"Calm down, dear father," the prince replied. "I never married my sister. The priest can testify to this."

Indeed, when the priest spoke and revealed the truth, there was great joy, and the king and queen were very happy to have their handsome son with them. Then they lived happily and content, and we can't even pay the rent.

10

THE INNKEEPER'S BEAUTIFUL DAUGHTER

Once upon a time there was a woman who ran an inn where travelers spent the night. She had a daughter who was extraordinarily beautiful, but because she was so beautiful, her mother could not stand her. Therefore, she kept her daughter locked up in a room so that no one could ever catch sight of her. Only one maid knew about her, and she was the one who brought her food every day.

Now one day the king happened to come by and wanted to stay over night at the inn. Just as he arrived, the maid was taking some food to the daughter. Because the maid was called to come quickly and prepare the king's room, she forgot to close the door to the daughter's room. When the innkeeper's daughter noticed this, she became curious and wanted to see the king just once. So she stuck her head through the doorway, and when the king came down the hall, she quickly pulled back her head. However, he had seen her and was completely dazzled by her beauty.

"Where is that beautiful girl whom I saw in the hallway?" he asked the maid who was serving him.

"Oh, your majesty," she replied, "that's the daughter of the innkeeper. She's just as good as she is beautiful, but her mother keeps her locked up so that no one has ever caught a glimpse of her."

The king was so delighted by her great beauty that he wanted to make the innkeeper's daughter his wife, but because he could not ask the mother right then and there for her daughter's hand in marriage, he called the maid and said, "I've decided to spend several days here.

42

I want you to speak to the daughter and see if she is willing to become my wife."

So the maid went to the innkeeper's daughter and said, "Just think, my little mistress, the king wants to marry you, and wants to know whether you will flee with him from this house, which only causes you misery."

"Oh," the poor girl answered. "How can I flee? My mother keeps such a close watch over me!"

"You let me worry about that," the good maid responded. Then she went to the king and said, "I know of only one way for you to succeed. Tomorrow you must depart as if you were returning home. Instead, stop at some spot nearby. At the same time, the daughter must pretend to be sick. Then I'll say to the innkeeper that her daughter's sickness is caused by her being locked up all the time, and she should let me take her for a walk outside. I'll bring her to you, but you must take me with you because I won't be able to return to the inn without her."

The king promised to do this, and the next morning he pretended to leave for home, but he only went a short distance and stopped at another inn in disguise so that he would not be recognized as king. Meanwhile, the daughter feigned an illness and said she could not eat anything and became thinner and thinner.

"What's wrong with my daughter? What's causing this sickness?" the innkeeper asked the maid.

"The poor child has no choice and will always get sick," the maid answered, "because she's always cooped up and never has any fresh air. Let me take her to mass tomorrow morning. If she goes for a short walk, I'm sure she'll get well again."

The innkeeper agreed, and the next morning the maid took her to mass. No sooner were they out of the mother's sight than they rushed to the king, who had a coach ready for them. He lifted the beautiful maiden into the coach and drove away. As for the loyal maid, he gave her so much money that she could move to another country with her entire family.

Now the king arrived at his castle and introduced the innkeeper's daughter to his mother.

"This is my dear bride," he said. "And now we want to celebrate a splendid wedding."

The maiden was so beautiful that the old queen took an immediate liking to her. There was a glorious wedding feast, and the king and his young wife lived happily and content together.

After a year had passed a war erupted, and the king had to depart for the battlefield. So he said to the old queen, "Dear mother, I must go off to war. I'm placing my precious wife in your hands. When she gives birth to our child, I want you to let me know about this right away, and I want you to take good care of her."

Upon saying this, he embraced his mother and his wife and set out.

Soon thereafter the young queen have birth to a baby boy, and the old queen took good care of her and sent the king a letter right away to inform him about the birth of his son. However, the messenger, who was to take the letter to the king, stopped to rest at the inn owned by the young queen's mother. He ordered some food, and while he was eating, the innkeeper asked him where he was coming from and where he was going. Then he told her that he was being sent to take the king good news about the birth of his son. When the innkeeper heard this, she decided to get revenge on her daughter because she had fled the inn. When the messenger laid down to sleep a while, she carefully pulled the letter from his pocket and stuck another one inside that said the young queen had been terribly unfaithful to him and deserved the most severe punishment. It was this letter that the messenger took to the king.

When the king read the letter, he became enormously sad because he loved his wife so much, but he wrote his mother that she should continue to take care of his wife and do nothing until he returned. The messenger took this letter and departed. When he passed by the inn, however, he stopped to eat something. The innkeeper asked him whether the king had sent back a reply.

"Yes, indeed," the messenger said. "The letter's in my pocket."

When the messenger took a nap after the meal, the innkeeper carefully drew the letter from his pocket and placed another one inside. This letter said that the old queen was to chop off the hands of the young queen, and afterward tie the child to the stumps of her arms and send her out into the wide world.

When the old queen received this letter, she began to weep bitter tears because she loved her daughter-in-law very much. But the young queen spoke to her with humility.

"I'll do whatever my husband and master commands."

So her hands were chopped off, and the child was tied to her arms so that she could suckle it. Then she embraced the old queen and wandered off far away into a dark forest. After she had roamed for a long time, she came to a little brook, and since she was so tired, she sat down beside it. "Oh," she thought, "if I at least had my hands, I wouldn't be so helpless. I could wash my baby's diapers and give him some clean clothes. If things continue this way, my innocent child will probably die very soon."

While she was speaking to herself and weeping, a venerable old man suddenly stood before her and asked her why she was crying. She explained to him why she was suffering so much grief and told him she was truly innocent and yet was being punished for something that she had not done.

"Don't cry," the old man said, "and come with me. Everything will go better for you."

He led her a little farther into the forest where he hit the ground with a cane. All of a sudden a castle appeared, and it was much more beautiful than the royal castle in which she had been living. There was also a garden that was better than the king's. Indeed, the old man was none other than Saint Joseph, and he had come to help the poor innocent queen.

Now the queen lived with Saint Joseph and her son in the beautiful castle, and since she was so virtuous, Saint Joseph caused her hands to grow back. Meanwhile, the child became tall and strong and more and more handsome with each day that passed. But let's leave the queen and her son for the time being, and see what's been happening with the king.

When the war was over he returned to his castle in great sadness, for his wife's unfaithfulness broke his heart in two.

"What did you do with my wife?" he asked his mother.

"Oh, you terrible man!" the old queen burst into tears and said, "How could you demand that your innocent wife be put through such terrible grief?"

"What" he cried. "Didn't you write to me that she was unfaithful and guilty of a terrible crime?"

"That's not what I wrote!" the queen replied. "I sent you the good news about the birth of your son, and you answered me that I should have her hands chopped off and sent into the wide world with her child."

"I never wrote that!" the king exclaimed.

They fetched the letters, and both insisted that they had not written them.

"Oh, my poor, innocent girl," the old queen moaned. "I'm sure that you are dead by now!"

There was great mourning in the castle, and the king became so melancholy that he was soon overcome by a serious illness. Eventually he recovered, but he continued to remain very sad. Then, one day, the old queen said to him, "My son, the weather is so beautiful. Don't you want to go hunting a little? Perhaps it will take your mind off things."

So the king mounted his horse and set out sadly into the forest without hunting, and because he was so sad, he did not pay attention to where he was going and lost his way in the dense forest. His entourage did not dare speak to him. When it was almost dark, the king wanted to turn around, but nobody knew the right way out of the forest, and so they rode deeper into the woods. Finally they saw a light burning in the distance and headed straight for it. Eventually they came to the beautiful castle in which the young queen was living. When they knocked on the door, Saint Joseph opened it and asked them what they wanted.

"Oh, good old man," the king answered, "could you please give us shelter for the night? We're lost and can't find our way back home."

Saint Joseph asked them to enter, gave them something to eat and drink, and showed them to some good beds. However, the queen and her child did not let themselves be seen.

The next morning, while the king was having breakfast, Saint Joseph went to the queen and said, "The king has spent the night here. Now the moment has come when all your sufferings will end."

So the queen dressed her son in nice clean clothes, and Saint Joseph told him to go to the king, kiss his hands, and say, "Good morning, papa, I'd also like to have breakfast with you."

When the king glanced at the handsome child, he was very moved and did not know why. Then the door opened, and the young queen entered with Saint Joseph and curtsied before him. The king recognized his dear wife right away and hugged her tightly in his arms, and he also embraced his son. Then Saint Joseph approached them and said, "All your sufferings are now at an end. Live happily and content, and if you have a wish, just call, for I am Saint Joseph."

Upon saying this, he blessed them and disappeared. At the same time, the castle vanished as well, and the king and the queen with her son and the entourage stood in the forest. In front of them, however, they saw the way that led out of the forest and to the king's castle. Soon they returned to the old queen, who was most grateful to see her dear daughter-in-law and her little grandson again. Then they lived happy and content, and we can't even pay the rent.

11

THE BEAUTIFUL MAIDEN
WITH THE SEVEN VEILS

O nce upon a time there was a king and queen who did not have any children, and yet they would have liked to have some very much. So the queen turned to Madonna del Carmine and prayed: "Oh holy Mother of God, if you grant me a child, I swear to you that I shall have a fountain built in the castle courtyard in his fourteenth year, and oil will flow from this fountain for an entire year."

Not long after this the queen became pregnant, and when her time came, she gave birth to a magnificently handsome boy who grew bigger and became even handsomer and stronger with each passing day. When he turned fourteen, his parents remembered their oath and had a fountain constructed in their courtyard. Once it was finished, oil began to flow from it. The prince liked to stand at the window and observe the people who came from far and wide in order to fetch some oil.

Now the year had passed, and the fountain had barely any oil left. An old woman heard about this and thought: "If I had only heard about this fountain sooner. Who knows if there is really any oil left flowing?" So she took a small pitcher and a sponge and set out toward the fountain. It had already stopped flowing, but there was some oil lying in the basin. The old woman took the sponge, soaked up the oil, and squeezed it out into the pitcher. She continued to do this until the pitcher was full. The prince stood on the balcony and observed everything, and in his arrogance he took a stone and threw it at the little pitcher so that it broke and the oil spilled out. The old woman became enraged and cursed him with a spell: "May you never marry until you've found the beautiful maiden with the seven veils."

From that day on the prince was melancholy and could think of nothing but the beautiful maiden with the seven veils. Then one day he went to his parents and said, "Dear father and mother, please give me your holy blessing, for I want to set out into the wide world and seek my fortune."

"Oh, my son," his mother cried, "what fortune do you want to seek? You have everything that you can possibly wish for. Stay with us, my son. You're our only child, and you were given to us only after we made a great oath."

But the prince could not be persuaded to change his mind and said, "Dear mother, if you refuse to give me your blessing, I shall have to depart without it. I can no longer remain here."

His parents heard these words clearly, and thus they granted him permission to depart and gave him their blessing. He took some money, mounted a beautiful horse, and rode away. He journeyed for a long time, straight ahead, for he was not certain where he might find the maiden with the seven veils. Finally, after many days, he came one evening to the edge of a large forest. At the edge of the forest stood a pretty cottage that housed a peasant, his wife, and children.

"I want to spend the night here," thought the prince, "and tomorrow I'll enter the forest." So he knocked on the door and asked for shelter, and the peasant and his wife kindly took him in. The next morning he thanked them, said farewell, and began riding to the forest. Just then the peasant's wife called after him: "Where are you riding, my handsome young man? Don't you dare enter the dark forest, for you don't know what dangers await you. There are terrible giants and wild animals in this forest, and they guard the beautiful maiden with the seven veils. You'll never be able to get through."

But the prince responded, "If this way leads to the maiden with the seven veils, then I am on the right path and must take it."

"I'm warning you," the peasant woman said. "You don't know how many princes and kings have entered this forest, and none of them have ever returned."

The prince would not let himself be persuaded to abandon his mission. This is why the woman finally said, "If you insist on trying your luck, then listen to some good advice. There's a pious hermit who lives deep in the forest about a day's journey from here. Go straight to him this evening and seek his counsel."

The prince thanked the good woman for her advice and rode into the forest, deeper and deeper, until he arrived at the hermit's cottage at dusk. When he knocked, a low voice asked, "Who are you?"

"I'm a poor wanderer who's looking for shelter," the prince answered.

"Keep out in the name of God," the hermit said and crossed himself.

"No, don't keep me out," the young man said. "I have been baptized."

Then the hermit opened the door, let the prince enter, and asked him where he was coming from and where he was going. When he heard, however, that the prince was searching for the beautiful maiden with the seven veils, he said, "Oh my son, let me warn you to return to your home right away. You'll be devastated if you continue your journey."

But the prince refused to listen to the hermit's warning, and the old man finally said, "I can't help you, but I'll give you some good advice. If you see a door that flaps open and shut, then bolt it down. Now go and rest. Tomorrow I'll show you the way to my brother who lives deeper in the forest about a day's journey from here. He can certainly help you. I can give you half of my bread to eat and some water. Each morning an angel comes from heaven to give me a pitcher of water and some pieces of bread that nourish me."

Then they shared the bread and water, and at daybreak the young man set out on his way. As it began to turn dark, he saw some light in the distance. When he approached it, he glimpsed the cottage of the second hermit, who kindly gave him shelter like his brother. He asked the prince what he was doing in such a wild region. After the prince told him everything, the hermit also tried to convince him to turn back, but the young man remained steadfast, and the hermit finally said, "My brother has given you some good advice, and now I'll tell you something more. When you see an ass and a lion, and the lion is holding the ass's hay in his mouth, and the ass has the bones that belong to the lion, then you are to go bravely to them and help them by giving each of them what rightly belongs him: the ass the hay, and the lion the bones. Now get some rest. Tomorrow I'll show you the way to my oldest brother who lives deeper in the forest about a day's journey from here."

The next morning the prince set out on his way, and at dusk he arrived at the third hermit's cottage. He was so old that his beard touched the ground. The hermit kindly gave him shelter and asked him what he desired. After the prince had told him everything, the hermit said, "Good. Now get some rest. Tomorrow I shall tell you what to do."

The next morning the hermit said to the prince, "Listen carefully to each and every word I tell you, for if you forget anything, you'll be lost. There are three things that you must take with you: some bread, a pack of brooms, and a bundle of feather dusters* to fan the fire. If you continue along this path, you'll first meet an ass and a lion. The ass will be holding the lion's bones in its mouth, and the lion the hay of the ass, and they will be arguing. Follow the advice of my second brother, and they will let you pass. Then you'll come across some giants who'll be hitting an anvil with enormous iron clubs. Wait until all of them lift their clubs at one time so that they cannot see you, and then run under the clubs as fast as you can. Next you will see a date tree standing along the way, and it will be bearing tiny meager fruit. Pick some of the dates, but don't throw them away. Instead you are to eat them and to praise the tree. After you have passed the date tree, you'll finally arrive at a large palace. This is where the horrible ogress lives who guards the three beautiful ladies with the seven veils. You must make your way into the palace, but there is a door that flaps open and shut, and it will prevent you from entering. Don't forget the advice of my first brother, and you'll be able to enter. Now some ferocious lions will rush toward you to eat you, but if you throw them some bread, they won't do a thing to you. Go up the palace stairs, and you will see the ogress's servants charging toward you. They'll be carrying large sticks because they don't have any brooms and they clean the floor only with sticks. Show them the brooms that you have and how to clean the floor with the brooms. Then they will no longer stop you. Once you are upstairs, the ogress's cooks will approach you. Give them each a feather duster, and they will let you pass because they don't have any. Finally you'll reach the ogress who will be sitting on a large throne. There will be three small caskets next to her elbows, and in each one of the caskets there is a beautiful maiden with seven veils. Give the ogress this letter, which she will read and then say to you that you must wait while she writes the answer in another room. She'll be going into that room, however, to sharpen her teeth so she can eat you. Therefore, don't wait for her. Instead, quickly grab one of the caskets and flee. It doesn't matter which casket you take, but don't take more than one. All the guards will calmly let you pass, but you must mount your horse and ride as fast as you can so that the ogress does not overtake you. Make sure that you do not open the casket until you have left the forest and are near a fountain because when you open the casket, the beautiful maiden will cry out: "Water!"

---

* Muscalori.

and if you do not have water right there for her, she will die. If you follow each and every one of my words exactly, perhaps you'll be fortunate and return here."

Upon saying this, the hermit blessed the prince and let him depart. The young man continued riding until he saw the lion and the ass arguing, just as the hermit had said they would be. So he went toward them and gave them what belonged to them. The angry beasts settled down and let him pass. When he rode further, he heard a terrible racket in the distance. It was caused by the giants who hit the anvil with their heavy iron clubs. So he waited until they all raised their clubs at the same time and then drove his horse beneath them so fast that they did not even notice him. After he had the good fortune of escaping the giants, he saw a date tree along the way that was full of fruit. He picked some dates, and even though they were small and puny, he ate them and said, "How sweet these dates are!" As he rode along, he came to the palace in which the ogress was living. The door was flapping back and forth, so he got off his horse and bolted the door with a strong hand, and then hacked through it. No sooner did he enter the palace than the raging lions rushed toward him and wanted to eat him, but he threw them some bread and they let him pass. Just as he began climbing up the stairs, the ogress's servants approached him. They were carrying large sticks and cleaning the stairs. When they caught sight of him, they wanted to beat him to death, but he took one of the brooms and called out, "Look, you should all have this kind of a broom. Then you wouldn't need so much time to clean all the steps." He began to sweep the stairs, and the servants were so happy about this that they took the brooms and divided them among themselves and no longer paid attention to the prince who continued along his way. He did not go very far, however, when the ogress's cooks came toward him. They did not have any feather dusters, and so they always had to fan the fire with their breath. When he gave them his dusters and showed them how to use them, they were very happy and let him pass without any trouble. Finally he came to a great hall where the ogress was sitting on a large throne and looked terrifying. Near her elbows were three little caskets. After the young man bowed, he gave her the letter, which she read.

"Wait here a moment, my handsome lad," the ogress said. "I'm going to write the answer."

But the prince knew that she was really going to sharpen her teeth, so he quickly grabbed one of the caskets and fled. He was fortunate to pass the cooks, the servants, the lions, and the door. Then he mounted his horse and rode away like the wind. Here, too, the date tree, the giants, the lion and the ass let him pass.

When the ogress came out of her room and saw that the prince had disappeared, she quickly counted the caskets and found that one was missing. "I've been betrayed! Betrayed!" she screamed and began running after the prince.

"Why did you let him pass?" she yelled at the cooks.

"We've served you so many years," they replied, "and you never gave us dusters to make our work easier. This young man was kind to us, and that's why we let him through."

Then she ran to her servants and said, "Why didn't you beat him to death with your sticks?"

"We've served you so many years," they answered, "and you never gave us a broom to make our work easier. This young man helped us, so why should we have beaten him to death?"

"Lions, why didn't you eat him?" the ogress screamed at the beasts.

"If you don't be quiet, we'll eat you. When did you ever give us bread like the handsome young man did?"

"Why didn't you stop him?" the ogress spoke to the door.

"I've locked your house for so many years," the door answered. "but it never occurred to you to bolt me down when I flapped back and forth."

"Oh, date tree," the ogress cried, "why didn't you stop him?"

"You've passed by me every day for so many years," the date tree replied, "and you've never taken a date and eaten it. But the handsome young man did this and praised my fruit."

Then the ogress ran to the giants and scolded them for not having killed the prince with their clubs. But they answered, "Why have you forced us to beat the anvil the entire day? When we raise our clubs, we can't see anyone who's passing by."

The ogress continued running and also scolded the lion and the ass for not having eaten the prince. "Be quiet," the lion responded. "Otherwise I'll eat you. You've passed by us for so many years, and you never thought to give either one of us the food that belongs to us, but the young prince did that."

So the ogress had to turn around and go back to her palace because nobody wanted to help her pursue the prince. In the meantime, the prince rushed through the forest with the casket, and as he passed the three hermits and the peasants, he thanked them all for their help. When he came out of the forest, he thought about opening the little casket. So he rode further until he came to a fountain. There he dismounted the horse and opened the casket.

"Water!" a voice cried out, and as soon as the prince poured some water into the casket, a magnificently beautiful maiden arose. She was so beautiful that her beauty shone through the seven veils that she was wearing, and she was wearing nothing but the seven veils. Then the prince said to the beautiful maiden with the seven veils, "Climb this tree and hide yourself in the thick branches. Just stay there while I rush home and get you some clothes to wear."

"Yes," she replied, "but don't let your mother kiss you. Otherwise you'll forget me and will only remember me after one year, one month, and one day.

The prince promised to do what she asked and rode home. When his parents saw him and approached him, he called out, "Dear mother, please don't kiss me, Otherwise, I'll forget all about my dear bride."

Since it was already evening, he thought he would spend the night with his parents and return to the beautiful maiden in the morning. He laid down to sleep, and while he was sleeping, his mother went into his room to look at him once more, and since she had such a great yearning to kiss him, she bent over him and kissed him. Consequently, he forgot his bride and stayed with his parents. Meanwhile, the beautiful maiden waited for him, and when he did not come, she became very sad and thought, "He must have certainly let his mother kiss him, and now he's forgotten me. Well, I'll just sit here in this tree for one year, one month, and one day, and wait for him."

After a year had passed, an ugly black slave happened to pass by the fountain one day in order to fetch some water. When she looked at the water, she saw the reflection of the beautiful maiden with the seven veils and thought it was her own. "Am I really that beautiful?" she cried. "If this is me, why should I have to go to the fountain with this pitcher?"* Well, she broke the pitcher and went home. When she returned to her mistress and was not carrying any water, her mistress scolded her and asked her where she had left the pitcher.

"I've seen my reflection in the water," the slave answered, "and since I am so beautiful, I'll no longer go to the fountain to fetch water."

Her mistress laughed at her and sent her immediately back to the fountain, this time with a copper pitcher. The slave looked into the water once again, and when she saw the beautiful reflection, she raised her eyes in astonishment and saw the beautiful maiden with the seven veils in the tree.

"Beautiful lady," she called, "what are you doing up there?"

---

* Sugnu tantu bedda, e vaju all' aqua cu a quartaredda?

"I'm waiting for my beloved," the beautiful maiden replied. "He is a handsome prince, and he will come to me in one month and one day to make me his wife."

"I'd like to comb your hair a bit," the slave said. So she climbed the tree and began combing the maiden's hair. She had a long needle with a black button, and she suddenly stuck the needle into maiden's head, but the beautiful maiden did not die. Instead, she turned into a white dove and flew away. Now the ugly black slave sat in the tree and waited for the prince, who was still with his parents and no longer thinking about his beautiful abandoned bride.

In the castle where the prince was now living, there was an ancient chambermaid who was so old that she could no longer speak correctly, and every time she spoke, the prince laughed at her. One day, when he laughed at her and was peeling an orange at the same time, he cut his finger, and a drop of blood fell on the white marble floor. The old woman cried out: "May you never marry unless you find a bride who is as white as the marble floor and as red as blood."

At this very same moment, a year, a month, and a day had passed and the prince called out, "Why do I have to look any longer? I already have a beautiful bride like this."

So he took a splendid coach and magnificent clothes and drove to the tree where he had left the beautiful maiden. However, when he arrived and caught sight of the ugly figure in the tree, he was horrified and cried out: "What's happened to you?"

In response, she said:

The sun came
and took my color.
The wind blew,
My voice has left me.*

"If I am to blame for what has happened," the prince responded, "I shall marry you no matter how you look."

Then she put on the beautiful clothes, got into the magnificent coach, and traveled to the royal castle. When the queen saw her, however, she said to her son, "This is the ugliest girl I've ever seen! Is this the beautiful maiden who caused you to suffer so much?"

---

* Vinni lu suli, mi cangiau lu culuri, vinni lu ventu, mi cangiau lu parlamentu.

"I abandoned her," the prince answered, "and the wind, the rain, and the sunshine have changed her looks. That's why I want to marry her no matter how she looks."

Therefore, a beautiful wedding was celebrated, and the prince married the deceitful slave. But the next morning when the cook was cleaning the antechamber, a white dove flew into the room and sang:

> Cook, cook, working away
> What's the prince doing with the slave?*

Then the bird flew away, but toward noon, as the cook was preparing the food for the royal table, the dove came once more and sang:

> Cook, cook, working in the kitchen,
> What's the king doing with the queen?†

This happened every day, and the prince gradually became angry and wanted to send the clumsy cook away. But the cook confessed the truth and told him how a white dove came twice a day and asked him how things were going with him and the queen.

"Very well," the prince responded, "tomorrow you are to line the window sill with glue, and when the dove comes, you are to call me."

When the dove came the next morning, the prince was already hiding in the kitchen and saw how the dove landed on the window sill and sang:

> Cook, cook, working in the kitchen,
> what's the king doing with the queen?

But when the dove wanted to leave, she was stuck to the glue and could not fly away. Then the prince jumped from his hiding place, took the bird in his arms, and stroked it. As he did this, he noticed the black button of the needle and thought, "You poor bird, who could have tortured you this way?" So he pulled out the needle, and as soon as he did this, the beautiful maiden with the seven veils stood before him. She had become even more beautiful and spoke, "I am the bride you abandoned in the tree. The black slave, whom you took for your wife, was the one

---

* Cocu, cocu ddi la sala, chi fa lu re cu la schiava?

† Cocu, cocu ddi la cucina, chi fa lu re cu la riggina?

who stuck the needle into my head so that I became a white dove. Then she took my place."

Then the prince had the beautiful maiden dressed in magnificent clothes and had her brought to the castle in a splendid coach, as if she had come from a long distance. Meanwhile, he told the slave, "A maiden from another foreign court has arrived. I want you to receive her with all the appropriate honors. She is to dine with us today."

The slave was content to do this, and when the beautiful maiden came, she did not recognize her. After they had eaten, the prince said, "Noble maiden, would you please tell us the story of your life."

Then the beautiful maiden told everyone what had happened to her, and the slave was blind to the truth and did not notice anything.

"Well, what do you think about all this?" the prince asked his wife. "What do you think this deceitful slave deserves?"

"She deserves nothing better than to be cooked in a kettle of boiling oil and then dragged through the city by the tail of a horse," the slave answered.

Then the prince cried out, "You've spoken your own sentence, and this is what will happen to you."

The slave was thrown into a kettle with boiling oil, and afterward tied to a horse's tail and dragged through the entire city. The prince, however, celebrated a splendid wedding and married the beautiful maiden with the seven veils. They remained rich and consoled, and we just keep sitting here and getting old.

12

THE MERCHANT'S CLEVER
YOUNGEST DAUGHTER

Once upon a time there was a merchant who had three daughters. The youngest, Maria, was very beautiful and at the same time smart and clever. One day the father had to take a trip, so he called his daughters and said, "Dear children, I must go away. Watch out for yourselves, for these are uncertain times. Be careful."

Upon saying this, he departed. For a while it was very quiet and peaceful. One day, however, a beggar came to the door and asked for alms. But this beggar was a robber in disguise.

"Don't let the stranger enter," Maria called to her sisters.

But when the beggar began to groan, "I'm so tired, my dear girls. It's been such a long time that I've had anything warm to eat or a decent rest," the two older sisters let him enter. After the beggar had eaten, he said, "Is it already dark? Where shall I find shelter? Oh, dear girls, please let me spend the night here."

"Don't do it," Maria warned, but her sisters did not listen to her. Instead they prepared a bed for him and told him to stay there. Maria could not sleep at all, for she suspected that he was really not a beggar, and she could not rid her mind of this suspicion. Now, when everything in the house was quiet, she got up, crept to the room where the beggar was sleeping, and hid herself nearby. It was not long before the door opened quietly, and the alleged beggar stepped out and cautiously looked around him. He sneaked down the stairs, opened the door, and whistled to his comrades to gather around him. Then they broke into the merchant's store. Maria immediately decided what to do. Like lightning she sprang through a back door into the open and ran to the police, who came running right away. They managed to seize the one robber who had disguised himself as a beggar. The others fled and left behind the merchandise. Then Maria went to her sisters, who were still sleeping. She woke them and said, "Just look at the consequences of your carelessness! Let me tell you what happened."

When their father returned, he heard how courageous and smart his daughter had been and was very happy, but the chief of the robbers could not accept that a young maiden had thwarted his plan, and he swore he would avenge himself. He took the most beautiful clothes from his treasures, mounted a splendid horse, and entered the city where Maria lived. Once there he posed as a grand and rich gentleman and occupied a beautiful house. Then he went to the shop owned by Maria's father, where he bought all kinds of stuff and had a friendly conversation with the merchant. He pretended to be the son of a rich baron and told the merchant all about his wealth and his beautiful castle. The next day he returned, and his visits continued until the merchant had taken a great liking to him. Now the robber asked permission to marry his youngest daughter, and her father went to her, very pleased by the great honor, and said, "Just think, my child, the young baron wants to marry you."

But Maria answered, "Oh, dear father, I feel very well here, and none of us knows this young man. How can we really be sure that he is what he says he is?"

However, her father was blinded by the robber's wealth and by the high rank of the young man, and he tried time and again to convince his daughter to marry him. Finally, Maria said, "Well, do what you want."

So a spectacular wedding celebration was arranged, and on the wedding day the bridegroom brought a letter from his mother in which she wrote to her son that she unfortunately could not attend the wedding, but she hoped that her son would come and visit her with his young wife. Therefore, after the wedding, the couple mounted their horses and rode off to visit the mother.

The road became steeper and steeper and more and more desolate. Maria realized that she was in a wild region that she did not know at all. All of a sudden the chief of the robbers turned to her and spoke in a rough voice: "Get off your horse now! Did you really believe that I was the son of a rich baron? I'm the chief of the robber band, and one of my men was hung because of you, and now I'm going to get my revenge."

Maria got off her horse and began to tremble.

"Now, take off your shoes and stockings," the robber continued, "and climb that mountain over there."

What could Maria do? She had to obey, and climbed the steep mountain with her tender feet. When they reached the top, the robber tore off her clothes, tied her to a tree, and began to whip her with a stick.

"Just wait," he exclaimed. "Now I'm going to call my comrades, and we'll whip you to death."

Upon saying this, he left her. Maria stood there tied to the tree and could not do anything to help herself. The whip lashes were so painful that she could do nothing but moan and groan. However, not far from the tree there was a narrow path, and on this path a peasant and his wife were riding to the market with some sacks of raw cotton. When they heard Maria's groans, they thought she was a ghost. They crossed themselves and wanted to move on as fast as they could, but Maria heard them and called out: "Oh, dear people, I'm a baptized soul like you. Don't leave me!"

So the peasant got off his mule, and when he saw Maria, he quickly took a knife from his pocket, cut the rope with which she had been bound, and set her free. However, what were they to do, for the robbers could appear at any moment! Thinking quickly, the peasant told Maria to get into one of the sacks, which she did, and the peasant stuffed as much cotton into the sack as he possibly could. Then he tied the sack on the mule, sat down on top of it with his wife, and rode away as fast as he could.

Soon the robbers appeared, but they were astonished to see that Maria was no longer there. The chief swore that he would kill her and set out after her. Shortly thereafter he caught up with her, the peasant, and his wife, and ordered them to stop with a grim voice. Because they were scared to death, they obeyed the robber, who took his sword, stuck it into the cotton, and wounded Maria many times. She did not make a sound, and because the sword had to pass back and forth through the cotton, the blood stains were wiped off, and the robber was fooled. He allowed the peasants to continue on their way. But after a short time he decided to pursue them and forced them to halt. When he stuck his sword into the sacks, he was foiled one more time and finally let the people continue on their way.

When they came to the next city, they stopped at a friend's house and said, "Please do us a favor, good mother. Give us your best bed, for we are carrying a poor wounded maiden, and we want to place her in your care."

So they put Maria in the bed, and because they had to move on, they entrusted her to the old woman. Maria remained with her until she had completely recovered, and when people in the city asked who she was, the old woman would always say, "She's my niece."

One day, when Maria was well again, she said to the old woman, "I'm healthy again and don't want to burden you any longer. See if you can find a job for me."

The old woman inquired and learned that the king was seeking a chambermaid. Maria applied for the position, and because she pleased the king so much, he took her into his employ. The more the king saw her, the more she pleased him, and one day he said to her, "You're to become my wife, and no one else!"

Then she had to tell him that she was married, and why she had been given away to the robber chief.

"Oh," the king declared, "if that's all there is to it, we'll catch him, and when he's hung you'll no longer be his wife."

So Maria was looked upon by all the people as the king's wife.

One day as she was sitting at her window, the chief of the robbers rode by.

"Oh no!" he thought, "you're still living, and you're even the king's wife! Just wait. I'll get you yet!" Then he went straight to a goldsmith and said, "Master, you must make me a silver eagle, hollow on the inside, and large enough so that I can stand inside it. I want it finished within three days."

The goldsmith promised to do it and gathered together a group of his apprentices who had to work day and night to finish the eagle. When the work was done, the robber called a porter and said to him, "I want you to walk back and forth with this eagle in front of the king's window until he feels an urge to buy it." Then he locked himself inside the eagle, and the porter carried him on his back and walked in front of the king's window. The king was standing with his wife Maria on the balcony once again, and as soon as he saw the beautiful silver eagle, he cried out, "Look, Maria! How beautiful! Let's buy it."

But Maria had recognized the robber as he had passed by the previous time. Therefore, she was suspicious and said, "Oh, your majesty, you already have so many beautiful things. Why do you want to give away your hard-earned money!"

However, the king liked the eagle so much that he bought it and had the porter bring it up into the castle and place it in his room. When the king and Maria were sleeping that night, the robber unlocked the eagle and stepped out. He carefully crept to the king's bed and placed a piece of paper on the pillow. As long as it laid there, neither the king nor the other people in the castle could wake up. Then he moved to Maria, grabbed her, and dragged her into the kitchen.

"You thought I wouldn't find you here!" he said scornfully, and he took the large kettle, filled it with oil, and set it on the fire. "I'm going to boil you in this kettle!"

Now Maria was in a bad situation, but she did not lose courage. Instead she said, "If I have to die, so be it! But let me fetch my rosary beads so that I can pray for the last time."

The robber permitted this, and Maria rushed into her room and called the king. But no matter how much she called, nothing happened. She kicked and pulled him, all in vain. In despair she grabbed hold of his beard and shook him. When his chin moved, it caused the sheet of paper to fall off the pillow. Suddenly the king and all the other people in the castle awoke. Maria led them into the kitchen where the robber was still stirring the fire. To his surprise, they grabbed him and threw him into the boiling oil. Afterward Maria married the king, and it was a spectacular marriage. She had her father and sisters attend the wedding, and they continued to live happy and content, but we were left without a cent.

13

MARUZZEDDA

Once upon a time there was a poor shoemaker, who had three beautiful daughters. The youngest, however, was the most beautiful, and she was called Maruzzedda.* The older sisters, however, did not like Maruzzedda because she was so unusually beautiful. The shoemaker was poor and frequently had to wander about the countryside for many days in order to earn money.

One day he said to his eldest daughter, "I want you to accompany me when I look for work. Perhaps I shall be a bit luckier. So his eldest daughter went with him, and he earned a tari. Then he said, "Listen, I'm very hungry. Let's eat ten pennies worth of food, and we'll take just ten pennies to the others."

So they bought something to eat and brought the others half of the money. The next day the shoemaker took his middle daughter and earned three carlini. Then he said, "Let's eat fifteen pennies worth of food, and we'll take the others just fifteen pennies."

So they bought something to eat and brought the others just half of the money. On the third day the shoemaker took Maruzzedda with him, and this time he earned two tari. "Listen, Maruzzedda," he said, "let's eat one tari worth of food, and we'll take the others just one tari.

---

* Diminutive of Maria.

"No, father," she replied. "I'd prefer to go home right away, and then we can all eat with one another."

When the father returned home, he told his other two daughters what had happened, and they said, "Just look at our ill-bred sister! Shouldn't she always do what you want?"

They used these words and more to stir their father against the innocent Maruzzedda. The next morning he took her with him again and earned three tari. "Listen, Maruzzedda," he said once more, "Let's eat three carlini worth of food, and we'll take the other three to your sisters."

"No, dear father," she said. "I'd prefer to go home right away. Why shouldn't we all eat together?"

When the father returned home, he told his older daughters about this once again, and they had even harder words for their sister. "Why do you want to keep that shameless person in your house any longer? Chase her out! Get rid of her!"

However, their father did not want to do this. So the sisters proposed: "Take her with you tomorrow, and leave her behind in some desolate spot so that she won't be able to find her way back home."

The father was blinded by their jealousy and let himself be duped by the sisters, and, so the next morning he took Maruzzedda with him. After they had wandered very far and had come to an unfamiliar region, he said to her, "Wait a moment and rest a while. I'll be right back."

So Maruzzedda sat down, and the shoemaker went away. She waited and waited, but her father did not return. The sun began to set, and the father still did not return. Finally, she was very sad and thought, "My father clearly wants to throw me out of the house. Well then, I'll set off into the wide world."

So she wandered away and continued to wander until she was tired and it had become evening. She had no idea where she might find shelter for the night. Suddenly, however, she saw a splendid castle in the distance. She went toward it, entered, and climbed the stairs, but she encountered nobody inside. She went through the rooms, which were lavishly decorated, and in one of them there was a table that had been fully set, but still there were no people. Finally she reached the last room, where she saw a beautiful maiden lying on top of a black frame used for coffins. She was dead.

"Well, since there is nobody here, I'm going to stay until someone comes and chases me away."

She sat down at the table, ate, and drank to her heart's content. Then she laid down in a beautiful bed to sleep. She lived this way for a long time, and no one disturbed her.

One day, however, her father happened to pass by while she was looking out the window. When he saw her, he greeted her, for he was sorry that he had abandoned her, and he asked her how she was doing.

"Oh, things are just fine," Maruzzedda responded. "I've found some work here as a servant, and they treat me well."

"May I come up for a while?" the father asked.

"No, no," she replied. "My master is very strict and has forbidden me to let anyone enter. Farewell, and greet my sisters for me."

The shoemaker went home and told his daughters that he had found Maruzzedda, and once again they deceived him with false words so that he became angry with the innocent Maruzzedda. After some days had passed, the jealous sisters baked a cake with some poison inside, and gave it to their father to take to the poor maiden.

During that very same evening, while Maruzzedda was asleep, the dead maiden appeared to her in a dream and called: "Maruzzedda! Maruzzedda!"

"What do you want?" Maruzzedda asked, half asleep, half awake.

"Tomorrow, your father will bring you a wonderful cake. But beware and do not eat it. Give the cat a piece. The cake has poison inside."

Maruzzedda awoke and saw that she was alone, and thought, "I must have probably dreamed this," and she fell back into a pleasant sleep.

The next day she saw her father coming. She allowed him to climb the stairs, but she would not let him enter.

"If my master should see you, he would discharge me from his service."

"Don't worry, my child," the shoemaker answered. "Your sisters have sent their greetings along with this cake."

"Tell my sisters that the cake is very beautiful," Maruzzedda responded, "and I thank them very much for sending it."

"Don't you want to try a little piece," the father asked.

"No, I can't right now," Maruzzedda answered. "I have work to do. Later, when my work is finished, I'll try a piece."

Then she gave him some money and told him to go. When he was gone, however, she gave the cat a piece of the cake, and the cat died immediately. Then she realized how true the dead maiden's warning had been and threw the cake away.

Meanwhile, the jealous sisters became restless at home because they wanted to know what had happened to Maruzzedda. Therefore, the shoemaker traveled to the castle again the next morning. When he knocked at the door, Maruzzedda came toward him, cheerful and in good health.

"How are things going, my dear child?" he asked.

"Everything is fine, dear father," she answered.

"Why won't you let me see the castle just one time?" he said.

"What are you thinking?" she replied. "That would cost me my job."

Then she gave him some money and sent him away. When the father arrived home and told his other daughters that Maruzzedda was completely healthy, they hated their poor sister even more than before. So they made a beautiful enchanted hat, and whoever put it on would become stiff and paralyzed. The father had to take this hat to Maruzzedda.

During the night, however, the dead maiden appeared to Maruzzedda in a dream once more and called out: "Maruzzedda! Maruzzedda!"

"What do you want?" she asked.

"Tomorrow morning your father will bring you a beautiful hat," the dead maiden said. "Beware, and don't put it on. Otherwise, you'll become stiff and paralyzed."

The next morning the shoemaker did indeed appear and brought his daughter a beautiful hat.

"Tell my sisters that the hat is very beautiful, and I thank them very much," she said to her father.

"Don't you even want to try it on so that I can see how it looks on you?" the father asked.

"No, no, I have to work now," she replied. "Later, when I go to mass, I'll put it on."

Upon saying this, she gave him some money and told him to go. She put the hat into a chest, but did not tear it up as she should have done. Meanwhile, her sisters were convinced that Maruzzedda had been destroyed by the hat, and they were no longer concerned about her.

About this time the dead maiden had been granted permission through God's grace to enter the heavenly paradise. She appeared to Maruzzedda for the last time in a dream and said, "God has permitted me to go to my final resting place, and I am leaving this castle and everything in it to you. Live a happy life, and enjoy all this splendor."

Upon saying this, she disappeared, and the black frame on which she had been lying was now empty.

Many months passed, and one day Maruzzedda decided to clean out all the chests and boxes in the castle. As she was doing this, she came upon the enchanted hat. Since she had received it so long ago, she had forgotten who had sent it to her and thought, "Oh, what a pretty hat! I'm going to try it on." No sooner did she put the hat on her head than she became stiff and paralyzed and could not move anymore. That evening the dead maiden appeared, for the Lord gave her permission to return to earth. She took poor Maruzzedda and placed her on the black frame. Then she flew back to paradise. Maruzzedda lay there as if she were dead, but she did not became pale or cold.

One day, after she had been lying like this for a long time, the king happened to go hunting, and the hunt took him into the vicinity of the castle. At one point he saw a beautiful bird, took aim, and hit it, but the bird fell right into the room where Maruzzedda was lying on the frame. The king wanted to enter the castle, but all the doors were locked, and nobody responded to his knocking. There was nothing else to do but climb through a window, and since the window was not very high, he ordered two of his hunters to climb through it. When they succeeded and saw the wonderful maiden, they forgot all about the bird and the king and kept staring at the dead Maruzzedda. The king became impatient and finally called out: "What are you doing inside there? Hurry up!"

The hunters went over to the window and asked the king to climb up. They told him there was a maiden inside, and that they had never seen anyone so astonishingly beautiful as she. So the king climbed through the window into the room, and as soon as he caught sight of Maruzzedda, he could not take his eyes off of her. When he bent over her, he noticed that she was still warm and cried out, "The maiden is not dead, just unconscious! Let's bring her back to life!"

They tried to wake her. They rubbed her and loosened her clothing, but it was all in vain—Maruzzedda remained stiff. Finally the king took off her hat in order to cool off her forehead, and all at once she opened her eyes and awoke from her slumber. Then the king announced, "You shall be my wife," and he embraced her.

However, the king had a mother, who was an evil sorceress, and consequently he was afraid to take Maruzzedda back to the castle with him. "Stay here," he said to her, "and I'll come to you as often as I can. From then on Maruzzedda lived in the castle and was secretly married to the king, and the king came and visited her whenever he went hunting. After one year she gave birth to their first son and called him Tamo.* After another year, she gave birth to a second son and called him Tamai.† And when she gave birth to a third son the following year, she called him Tamero.‡

---

* T'amo. Translation: I love you.

† T'amai. Translation: I loved you.

‡ T'amerò. Translation: I'll love you.

The old queen had gradually noticed, however, that her son often went hunting and stayed away from the castle for a long time. When she investigated things, she learned about his marriage. So she called a loyal servant and said, "Go to the castle where the king's wife is living and say to her: "My majesty, the queen, will grant you a pardon when you send your oldest son to her today.""

The servant did this, and poor Maruzzedda was fooled and gave the man her eldest son. The next day the old queen had the second son fetched, and soon afterward, the third son. When she had the three children in her castle, she called her cook and said to him, "You must kill these three children and bring me their hearts and livers as proof that you have followed my orders."

The cook had children himself, and his fatherly heart took pity on the poor innocent children and he did not kill them. Instead, he took them to his house and hid them there. As for the queen, he brought her the heart and liver of three billy goats.

Meanwhile the king became sick and laid in his bed. The queen sent another messenger to Maruzzedda and told him to say: "Your husband is sick. You are to go to him and take care of him."

Maruzzedda put on three dresses, one on top of the other, and went to the castle. When she entered the courtyard, there was a huge fire burning, and the old queen was standing beside it and called out, "Throw the girl into the fire!"

"First, let me take off my clothes," Maruzzedda requested, and she took off the first dress, threw it into the fire, and cried with a loud penetrating voice, "Tamo!"

But the queen had placed a group of musicians in front of the king's door, and they had been ordered to play their instruments with all their might so that the king would not be able to hear what was happening in the courtyard. However, he heard his wife's cry, even if it was very weak.

"Stop playing your music," he said, but the musicians continued to play as loudly as they could. Then Maruzzedda threw off the second dress and cried out even louder: "Tamai!"

This time the king heard it much better and called out: "Stop your music!"

But the musicians had received orders not to obey him and continued to play. Then Maruzzedda took off the third dress and yelled from the bottom of her anxious heart as loudly as she could, "Tamero!"

The king heard the cry, jumped out of bed, and ran down into the courtyard. Just as he arrived, the servants were about to throw poor Maruzzedda into the fire. He commanded them to stop and to tie up the queen instead and to throw her into the fire. Then he embraced his wife and said, "Now you will be the queen."

"Oh," she responded, "before anything, take me to my children."

"Where are the children?" the king asked.

"What? They're not here?" the poor mother cried. "Oh my children, my dear children!"

Then she told the king how his mother had sent messengers to fetch the children, but nobody knew anything about this, and there was great sadness in the castle. Then the cook asked to see the king and said, "Your majesty and my queen, console yourselves! The old queen had ordered me to kill your children, but my heart took pity on them, and I let them live."

Then the three children were brought to them, and they embraced them with great joy. The king and queen celebrated with a splendid feast and gave rich gifts to the cook.

And so they lived happy and content,
But we can't even pay the rent.

14

ARMAIINU

O nce upon a time there was a king who had three beautiful daughters. One day, while the princesses were enjoying themselves in the garden, three frightening giants broke in and made off with the maidens. Consequently, the king had it proclaimed throughout his realm that whoever brought his daughters back to him could choose one of the princesses for his wife and would become king after him. Many men arrived and set out to find the princesses, but none of them ever returned from their quest.

Now one day, three princes arrived. They were brothers and had themselves announced to the king.

"Your majesty," they said, "we've come to rescue the princesses."

"Oh," answered the king, "many men have set out on this quest, and none have returned. Let's hope that you'll have better luck."

So the three princes began their journey and continued to wander for one year, one month, and one day until they came to a large beautiful castle that lay in the middle of a huge estate. By this time they had lost the courage to travel any farther and said to each other, "Let's stay here until we learn something more concrete about where we might find the princesses. This estate is beautiful, and there's more than enough game to hunt so we can feed ourselves."

So they remained there, went hunting, and led a splendid life in the beautiful castle. Meanwhile the king continued to wait for his daughters and their rescuers, and because no one came, he finally thought,

"They've certainly gone missing like the others," and became very sad. However, he had an old gatekeeper who had once been a soldier, and because he had lost an arm and a leg in a war and could not work, he had become the king's gatekeeper and was called Armaiinu. Well, this man went to the king and said, "Your majesty, I'm going to set out and search for the three princesses and the three princes and bring them back to you."

"Oh Armaiinu!" the king laughed and said. "If so many strong young men have been destroyed trying to find my daughters, how do you expect to succeed?"

But Armaiinu would not let himself be dissuaded from going on this quest, and the king finally granted him permission to leave. So Armaiinu set out on foot and carried a small sword that caused people to laugh when they saw it. However, it was a magic sword, and whoever owned it could not be stopped. Armaiinu wandered and wandered, and since he was old and lame, he needed two years, two months, and two days until he came to the castle where the three princes were staying. Finally he reached it, entered, greeted the princes and said, "I've come to look after you and to help you recover the princesses."

The princes laughed, but they also gave him a hearty welcome.

"All right," said Armaiinu, "let's stay here for another few days, and one of us will take a turn and stay in the castle and cook while the others go hunting."

The princes agreed, and on the first day the eldest brother remained in the castle. As he began plucking a wild duck, a powerful giant burst into the castle and asked him with a threatening voice, "Who gave you permission to live in my castle?"

"We've been living here already for two years," the prince answered. "Why has it occurred to you just now to see who's living here?"

"Is that the way you answer me?" the giant shouted and lifted a large club and beat the prince until he lay on the ground half dead. When the others returned, the duck was only half plucked, and the prince was lying on the ground and groaning.

"I felt such a terrible pain in my body," he said, "that I couldn't finish my work."

On the second day the middle brother stayed behind, and things did not go any better for him. While he was plucking a wild duck, the giant appeared and asked him who had allowed him to live in the castle, and because he gave the same answer as his brother, the giant beat him as well and left him lying on the ground half dead. When the others returned, they found the duck only half plucked and the prince on the floor.

71

"Ohhh!" he groaned. "All of a sudden I had such a terrible headache that I could not continue working."

Consequently, they had to go to bed on empty stomachs again. However, the eldest brother said to the middle one, "Tell me, did the giant perhaps beat you?"

"Yes," answered the other. "But let's not tell the others. If we received a beating, why shouldn't they as well?"

The next morning the youngest brother remained at home, and things did not go any better for him. When the others came home, the duck was only half plucked, and the prince lay on the ground and groaned, "Ohh, I suddenly didn't feel so well. That's why I couldn't make anything."

"Well, that's real nice!" said Armaiinu. "The three of you are strong young men, but we've had to go to bed hungry three nights in a row. One of you felt a terrible pain in his body, the other had a headache, and the third felt sick. I see now that tomorrow your poor Armaiinu will have to remain home and do the work for all three of you."

"Yes," thought the brothers. "Now you'll be home to get the beating that we had to taste."

So on the fourth day Armaiinu remained at home, and just as he was plucking the duck, the giant appeared and said with a threatening voice, "Well, are you still here? Just wait! I'm going to murder you today!"

But Armaiinu pulled out his magic sword and attacked the giant. With one fell swoop, he lopped off the giant's head. Then he roasted the duck, and when the others came back, he was waiting for them by the door in good spirits.

"You've come just at the right time," he called out to them. "Dinner's ready."

The brothers were very astounded and asked him whether anyone had come to the castle.

"Oh yes," Armaiinu responded. "A man came, and since he was so impolite, I cut off his head."

The princes became frightened and thought, "Something strange is going on here!"

The next morning Armaiinu said, "Let's go now and rescue the princesses. Behind the castle there's a large cistern. One of us will have to be let down into it because the poor maidens are being held captive there."

"Good," answered the eldest prince. "I'll try it."

So they took a large basket and tied it to a rope. Then the prince got into it and took a little bell with him. They agreed that whenever he rang the bell, he would be pulled up by the others. However, to land on the floor of the cistern he had to confront a huge wind, a great deal of fire, and lots of water. As soon as the prince encountered the wind, he became so scared that he rang the bell and had himself pulled up.

Now the middle prince wanted to try his luck and was brave enough to make it through the huge wind, but when he felt the water on his feet, he lost his courage and had himself pulled up. Next in turn was the youngest prince, who went courageously through the wind and water, but when he felt the fire, he did not want to go any further and had himself pulled up.

"Now your poor Armaiinu will have to try his luck," the old man said. Then he stepped into the basket and had himself lowered into the cistern. Fortunately he was able to make his way bravely through the wind, water, and fire and landed at the bottom. Once there he climbed out of the basket and wandered a while in a dark room until he saw a door with a light shining beneath it. When he opened it, he saw a beautiful salon in which the eldest princess was sitting before a magnificent mirror. In front of her lay a giant whose head was on her lap. Armaiinu drew out his magic sword and chopped off the giant's head before the monster could awake. Then the princess pointed to a door, and when he opened it and went through, he came to a second salon, in which the second princess was sitting before a mirror. In front of her lay the second giant with his head on her lap. But Armaiinu slashed his head off and went through a door into the third salon where the youngest princess sat like her sisters in front of a mirror holding the giant's head on her lap. Once again Armaiinu chopped off the head of this giant, and thus he liberated all the princesses. Then he led them to the place where the basket was still hanging and rang the little bell. The princes pulled the first princess up to the top and let the basket down again. Armaiinu put the second princess into the basket, and after the basket returned, he set the youngest in it. After the three princes had pulled all the daughters to the top, they talked with one another and said, "Let's leave the old gatekeeper to sit there. Then we can share the reward for rescuing the princesses just among ourselves."

They threatened the maidens and said that they would murder them if they did not swear a holy oath to keep quiet and left the place as fast as they could. When they arrived at the king's court, they said, "Your majesty, after a long battle and great difficulty, we succeeded in freeing your daughters and killing the giants."

The king was extremely happy when he heard this news. Afterward he arranged for a magnificent wedding, and each prince married a princess. In the meantime Armaiinu waited in the cistern for a long time and kept ringing the little bell, but the basket did not reappear. Finally he realized that the princes had betrayed him. He went back into the beautiful salons and looked at all the treasures that had been gathered there, but felt only anger because he thought that none of the treasures could help him so long as he was trapped in the cistern. As he stood before the mirror the oldest princess had used, he was so overcome by his rage that he took a large stone and threw it against the mirror, which broke into a thousand pieces. To his surprise, however, a splendid emperor's robe and crown fell out of the mirror.

"What use are this beautiful robe and crown if I can't get out of the cistern?" he cried as he ripped the robe into a thousand pieces. Then he went into the second salon and smashed the other mirror. All at once another emperor's robe and crown fell out of the mirror, and they were even more splendid than the others. Armaiinu wanted to tear apart this robe as well, but when he saw how superbly embroidered it was, he did not want to ruin it. He went to the last salon, where he broke the third mirror. All at once a small flute fell out, and when he put it to his mouth and blew it, a voice cried out: "At your command!"

"I wish to become a handsome young man," Armaiinu responded, and suddenly he was transformed into a gorgeous young man. Then he put on the robe, set the crown on his head, and looked like a powerful emperor. So he whistled again and wished himself out of the cistern, and within seconds he stood in free air. Next he wished for a large retinue and a coach with six horses, and he drove to the king's court.

When the king heard that the emperor of the world* was coming to his realm, he rushed out to meet him and fell at his feet, but Armaiinu lifted him up in a friendly fashion and said he wanted to dine with the king.

So a magnificent dinner was prepared, and after the meal each person was to tell a story.

"I want to tell you the story about a poor gatekeeper," Armaiinu said and began to tell his own story. The three princes, who were sitting at the table with their wives, became very frightened when they heard this story, and Armaiinu cried out, "Yes, your majesty, and I am that poor Armaiinu, and these three princes are the traitors who deserted me, and if you need some proof, just look at how all three are twisting in their seats and have become so pale."

The king ordered the three princes to be led out of the room and to be hung. Afterward he said to Armaiinu, "Choose one of my daughters, and after I die, you will become king."

---

* L'imperaturi di tutto lu munnu.

"No, your majesty," Armaiinu responded, "your daughters deserve to marry three princes. I wish nothing more than to die in your service as your faithful Armaiinu just as I was before."

So he wished himself back into his former shape and became the lame, one-armed Armaiinu he had previously been and remained the king's gatekeeper until he died. As time went by, the three princesses married three princes and remained happy and content, but we did not receive one cent.

15

THE GOLDEN LION

Once upon a time there was a rich merchant who had three sons. One day the eldest said to him, "Father, I want to set out to see the world. Give me a beautiful ship and a lot of money, and let me go."

So the father ordered a beautiful ship to be equipped for his son, and the son sailed off. After he had traveled for some time, he landed at a magnificent city where he saw a proclamation written by the king that said, whoever could find his daughter within a week could have her for his wife. But if he did not succeed, it would cost him his head.

"Well," thought the young man, "this shouldn't be all too difficult."

So he went to the castle and informed the king that he wanted to find the princess within a week.

"Good," the king answered. "You can look in the entire castle. If you don't find her, you will lose your head."

So the young man stayed in the castle and had everything he wanted to eat and drink, and he was allowed to go anywhere he desired to go in the castle. Yet no matter where he searched, in each and every corner, and no matter how many closets he opened, he could not find the princess, and after a week he was beheaded.

When he did not return home, the second son said, "Father, give me a ship, too, and a large sum of money. I want to set out and search for my brother."

76

So the father ordered a second ship to be equipped, and the son set sail. The winds led him to the same shore where his brother had landed, and when he saw his brother's ship still anchored in the harbor, he thought, "Well, my brother can't be far from here," and he went on land. All at once he saw the same proclamation by the king, who announced that whoever could find his daughter within a week could have her for his wife, but whoever did not succeed would lose his head. "I'm sure my brother tried to find the beautiful princess and lost his life," the young man said to himself. "Now I'll try, and I'm sure I'll succeed."

So he had himself announced to the king and tried to find the princess, but he had no better luck than his brother. No matter where he searched he could not find the beautiful princess, and on the eighth day he was beheaded.

Now only the youngest son remained at home. When he saw that his brothers did not return, he, too, had his father give him a ship and a large sum of money and set out to search for his brothers. The winds drove him to the same shore where he saw his brothers' two ships. When he landed, he entered the city and saw the king's proclamation. "So," he thought, "whoever can find the king's daughter is to get her for his wife? I'm sure my brothers tried to find her and lost their heads. Now I'm going to try my luck."

While he walked toward the castle with these thoughts in his head, a poor woman came up to him and begged for some money: "My handsome lad, give an old woman some alms."

"Leave me in peace, old woman," he responded.

"Oh, please don't turn me away," the woman said. "You're such a handsome young man. You certainly wouldn't refuse to give an old woman some alms."

"I'm telling you, old woman, leave me in peace."

"Do you have some troubles?" the old woman asked. "Tell them to me, and I'll help you."

He told her that he was searching for the beautiful princess and was trying to think of a way to find her.

"Well, I can help you," the old woman said, "but only if you have a good deal of money."

"Oh, I've got plenty," the young man replied.

"Well then, let a goldsmith make a golden lion for you," the old woman said. "It should have crystal eyes and be able to play a pretty song. After that I'll help you some more."

So he had a golden lion made, and it had crystal eyes and played a merry little song. When the old woman came, she stuck the young man inside the lion and took it to the king. Since the lion pleased the king so much, he asked the old woman whether she would sell it to him.

"The lion doesn't belong to me," she answered, "and my master refuses to sell it at any price."

"Well, at least let it stay here for a short time until I've shown it to my daughter," the king responded.

"Yes, I can do that," the old woman said. "But tomorrow my master must have it back."

When the old woman went away, the king took the golden lion into his room, and at a certain spot, he lifted up part of the floor. Then he climbed down some stairs with the lion in his arms, opened a door, and then another one and another one until he had opened seven, each one with a special key. Meanwhile, the young man who was hiding in the lion saw everything. Finally they came to a beautiful hall in which the princess was sitting with eleven playmates. They all looked exactly like the princess, and they all wore the same clothes.

"How unlucky I am!" thought the young man. "Even if I make it to here, how am I going to tell the princess apart from all the others? They all look alike."

The princess was very pleased by the golden lion and asked, "Dear father, let the cute animal stay here for the night so that we can enjoy it."

After the king had locked her in the hall again, the maidens continued to have fun with the pretty golden lion and then laid down to sleep. But the princess took the golden lion into her room and placed it next to her bed. After a while the young man began to speak: "Oh beautiful princess, just look and see how much I've suffered in order to find you."

Then she started to scream, "The lion! The lion!"

However, her friends thought she was screaming in her sleep and did not move.

"Oh, beautiful princess," the young man spoke again. "Don't be afraid. I'm the son of a rich merchant and wish to become your husband. I've only hidden myself in this golden lion in order to find you."

"What's the use of it all?" she responded. "Even if you get this far, you won't be able to tell me apart from my companions, and you'll still lose your head."

"You can take care of that," he suggested. "I've already done a lot for you. Now you can do something for me."

"All right then," the princess said. "Listen to me. On the last day of the week I'll wrap a white sash around my hips. Then you should be able to recognize me."

The next morning the king came and took the golden lion away and returned it to the old woman who was already at the castle. Then the old woman carried the lion out of the castle and let the young man out. As soon as he was out of the lion, he went to the king and announced that he wanted to find the beautiful princess.

"Good," the king answered, "but if you don't find her, it will cost you your head."

So the young man stayed in the castle, ate and drank, and pretended every now and then to search for the princess. On the eighth day he entered the king's room and gave an order to his servants: "Rip open the floor at this spot."

The king became frightened and said, "Why do you want to rip open the floor? She's certainly not hiding beneath it."

However, the young man did not let himself be misled. Instead, he gave the order a second time for the floor to be ripped open. Then he climbed down the stairs, and when he came to the door, he called out, "Where is the key to this door?"

Then the king had to unlock the door, and also all the other doors, and when they entered the hall, the twelve maidens were standing in a row, and they all looked so much alike that one could not tell them apart. But the princess quickly wrapped a white sash around her hips, and the young man went right toward her and cried out, "This one is the king's daughter, and I very much want her for my dear wife."

Since he had made the right guess, the king could no longer say no, and he organized a splendid wedding. After the wedding the king heaped treasures on him, and the young man took his beautiful wife and sailed home to the old merchant. Before they left, however, they gave a splendid gift to the old woman. In the end they remained man and wife, but we sit here and stare at one another without much life.

16

THE TWELVE ROBBERS

Once upon a time there were two brothers who were both poor and miserable. They had many children and little money. One day, one of the brothers said to his wife, "I want to go into the country to see if I can find some work. Perhaps I'll be able to earn some money."

So he set out on his way and traveled straight ahead until he came to a tall mountain. Then he sat down and began thinking about his sad fate. As he was sitting there, he suddenly saw twelve robbers coming toward him. "Oh, how unlucky I am!" he thought. "If they find me here, they'll murder me." Fortunately, he saw a thick bush nearby where he decided to hide himself until the robbers rode by. However, instead of moving along, the robbers began to climb the steep mountain and were carrying treasures with them. When they reached a large rock, the first robber said, "Open up, door!"*

As soon as he said these words, a door in the rock opened, and all twelve robbers went inside. Then the rock closed itself behind them. After a while they came back out, and the last robber said, "Close, door!"† And the door closed behind them.

---

* Gràpiti, cicca.

† Chiuditi, cicca.

"Oh," thought the poor man, "there are things I can fetch in that cave!" And when the robbers had disappeared, he crawled out from the bush, climbed the mountain, and stood in front of the rock.

"Open up, door!" Immediately the door opened so he could enter. "Close, door!" Immediately the door closed behind him. Then he saw all the treasures of the world that were stored there because the robbers brought everything they stole to this cave. Indeed, the poor man kissed the ground when he saw all the gold and so many treasures. Then he filled his pockets with as many gold coins, as he could carry and said, "Open up, door!" The door to the rock opened, and he went out and said, "Close, door!" so the rock would close again. Then he went home delighted and said to his wife, "God has sent us an abundance of good things so that we can now live comfortably and without worries."

So he set up a small business with the money, and God blessed him so that everything went well for him. But when his brother saw how well things were going for him, he went to him and said, "Dear brother, how did you manage to get all this money? Tell me so that I can also go there and fetch a little.

"Let me tell you what happened to me," said his brother, who began to tell his story. "If you want to go there, you'll still find a huge pile of gold, but you must pay attention to one thing. When the robbers enter, you must count them, and when they come out, you must count them again so that you know whether any one of them has remained inside."

The brother set out and soon came to the tall mountain where the robbers lived. He hid behind a bush, and shortly thereafter the robbers came. He counted them, and there were eleven. When they had returned home some time before, they had found that some of their money was missing, and the captain of the robbers had said, "From now on, one of us will remain at home because the rascal who stole from us will probably come a second time."

 Neither of the two brothers could have known this, and when the poor brother who hid himself behind the bush saw the robbers come out again, he counted them once more, and there were eleven again. "Well," he thought, "eleven went inside, and eleven have come back out. So now I can safely go inside."

He took a place in front of the rock and said, "Open up, door!" The door opened up, and he went inside, where he found the gold in great piles. No one could be seen, so he filled his pockets with gold. However, when he wanted to go back outside, the twelfth robber suddenly sprang out at him and killed him.

After the robbers came back home and saw the murdered man, they said, "Well, you scoundrel, now you've received your payment."

Meanwhile, the other brother continued to wait for his poor brother, and when his brother did not come, he thought, "I'm sure the robbers caught him and killed him." So he asked the wife of his brother and their children to come and live with him and looked after them. He remained happy and content, and the old woman sits there without a toothpick or a tooth to pick.

17

THREE GOOD PIECES OF ADVICE

Once upon a time there was a man who had a wife, whom he loved with all his heart. When his wife became pregnant, she said to him one day, " My dear husband, I have such a great craving for a piece of liver. If only I could have some liver!"

"If that's all you want, just a piece of liver," her husband answered, "I'll easily get it for you."

So the man went to a relative who was a butcher and said, "Cousin, be so kind and give me one and a half pounds of liver. My wife has a great craving for some liver."

"I'll be with you right away, cousin. Wait a moment until I've finished serving these other customers."

The man waited and waited. The customers went away, and others came, and his cousin still did not give him a piece of liver.

"Cousin, please wait on me. My wife is sitting at home and cannot sit still because she's got such a great craving for a piece of liver."

"Wait a moment, cousin, until I've finished serving these customers," the butcher answered and continued to serve the other customers one after the other, keeping his own cousin waiting. Finally his cousin lost his patience.

"Is my money not as good as these other people?" he thought, and all at once he grabbed a club and split the butcher's head in two so that he fell dead to the ground. When he saw the butcher lying dead on the ground, he became scared and ran home to his wife.

"Dear wife," he said, "I must get away from here, far away from here. I've met with some bad luck.* My cousin kept serving all the other customers and put me off. But I was thinking of you and felt sorry that you had to wait so long. Finally I lost my patience and hit him with a club and split his head in two. That's why I've got to go off into the wide world and leave you alone."

His wife moaned and wept, but what use was it? In her condition she had to remain alone, and her husband set off into the wide world. As he roamed about, he came to Rome and thought, "Better here than anywhere else. I'll stay here and enter the pope's employ."

So he took a job with the pope and served him faithfully for forty years, and the pope became very fond of him. When the forty years were over, he thought one day, "I've been away from home so long and don't know whether my wife is still living, or whether I have a son or a daughter. I want to return to my hometown. I'm sure that nobody will remember the dead butcher anymore."

So he went to the pope and said, "Your excellency, I have served you faithfully for forty years. Please let me now go back home."

"Good," said the pope, "and since you have served me so faithfully, take this money."

Upon saying these words, he gave him three hundred ounces of gold. The man thanked the pope, put the money in his pocket, and kissed the pope's hand. When he was about to leave the pope called him back and said, "I have a piece of good advice for you. Will you give me a hundred ounces for it?"

"Excellency, take what you would like," the man answered and gave him back a hundred ounces.

"Just remember," the pope said, that this piece of advice has cost one hundred ounces, so pay attention. When something unusual happens to you on your way home, do not say anything about it."

The man promised to do what the pope advised, kissed his hand, and wanted to go, but the pope called him back a second time and said, "If you give me another hundred ounces, I'll give you another piece of good advice."

"Excellency, do whatever you please," the man answered, and put another hundred ounces on the table. Then the pope said, "Just remember that this piece of advice has cost one hundred ounces, so pay

---

* In Sicilian, ci succidìu una disgrazia; in German, mir ist ein Unglück begegnet.

attention to my words. You are to take the exact same path home that you took forty years ago when you first came here."

The man kissed the pope's hand and wanted to leave, but the pope called him a third time and said, "Give me another hundred ounces, and I'll give you a piece of good advice."

"Excellency, take what you want," the man answered and gave the last hundred ounces back to the pope. Then the pope said, "Listen carefully to my words, and don't forget that this advice has cost you one hundred ounces. Let the anger that grips you in the evening rest until the next morning. If you are gripped by anger again in the morning, let it rest until the evening. Remember my words. They will serve you well. And now that you have served me for forty years, you can stay with me for one more day and bake me a whole oven full of bread."

So the man went into the kitchen and kneaded a beautiful white bread, and the pope had the three hundred ounces of gold secretly stuck into the largest loaf and baked with the rest of the bread. When the man came the next day to say farewell, the pope gave him the largest loaf of bread and said, "Take this beautiful white bread with you and eat it only when you are in good spirits."

Then he blessed him and let him depart. The man wandered straight ahead to his hometown. One day, as he was moving along, he became hungry, and since there was an inn along the way, he entered and ordered something to eat. The innkeeper brought him some fish with bread and wine and placed everything in front of him. He also set a dead skull next to him. The man wanted to ask what it meant, but then he remembered what the pope had said: "When you encounter something extraordinary, you should not say anything," and so he kept quiet. After he had eaten the innkeeper said to him, "You're the first person who did not ask me why I set the skull next to him, and this has saved your life. Let me show you what's happened to all those who could not control their curiosity."

Upon saying these words he led him into a drab cellar, where there were many corpses and bones. They were the corpses of those people who had asked the innkeeper why he had placed a skull next to the food. So the man thanked the pope in his heart for the good advice and thought, "To be sure it cost me a hundred gold ounces, but the advice has saved my life."

Now he continued his journey and wandered for many days again. One day he met a lot of workers, who were going into the countryside to pull out the flax, and they said to him, "Do you want to go to Catania? Why are you going that way? Come with us. We're taking a much shorter way."

The man thought about the second piece of advice he received from the pope that he was to take the very same path back that he had taken to reach Rome, and so he answered, "You go your way, and I'll go mine."

He was about a mile away when he heard loud screams. The poor workers were being attacked and murdered by robbers. So he thought: "The pope's advice cost me one hundred ounces of gold, but it saved my life. Blessed is he who gave me this advice!"

Finally, after some days had passed, he arrived late in Catania and went straight to the house where his wife had lived forty years ago. Now, she had given birth to a son at that time, and he had become a priest and lived with his mother. When the man knocked on the door, the son ran down the stairs, opened the door, and asked him what he wanted. When the man saw the priest, he was overcome by great anger and thought, "Who's this cleric living with my wife?"

It would not have taken much for him to murder the priest, but the man thought about the good advice that the pope had given him: "Let the anger that grips you in the evening rest until the next morning." And he answered, "I'm just a poor pilgrim. Could you please give me shelter for the night?"

So his son led him inside, and his wife, whom he had not seen for such a long time, was sitting in the living room.

"Come in, poor man," she said. "Rest a while until I've finished making dinner."

Then she set the table for the evening meal and invited him to eat with them. During the meal the pilgrim said, "Tell us a story, good woman. I'm sure you know many."

"Oh," she answered, "What other story should I tell you but my own sad tale about how I lost my husband shortly after my marriage."

"How did that happen?"

"I was pregnant, and one day I said to my husband that I had a craving for a piece of liver. So he went to the butcher shop to buy it, but because the butcher kept him waiting so long, he picked up a club in anger and split the butcher's head in two. Therefore he had to flee, and I haven't heard from him in forty years. When the time came for me to have my baby, I gave birth to this son, who has become a priest."

When the man heard that the priest was his own son, he thanked the pope in his heart for his good piece of advice. "I might have done something unfortunate in my anger," he thought to himself, and then he spoke to the woman, "It's remarkable! My story is similar to yours, good woman. I had been married only a short time, and my wife was pregnant. One day she said to me, 'Oh, dear husband, I've got a craving for a piece of liver. If only I could have a piece of liver!' So I went to the butcher to buy it, but the butcher served all the customers except for me so that I finally lost my patience and split his head in two. Then I had to flee and leave my poor wife behind. Since then I have heard nothing about her, and now, after forty years, I've returned to see whether she's still living."

As he told his story, his wife kept looking at him, and she could not take her eyes off him. When the story ended, she recognized him and embraced him with many tears and great joy. Then he embraced his son and was glad that he had become such a tall handsome man.

After they had calmed down somewhat and wanted to eat some more, the man took the bread out of his backpack and said, "This bread is all that I've brought for you, and the pope told me that I should eat it when I was in good spirits. When could I ever be happier than I am now that I've found you again? So let's eat this bread."

Upon saying these words, he sliced the bread, and just imagine— three hundred ounces of gold fell out. He was now a rich man and lived many more years with his wife and son in happiness and without any worries.

18

TOBIÀ AND TOBIÒLA

Once upon a time there was a man named Tobià, and his wife was called Sara and his son Tobiòla. Tobià was a pious, God fearing man, and he used all his money and possessions to do good for the poor. All the poor people who died were brought to his house, and then he carried them outside the city on his back and buried them at his own cost. His wife often reproached him for this: "Oh, Tobià, what will happen to us when you give all your money and possessions to the poor? You'll see, there'll come a time when we ourselves will have to go and beg."

"Let it be, dear Sara," he answered. "Whoever does good, will have good done to them."*

Now one day Tobià happened to hear that a poor man had died in the city.

"Bring him here to me," he said. "I'll bury him this evening."

So the people brought the dead man and laid him under the bed. In the evening Tobià took the dead man on his shoulders and carried him outside the city. After he had buried him, he became so tired that he laid down to sleep beneath a tree. Now a swallow happened to have her nest in this tree. While Tobià slept under the tree, some of the refuse from the swallow fell down into his eyes so that he became blind. When he

---

* Cu beni fa, beni trova.

awoke, he could not see anything, and it was only with great effort that he made his way back home. When his wife saw him coming in this condition, she raised her hands to her head and moaned and groaned, "Oh, Tobià, what's happened to you?"

"There's nothing I can do about it," Tobià said. "I laid down to sleep beneath a tree to rest for a while, but there was a swallow that had built her nest there, and some of her refuse fell into my eyes, and I became blind."

"Oh, how unlucky we are! What's going to happen to us now that you can't work, and now that you've given all our money and possessions to the poor?"

"Calm down," Tobià said. "Whoever does good will have good done to him, and God does not abandon the just."

Tobià was now faced with a difficult time because he could no longer work, and soon he ran out of money. So, one day he said to his wife, "Dear wife, we have no more money. Not far from here there's a city where an acquaintance of mine is living, and I loaned him some money some time ago. Let's send our son Tobiòla to him and ask him to repay the loan."

So Tobià called his son Tobiòla and said to him, "My son, you must go to the city where my acquaintance lives and fetch the money that I loaned to him. However, I don't want you to travel there alone. Go to the marketplace and see if you can find a traveling companion."

So Tobiòla went to the marketplace and saw a handsome, slender young man, who asked him, "Tobiòla, are you taking a trip?"

"Yes, to the city over the mountain."

"I've got to go there, too. We can travel together."

Tobiòla was very pleased when he heard this, and he took the young man to his parents and said, "Dear father and mother, I've found a traveling companion. Give me your holy blessing, and let me depart."

So Tobià and his wife blessed their dear son and embraced and kissed him. Soon after Tobiòla set out with the young man, but the city to which they were traveling would take many days to reach.

One day, as they were on their way, they came to a river in which a fish was swimming, and it swam close to the bank.

"Tobiòla," the young man said, "grab the fish and cut out its gallbladder and liver. They'll be useful to you."

Tobiòla did what the young man told him to do. He grabbed the fish, cut out its gallbladder and liver, and put them in a tin can. Soon they reached their destination, where Tobiòla was to fetch the money.

"Where are you going to spend the night?" the young man asked him.

"My father has an acquaintance here, and he's a relative. So I'm going to stay with him," Tobiòla said.

Now this relative had a daughter who was very beautiful, and had already had seven husbands, but they all died during the wedding night. When Tobiòla and the young man went to the relative, Tobiòla said, "Uncle, I'm the son of your cousin Tobià and his wife Sara."

"Oh nephew, what a pleasure!" the man exclaimed. "Come into my house and stay with me, you and your companion."

Tobiòla and the young man entered, and the beautiful uncle's daughter brought them something to eat and drink.

"Do you know what I've thought, Tobiòla?" the young man asked. "I want you to marry the beautiful maiden."

"Oh, my brother,"* Tobiòla answered, "that will be the death of me. This maiden has already had seven husbands, and they were all found dead in bed the morning after the wedding."

"Just calm down, Tobiòla. If you do what I tell you to do, nothing will happen to you."

After the young man said this, he went to the uncle and said, "Good friend, my companion Tobiòla wants to marry your beautiful daughter. Please allow him to have her, and let us return to our home."

The father refused and said, "Don't you know that my daughter is burdened by this terrible fate? She has already had seven husbands, and they all died during the wedding night."

"Who knows," the young man answered, "perhaps Tobiòla won't die. Give him your daughter."

The father finally agreed, and the wedding was celebrated. After the wedding, Tobiòla's companion took him aside and said, "Listen to my words and follow them exactly as I tell you. Tonight, when you are led into the room with your young wife, lock all the doors and windows, and place the gallbladder of the fish on the coal stove so that it burns and you and your wife inhale it. Then you and your wife are to throw yourselves down on your knees, and do atonement for three hours because your wife is plagued by a devil named Romeò. This devil has possessed her because her other seven husbands never atoned for their sins."

Tobiòla remembered everything the young man told him, and when he was led into the room with his wife, he closed all the doors and windows so that the smoke could not get out. Then he took the gallbladder out of the tin can and burned it on the coal stove, and the smoke filled the entire room. Tobiòla and his wife threw themselves down on the ground and did atonement for three hours, and the beautiful maiden

---

* Fatri meu.

wept bitterly. Indeed, her heart was full of anxiety. After three hours they went back to bed and slept peacefully until morning.

When daybreak came, the uncle and his wife got up and were filled with worry.

"Go into the room," the man said to his wife, "and see whether the unfortunate Tobiòla is still alive."

When she entered the room, she saw that the two of them were still sleeping peacefully and soundly. All at once there was great joy in the house, and everyone praised God and thanked him for his mercy. Tobiòla remained a few more days in this city, and after he received his father's money, he said to his uncle, "Dear father-in-law, I must return home to my parents. Give us your blessing and let us depart."

So the uncle loaded the dowry of his daughter on a few mules, blessed his daughter and son-in-law, and let them depart.

At home, Tobiòla's mother Sara still wept because her son had been away for such a long time and she had heard nothing from him. Every evening she had climbed a high mountain to see if he might soon be returning home. When she returned to the top of the mountain on this particular evening and stood there with tears in her eyes looking for Tobiòla, she suddenly saw two men and a woman coming with many packed mules, and when she took a second clearer look, she saw that one of the men was her son Tobiòla.

"God be praised!" she exclaimed full of joy. "My son is coming, and what a beautiful maiden he has with him! That's a certain sign that things went well."

When Tobiòla recognized his mother, he ran toward her and kissed her hand, and the beautiful maiden also kissed her hand, and so they continued on their way home in good spirits.

Now just imagine the joy of the old, blind Tobià when he heard that his son had returned! Meanwhile, the young man said to Tobiòla, "Now take the liver of the fish and rub your father's eyes with it. Then his sight will be restored."

So Tobiòla took the liver of the fish out of the can and rubbed his father's eyes with it, and as soon as he did this, his father could see again. While they were rejoicing about this miracle, the young man transformed himself into a handsome angel and said, "I am the Angel Gabriel and was sent by God to help you because God saw how pious and God-fearing you are. Lead a holy life, and you will be happy, and when you die, God will receive you in his paradise."

Upon saying this, he blessed them and flew back to Heaven. Afterward Tobià and his family continued to lead a holy life, and when their time came, they died, and God took them in his arms.

19

JOSEPH THE JUST

Once upon a time there was a great king who had three sons, and the youngest was called Joseph. The king was more fond of this son than the others, and they became filled with envy. Now the king had large estates in Chiana and had to send his sons there frequently to inspect how the wheat was doing as well as the oxen and the horses. However, he sent only his two elder sons. The youngest he kept with him.

Now one day his elder sons said to him, "Father, we're the ones who always have to go to Chiana while Joseph stays peacefully at home. Why don't you let him accompany us once? Otherwise, if you don't, it's a sign that you love him more than you love us."

"My sons," the king answered, "I love you all the same because you are all my children, but your brother is still young, and I fear that the wild animals might eat him."

"And you're not afraid that the same thing might happen to us? Now we clearly see that you love our brother more than you love us!"

What could the king do? In order to satisfy his elder sons, he called little Joseph to him and said, "Your brothers must travel to Chiana again, and you, my son, must accompany them."

So the three brothers set out together for Chiana. However, the hearts of the two elder brothers were filled with envy and anger, and the eldest said to the second one, "I can't stand the sight of our brother anymore. Let's throw him down into the empty well over there, and he'll die of hunger."

So, they tied poor Joseph on a long rope and let him down into the well and waited on top and waited for him to die. While they were waiting there, a powerful king came riding by, much more powerful than their father, and he asked them, "What are you doing at this well?"

"We have to guard the boy down there," they answered. "He's supposed to die."

When the king looked down into the well and saw the marvelously handsome boy, he felt pity for him and said, "Pull him up. I'll buy him from you."

So the princes pulled their brother up, and the king gave them some money and took poor Joseph with him. Meanwhile, the brothers took his shirt away from him, slaughtered a goat, and dipped the shirt into the blood. When they returned home, the king asked them right away, "Where's your brother Joseph?"

"Oh, father!" they cried out. "Wild animals ate him. Look, here is his bloody shirt."

Just imagine the grief of the poor father! He beat his chest, pulled out his hair, and moaned. "Oh, my son, my dear son, the wild animals have eaten you!"

Now let's leave the father and see what happened to his son.

The powerful king took Joseph with him to his land and had him instructed in everything. Joseph continued to grow and became the wisest and most just man in the country, and the king placed him in charge of all his estates and named him Joseph the Just.*

Many years passed, and one day Joseph went to the king and said, "Your majesty, listen to my words, and follow my advice. Seven years will come, and they will be so fruitful that your people will not know what to do with all the wheat and corn. During these seven years you are to order great warehouses to be built and filled with the wheat and corn because seven bad years will come after, and everything will be ruined. If you don't collect and save wheat and corn before this, you and your people will starve to death."

And everything happened just as Joseph had prophesied.

Seven years came in which everything flourished, and so much wheat and corn grew that they barely had room to collected everything. The king ordered large warehouses to be built and filled them with the wheat and corn, as Joseph had recommended. After the seven fruitful years came seven years that were so bad that nothing ripened. No wheat,

---

* Giuseppi Giustu.

no barley, no fruit. Nothing. There was a great rise in the price of food in all the countries, and the king placed his loyal Joseph in charge of the food stocks and let it be known that there was still a great deal of wheat and corn in his country. Many people came from other countries to buy wheat and corn.

At this time the other king, Joseph's father, spoke to his sons, "Dear sons, there is no more wheat and corn in our country. Therefore, I want you to go to the realm where the king has collected and saved wheat and corn and buy some for our country."

The two sons set out for the other realm. When they were led before Joseph the Just, they did not recognize him, but he recognized them.

"What do you want?"

"Your highness, we've come to buy wheat and corn."

So Joseph had their sacks filled with the most beautiful wheat and corn. Then he invited them to dine with him and gave them something to eat and drink. Indeed, he was extremely friendly to them. After they had eaten, the brothers said, "Now we must return to our father in our country."

When they were not looking, Joseph secretly stuck a gold cup in one of the sacks of wheat and let his brothers depart. When they were scarcely a mile away, he pursued them with his servants, and when he had overtaken them, he said, "What have you done? Is this the way you repay my hospitality? I received you as though you were my best friends, and then you stole my gold cup!"

The brothers were extremely shocked and said, "Oh, my lord, we didn't steal anything from you. We are honest people. If you want, you can search our sacks."

"You can be sure I'll do that!" Joseph exclaimed, and he examined the sacks himself and found the gold cup in the very first sack.

You can imagine how shocked the princes were, but Joseph cried out, "You see yourself how you've paid me back! Therefore, one of you shall sit in prison, and the other will return home and fetch your father here so that I can speak to him."

So one of the princes was taken to the prison, and the other returned to his home country. When the king saw him return alone, he asked him immediately, "Where is your brother?"

The son told him everything that had happened, and the king began to weep and moan very loudly.

"Am I to lose all my children? One of them was torn apart by wild animals. The other's sitting in prison. Oh, how unlucky I am!"

Soon he set out and traveled to the country where Joseph was living. When he was led before Joseph, he wanted to fall at his feet, but Joseph lifted him, and his heart was trembling when he saw his old father again. Then the king told him how he had lost his first son, and how he was so unfortunate to see his second son in danger, and he pleaded for his life. However, Joseph could no longer control himself and cried out, "Do you wish to see your youngest son Joseph again?"

"Oh, if only God would permit that!" the old king answered.

"Dear father!" Joseph exclaimed. "I am your youngest son, Joseph! Wild animals did not eat me. My brothers sold me to the king of this land, and I am in his service."

When his brothers heard this, they fell to their knees because they thought that Joseph would take revenge on them, but he lifted them up, embraced them, and forgave them for everything they had done. Then he went to the king of the country and told him how he had found his father again and wanted to return home with him. So he took his leave, and they returned to their home country and lived happy and content, and we were left without a cent.

20

THE TWO BROTHERS

Once upon a time there were two brothers who were both very handsome. However, they were poor and led a wretched existence. Indeed, they barely supported themselves through fishing. Now one day they happened to go out to sea in their boat, and they caught a tiny fish.* So the older brother said, "What a miserable voparedda this is! When I return home, I'll cook it and eat it myself."

"Let me live!" the little fish cried out. "Throw me back into the sea, and I'll bring you good fortune."

"What do you think I am, you dumb fish!" the young man responded. "I caught you, and now I'm going to eat you."

But the younger brother intervened and said, "Oh, why don't you let the little fish live? What use will it be to you if you eat it. It's so small that you'll swallow it in one bite. Do what it wants and throw it back into the water."

"If you let me live," the voparedda said, "you will find two splendid horses on the seashore tomorrow, and they'll be carrying everything you need to become fine knights and to set out into the world."

"All this is so stupid!" the older brother cried. "How do I know that you're telling the truth?"

---

* Voparedda, which is a poor kind of small fish.

"Let the fish live," the younger brother pleaded with him. "Even if it's not telling the truth, we'll most likely catch it again. But if it's really telling the truth, we'd be throwing away our good fortune if we killed it."

So the older brother let himself be persuaded, and he threw the voparedda back into the sea. When they went to the seashore the next morning, two splendid horses, already saddled and bridled, were standing there, and next to them were gorgeous clothes and armor, two swords, and two large purses filled with money.

"Do you see?" the younger brother said. "Weren't we lucky that we didn't kill the little fish? Now we can set out into the wide world and seek our fortune. You go that way, and I'll head off in this direction."

"All right," the older brother responded. "But how are we to fix things so we know whether the other is alive or not?"

"Do you see that date tree over there?" the younger brother said. "If we want news of one another, we'll come here and take a slice of the trunk of the tree with our swords. If milk flows from the tree, it will be a sign that the other is still alive. If blood flows from the tree, then the other is either dead or in danger of dying."

So the two young men put on their armor, fastened their swords, and attached the money purses. Afterward they embraced each other with tenderness, mounted their horses, and rode off into the world, one brother in one direction, the other in another direction.

The older brother rode straight ahead until he came to a foreign realm. When he crossed the boundary, he reached a river, and alongside sat a lovely maiden. She was bound and weeping bitter tears, for there was a wicked dragon with seven heads that lived in this river, and every morning the king sent one of his people to the river for the dragon to eat. If the king did not do this, the dragon would devastate the entire realm. Because the king had already sacrificed nearly all the people, he finally had to send his own daughter to the dragon. When the young man saw the beautiful maiden weeping bitterly, he asked, "Why are you crying, beautiful maiden?"

"Oh," the princess answered. "I've been tied up here so that a wicked dragon with seven heads can come and eat me. You'd better flee, my handsome young man! Otherwise, the dragon will devour you, too."

"I'm not going to flee," the youth responded. "I'm going to rescue you."

"Oh, how's that possible? This monster is terrible! There's nothing you can do against it."

"Let me worry about that, beautiful maiden," the young man declared. "Just tell me from what direction the dragon will be coming."

"All right, if you insist on freeing me, then at least listen to my advice. Stand back a bit when the dragon rises from the water, and I'll say, 'Oh, dragon, today you can eat two humans. Take that young man over there first because I'm tied up and can't get away from you.' Perhaps then you'll be able to defeat the dragon."

The young man took some steps backwards. Soon the water began to roar, and a terrible dragon rose out of the river and wanted to hurl itself at the princess to eat her. But she cried out, "Oh, dragon, today you're getting two humans to eat. Take the young man over there first because I'm tied up and can't get away from you."

So the dragon charged at the young man and tried to swallow him, but he took out his sword and fought until he finally defeated the dragon with the seven heads. After he made sure the dragon was dead, he untied the princess, and she embraced him with great joy and said, "You've rescued me from the dragon, and now you'll become my husband. My father had announced that whoever killed the dragon could have me as his wife."

However, the young man answered, "I can't become your husband now because I must continue my journey. Wait seven years and seven months for me. If I don't return by then, you can marry someone else. Just so you will recognize me again, I'll take the seven tongues of the dragon with me."

So he cut out the seven tongues of the dragon, and the princess gave him an embroidered scarf in which he wrapped the tongues. Then he mounted his horse and rode off.

Soon after he departed, one of her father's slaves arrived. He had been sent by the king to see what had happened to his poor daughter. When the slave arrived, he found the princess alive and well. At her feet lay the slain dragon.

"If you don't swear to your father," he said, "that it was I who killed the dragon, I'll murder you on the spot."

What could the poor maiden do? She promised the slave to do as he demanded, and he took the seven heads and led the princess to the king. Just imagine how happy the king was when he saw his daughter again, for he believed that she was dead. The entire city rejoiced, and when the slave told everyone that he was the one who had killed the dragon, the king cried out, "Now you may have my daughter as your wife."

However, the princess threw herself at her father's feet and said, "Father, you have given your royal word, and therefore you must keep it, but I beg you to grant me a favor and let me remain single for another seven years and seven months. Then I'll marry the slave."

The king granted her request, and she waited seven years and seven months for her bridegroom, and she wept day and night for him.

Meanwhile, the young man had traveled around he entire world, and when the seven years and seven months were up, he returned to the city where his bride was living. To be exact, he arrived in the city a few days before the wedding between the slave and the princess was to take place. The true bridegroom had himself announced to the king and said, "Your majesty, it is me who deserves your daughter, for I was the one who killed the dragon. Just look at the seven tongues of the dragon and your daughter's embroidered scarf."

"Yes, dear father," the princess spoke, "this young man is telling the truth and is my bridegroom, for the slave made up his story. Still, I think you should pardon him."

"I find it impossible to pardon such a traitor!" the king cried out. "Off with his head! And I mean immediately!"

So the deceitful slave was beheaded, and the king arranged a glorious wedding celebration. The princess married the handsome young man, and they lived happy and content with one another.

Now one evening it so happened that the young man was looking out the window and saw a large bright light on top of a mountain.

"What's that bright light doing over there?" he asked his wife.

"Oh," she answered, "don't look at the light. An evil sorceress lives up there, and no one has been able to defeat her."

He soon began feeling the urge to set out and defeat the wicked witch, and the next morning he mounted his horse. No matter how much the princess cried and complained, he rode off toward the mountain where he had seen the bright light. He had to ride for a long time, and it became dark before he arrived so that he could no longer see his way. Nevertheless, the light was so bright that he rode straight toward it. Finally he came to a beautiful castle, and the bright light was beaming from the windows. He entered and climbed the stairs. All at once he saw an ugly old woman, who was sitting in a room.

"With just one hair from my head I can change you into stone," she said.

"I don't believe you," the young man cried. "Be quiet, you old woman! Do you think your hair can really harm me?"

In response the witch touched him with one of her hairs, and he was immediately turned into stone and could no longer move.

About this same time his brother happened to think about him and said, "I'm going to return to the date tree to see whether my brother is still alive."

So he went to the date tree and stuck his sword into it, and suddenly he saw blood gush out of the trunk.

"Oh, I feel so terrible! My brother is either dead, or his life is in danger. I must go and search for him throughout the world."

So he mounted his horse and said, "Get going, horse. Run like the wind!"

And he searched the entire world until one day he came to the city where his brother had married. The poor princess was still waiting for her husband and wept bitter tears because he was gone. On this particular day she was standing on her balcony, looking for her husband. All at once she saw his younger brother riding through the city, and since this young man looked just like the older brother and wore the same armor, she thought he was her husband and ran toward him full of joy and cried out, "Oh, you've finally returned! My dear husband! How long I've waited for you!"

When the young man heard this, he immediately thought, "My brother must have been here, and this beautiful maiden is my sister-in-law."

However, he did not say anything. Instead, he let her believe that he was her husband. Meanwhile she led him cheerfully to the old king, and he, too, was very happy to see his son-in-law again, and they ate and drank together. In the evening the young man had to go with the princess to her room. When he got undressed, he took his double-bladed sword and placed it between himself and his brother's wife. She was frightened when she saw the double-bladed sword, but did not dare to ask him why he had done this. So it went for many more days.

One evening, while the young man was looking out of the window, he also saw the bright light on top of the mountain,

"Oh!" the princess cried out. "Are you looking at that light again? Do you want to set out again to defeat the wicked witch?"

All at once he realized that his brother must be in the power of a sorceress, and the next morning he mounted his horse and said, "Get going, horse. Fly like the wind!" And he secretly rode off.

Just like his brother, he had to ride the entire day. Toward evening he encountered a little old man, who was in truth St. Joseph.

"Where are you going, handsome young man?" he asked.

"I want to rescue my brother," the youth told him. "A wicked witch has him in her power."

"Do you know what you must do?" the saint asked. "The witch's power lies only in her hair. Therefore, when you speak to her, jump at her and grab her by the hair, and she will lose her power. Make sure, however, that you don't let go of her. Take her to your brother and force her to revive him. She has a salve that can wake up the dead. As soon as she restores your brother to life, cut off her head because she is an extremely evil witch."

The young man thanked Saint Joseph and continued to ride until he came to the castle. Then he entered and climbed the stairs and saw the same ugly old woman, who called out to him, "With one hair of my head I can turn you into stone."

In response he jumped at her, grabbed her by the hair, and said, "You wicked old woman! Tell me right away where my brother is. Otherwise, I'll cut off your head on the spot."

Because the witch no longer had any power over him, she said, "I'll lead you to your brother, but you must let go of me. I can't walk this way."

"Don't think about it, you ugly witch!" the young man cried out and did not let go of her. So she led him into a room in which there were many petrified people.

"There's your brother," she said.

He looked at all the people and said, "My brother is not here. Beware, old witch! Otherwise, I'll cut off your head!"

So she led him through many other rooms, and in each one she said, "Here's your brother."

But he did not let go of her. Rather, he kept saying, "My brother is not here. Lead me to him or I'll cut off your head."

Finally, in the last room, he saw his brother lying on the ground. Then he said. "This is my brother. Now bring the salve that you use to wake the dead."

She went to a closet in which there were many salves and potions, while he kept a tight hold on her hair. Whenever she showed him a false salve, he threatened to kill her. Finally she showed him the right one, and he forced her to rub the salve on his brother. When his brother opened his eyes, he sliced off the witch's head. Meanwhile, his brother rubbed his eyes and said, "Oh, how long have I been sleeping? Where am I?"

"The wicked witch kept you prisoner here," his brother said, "but now she's dead, and you're freed of her power. Now let's go and revive all the other knights whom she cast under her magic spell."

So they rubbed the salve on all the other petrified knights, and they became alive again, were happy, and thanked their rescuers. Then they divided the treasures and precious things that the witch had amassed and returned to their homes. The older brother kept the healing salve and set out with his brother to return to his castle.

As they were riding side by side, the younger brother said, "Oh what a fool you were to ride out and defeat a witch while you left such a pretty wife alone at home! When I arrived, she mistook me for you, and I even shared her bed with her."

When his brother heard this, he exploded violently with jealousy, took out his sword, and cut off his brother's head. Then he entered the city where the princess had been weeping for him day and night. When she saw him coming, she ran toward him full of joy, embraced him, and said, "Oh, how long I've been waiting for you! Now I won't let you set out on another adventure again!"

She led him to the old king, and the entire realm rejoiced because of his safe return. In the evening, as he prepared to go to bed, his wife said to him, "Why did you lay a double-edged sword between us every evening after your previous return?"

All at once he realized how faithful his brother had been, and when he thought how he had killed him, he began to groan very loudly and wanted to ram his head against the wall. Then, suddenly, he remembered the salve that he had brought with him, and he stood up and rushed to the place where he had left his brother. Once there, he rubbed the salve on his neck, set his head on his shoulders, and brought him back to life. The two brothers embraced each other full of joy and returned to the city and held a great banquet. And so they remained rich and consoled, while we just sit and continue to get old.

21

THE SEVEN BROTHERS WITH MAGIC TALENTS

Once upon a time there was a king who had an only daughter, and he loved her with all his heart. One day he summoned an astrologer, who was to predict the princess's fortune.

"When the princess turns fifteen," the astrologer said, "a giant will come and steal her away."

So the king had the princess carefully guarded so that nobody could make off with her. When the princess became fifteen, however, she was standing at her window, and a giant came by and pulled her to him with his breath. He took her in his arms and fled so fast that no one could catch up with him. The king became very despondent and issued a proclamation throughout the entire realm that whoever brought his daughter back to him could have her for his wife and become king after him.

A poor old woman happened to hear this. She was the mother of seven sons, all endowed with magic talents.* So she called the eldest and said, "If you tell me what your talent is, I'll have a new suit made for you."

"I can take ten men in my arms," he replied, "and can run as fast as the wind."

---

* Actually, they were enchanted, *erano infatati*.

104

Then the mother called the second son and asked him what his talent was.

"When I put my ear to the ground," he answered, "I can hear everything that's happening in the world."

The woman continued to ask all her sons, and each one had a special talent. The third son could break through seven iron doors with one blow of his fist. The fourth could steal something from the arms of people without them noticing a thing. The fifth could build an iron tower with one blow of his fist. The sixth had a rifle, and he could hit anything he aimed at with this weapon. Finally, the youngest could wake the dead when he played his guitar. With these seven sons the mother went before the king and said, "Your royal majesty, my sons want to bring back your daughter."

The king was very happy about this and had a new suit made for each one of them, and so they wandered off together. When they were outside the city in a forest, the second brother put his ear to the ground and said, "I hear the princess weeping. She's sitting in a tower with seven iron gates, and the giant is holding her in his arms."

Then the oldest grabbed all seven of his brothers together and ran with them up to the tower in which the princess was being held.

"Now it's your turn," they said to the third brother, who hit the seven iron gates with such a powerful blow of his fist that they all collapsed. The fourth brother crept into the tower, and while the giant slept, he stole the princess from his arms and brought her out to his brothers. Once again the oldest grabbed all his brothers and the princess together and ran from there as fast as the wind.

When the giant awoke and did not find the princess in his arms anymore, he set out after the brothers, and since he could run faster than the eldest brother, he soon caught up with them. So the brothers called out to the fifth brother: "Now it's your turn."

And when he hit the ground with his fist, a tower appeared in which all eight of them could hide. The tower was so strong that the giant could not destroy it. Therefore he set up camp before the tower and continued to yell: "If you give the princess back to me, I'll let you all go free."

The brothers refused, and finally he said, "Let me just see her pinky. Then I'll let you all leave without harming you."

The brothers thought, "That's something we could do," and they made a small hole in the tower and let the princess stick out her pinky. No sooner did the giant see it, than he pulled her to him with his breath, took her in his arms, and started to run away as fast as he could.

"Quick, shoot him dead," the brothers spoke to the sixth one, who took his rifle, aimed, and shot the giant dead. As they ran to the spot, they saw that he had also shot the princess. All at once the youngest brother took his guitar and began to play. Soon the princess opened her eyes and was revived. Now the oldest took them all in his arms and ran back to the king's castle.

There was great joy in the castle, and the king said, "Which one of you is to have the princess for his bride? Let me hear who performed the greatest feat."

"That was me," the eldest cried, "because I was the one who carried my brothers and the princess together in my arms, and I ran as fast as the wind."

"No, it was me," the second said, "because you would not have known where the princess was without me."

"No, I deserve the princess," interrupted the third brother. "I was the one who knocked down the seven iron doors."

"What use would all that have been if I hadn't stolen the princess from the giant's arms?" asked the fourth brother.

"And if I hadn't built an iron tower," the fifth brother declared, "the giant would have killed us all."

But the sixth brother explained, "No, I deserve the princess because I shot the giant dead."

"And the princess as well," cried the youngest. "And if I had not recalled her from the dead with my guitar, she would still be dead."

"Yes," announced the king. "You're the one who performed the greatest feat, and you shall marry my daughter."

So a splendid wedding was celebrated, and the youngest son married the princess. However, the king was very generous with gifts to the other brothers, and he invited them, along with their mother, to stay in the castle. Indeed, they lived there happy and content, and we don't have one single cent.

22

THE PIOUS YOUNG MAN
WHO WENT TO ROME

Once upon a time there was a poor washerwoman who had an only son, and to be sure, he was very dumb, but he was also good and pious deep down in his heart. The poor woman used to send him into the woods with her mule, and he would search for firewood to sell in the city. This was their miserable existence.

Now one day her son happened to pass by a small church with his mule loaded with firewood. A sermon was being given just at that time, and he tied the mule outside and went into the little church and heard the priest say, "My friends, listen to what the Lord says: Whoever gives to the poor in my name will be repaid a hundredfold." When the young man heard this, he went outside, sold the wood and the mule, and gave the money to the poor.

"Now the Lord must repay me a hundredfold," he thought, and he returned to the church and sat down in a corner where nobody noticed him. When all the masses had been held, the sacristan closed the church and did not realize that the young man had remained behind. The young man waited until everything was quiet and climbed up to the altar where there was a large crucifix, and he began speaking to it with the following words. "Hey, listen to me, you!" (Notice how simple-minded he was, for he took the liberty to address Jesus in a very familiar way.) "Listen you," he said, "I carried out your commandment, and I gave everything that I sold to the poor. Now you must repay me a hundredfold. Otherwise, I won't have anything at all to take to my mother."

He spoke to the crucifix this way for a long time, and finally the Lord answered him, "I myself am poor and cannot give you any money. But go to Rome—my brother lives there in the greatest church. He is much richer than I am. Perhaps he can give you the money."

"That's true," said the young man. "You must be very poor because you're completely naked."

So he went back to his corner and waited until the sacristan opened the church the next morning so he could leave. Then he set out for Rome without telling his mother anything. He wandered the entire day until it became dark and he came to a monastery.

"Perhaps I can stay here for the night," he thought, knocked on the door, and asked for shelter. He was granted permission to enter, and he and the prior conversed for a while.

"Where are you going, my son?" he asked.

"I must go to Rome and speak with the Lord about a sum of money that he owes me."

At first the prior thought that the peasant boy wanted to make a fool of him, but as soon as he realized how simple-minded he was, he said to him, "You could do me a favor. My monks always have an argument after supper and bash each other's heads until they are bloody. Otherwise, they are very pious and behave themselves. It's as though some evil spirit took possession of them after supper. When you speak with the Lord, ask him where all this comes from, and if you bring me the right answer on your return, I'll give you a gift of one hundred ounces of gold."

The young man promised to do this. Then he rested the entire night in the monastery, and the next morning he set out again on his way to Rome. He wandered the entire day until evening when he came to a small city. All at once he saw a pretty cottage, knocked at the door, and asked for shelter, and the owner granted it to him. This man was a merchant and had three beautiful daughters. When the merchant began talking to the young man, he asked him where he was going.

"I have to go to Rome and speak with the Lord because of a sum of money that he must give me."

The merchant thought he wanted to make a fool out of him, but when he realized how naive the peasant boy was, he said to him: "Do me a favor. I have three beautiful daughters and have not been able to marry off one of them, even though I'm rich. When you speak to the Lord, ask him why this is so, and if you bring me the answer, I'll give you one hundred ounces of gold."

The young man promised to do this, and the next morning he continued his journey. When it turned evening, he came to a farmhouse, knocked on the door, and asked for lodging for the night. The farmer received him in a friendly way, invited him to dinner, and asked him, "Where are you going?"

Once again the young man explained that he was going to Rome to speak to the Lord about a certain sum of money.

"You could do me a great service," the farmer said. "I have a lot of beautiful land, and previously I grew a great deal of fruit on it. But for some years now, the trees have all become barren, and I can no longer grow dates or cherries. When you speak with the Lord, ask him why this is happening. If you bring me the right answer, I'll give you a hundred ounces of gold."

The young man promised to do this, and the next morning he continued his journey. Finally he came to Rome and immediately found the greatest and most beautiful church in which a mass was being held. As soon as he saw the many silk and gold garments of the priests and the gold monstrances covered with precious stones, he thought, "The Lord was right. His brother is much richer. He can certainly give me my money."

So he hid in a corner and waited patiently until the sacristan closed the church door. Then he climbed up to the altar and said, "Listen, you. Your brother sent me to you. He was supposed to give me a large sum of money, but he's too poor, and he told me to tell you that you should give me the money instead of him."

The Lord let him keep making this request for some time, and then he answered him: "Good, my son. Just return home, and along the way you'll receive your money."

"All right," the young man said, "But I still must ask you something. About a half a day's journey from here there's a farmer who owns some land that used to produce a lot fruit. But for some years now the trees have become barren. Why is that happening?"

"Before this," the Lord responded, "the farmer had not built a wall around his property, and when a poor person came by and needed something to eat, he stuck out his hand and took a pear or some other fruit to fill his stomach. But the farmer was greedy and refused to grant the poor people some fruit. That's why he had a wall built around his land, and since then the trees have become barren. If he tears down the wall, the land will once again produce the fruit he wants."

"Tell me something more," the young man continued. "There's a merchant living in a city nearby, and he has three beautiful daughters. Even though he's rich, he's not been able to marry off any of them. Why's that so?"

"The girls are much too interested in their dresses and want to attract men by the clothes they wear. If they were nice and proper and would go to church without makeup, they would soon find husbands."

"Now, I'd like to know one more thing," said the young man. "There's a monastery not too far from here, and the monks are well-behaved and pious the entire day. But when they eat in the evening, they begin to argue and make a racket. Why's that happening?"

"The devil is their cook," the Lord answered. "He's cast a spell over their food so that it causes them strife."

The young man thanked the Lord, and the Lord took something from his side and gave him a stone upon his departure and told him to keep it somewhere safe. The young man hid in the corner again, and when the sacristan came the next morning, the peasant boy went out and began his journey back home.

When he came to the farmer, the man asked him, "Did you speak with the Lord?"

"Yes," he answered, "the trees on your property are barren because you built a wall around your entire land. When the wall is torn down and does not keep the poor from taking fruit from time to time, your land will produce fruit again."

"Wonderful," said the farmer. "I'll try this right away. But you must stay here until the trees bear fruit again, otherwise I won't give you the hundred ounces of gold."

So the young man remained there, and the farmer tore down the wall, and just imagine, in a few days the trees were covered with blossoms! So the farmer gave the young man the hundred ounces of gold, thanked him, and let him go.

Then the young man went to the merchant, who also asked him whether he had spoken with the Lord.

"Yes," he answered. "Your daughters won't get married because they think about make-up and clothes too much. If they were to go to church and be nice and proper, they would soon find husbands for themselves."

"Stay a few days with me so I can see whether your advice is really good," said the merchant. "Then I'll give you the hundred ounces of gold."

So the young man remained there, and the merchant took the make-up and beautiful clothes away from his daughters and sent them to church dressed in a modest and proper way. And just imagine, after a few days, there were so many suitors who wanted to marry the merchant's daughters that the merchant had a large choice to select from! Consequently, he gave the young man the hundred ounces of gold, thanked him for his good advice, and let him depart.

In the evening the young man came to the monastery and was led to the prior, who asked:

"Have you spoken with the Lord?"

"The devil is the cook in your monastery, and he casts a magic spell over the food that causes strife among the monks," the young man answered.

"If that's true," the prior said, "I shall make this sinister spirit disappear right away."

So he took some holy water and dressed himself in holy robes, went into the church, and cast the evil spirit out of the monastery through his sacred acts so that the monks were left in peace from then on. The prior thanked the young man, gave him one hundred ounces of gold, and let him depart.

When he approached the city, the stone, which he had been carrying in a pocket next to his chest, began to illuminate and send such bright wonderful rays that one could see them from miles around. When news reached the priests, they set out ceremoniously and marched toward the wondrous stone. Then the young man told them everything, and because he was found to be worthy of speaking with the Lord, he was also to carry the stone and walked beneath the canopy of the holy procession with the stone in his hands. When he went into the church and placed the stone on the altar, he fell to the ground and was dead, but his soul flew up to heaven. His mother happened to be in the church and recognized her son, and when she saw him sink to the ground, she rushed to him and took him in her arms. All at once she found the three hundred ounces of gold and took them and led a pious life by doing much good for the poor. And when she died, she was reunited with her son in heaven.

23

SABEDDA AND HER BROTHER

Once upon a time there was a man whose wife died and left behind two children, a son and a daughter. The daughter was very beautiful, more beautiful than the son, and was taught by a teacher in a school. This teacher had a daughter, who was dark and ugly—uglier than debts. Since the teacher was a shrewd woman, she gave the beautiful girl sweets and said to her, "Tell your father he should marry me, and then I'll give you sweets every day, and you'll lead a good life."

So the child asked her father to marry the friendly teacher, but the father always answered, "Sabedda,* you don't know what you're saying. You'll see. You'll regret this one day."

But Sabedda continued to ask until he lost his patience one day and said, "Good, I'll do what you want, but when things go bad for you, don't come to me and complain."

So the father married the teacher, and at first the stepmother was friendly with Sabedda and her brother. But it did not take long before she became unfriendly, and Sabedda had to do all the hard work: look for wood and carry the water. Moreover, she often received beatings and little to eat. On the other hand, the woman was friendly toward her own

---

* Isabella.

daughter and let her do what she wanted. When Sabedda became sad, her father said to her, "You see. Why didn't you listen to me? I told you that you would regret it. Now I can't help you."

One day, after the stepmother had cruelly beaten the poor Sabedda once more, the girl said to her little brother, "Come, let's set out into the wide world and try our luck. I can't hold out any longer the way our stepmother is treating me."

Her brother agreed, and so they stole away and wandered into the wide world. After they had traveled for a long time, the brother became so thirsty that he was wasting away, and when they came to a brook, he said, "Sabedda, I'm so thirsty. I want to have a drink."

But Sabedda listened to the murmuring water of the little brook, "Whoever drinks my water will be turned into a sheep with gold horns."

However, her brother had already bent over the brook, and no sooner did he take a swig of water than he was transformed into a cute little sheep with pretty gold horns. All at once Sabedda began to weep and continued sadly on her way with the sheep running next to her. On this very same day, the king happened to go on a hunt, and while he was chasing a deer, he encountered the weeping Sabedda, who was so beautiful that he could not take his eyes off her. Then he asked why she was crying, and she answered, "I'm a poor child and have a wicked stepmother at home. She always beats me so much, and that's why I ran away."

"Do you want to come to my castle and become my wife?" the king answered.

"Yes," answered Sabedda, "but my sheep must also come with me."

The king took her up on his horse, and a servant led the little sheep, and so they went to the castle. The king had Sabedda dressed in royal clothes, and a magnificent wedding was celebrated. But Sabedda always looked after her little sheep first, and the animal also had to sleep in her room.

After a year the queen gave birth to a lovely boy who was the great joy of the castle. However, about the same time, the deceitful stepmother heard that Sabedda had not died and had instead become a queen. Therefore, she became completely green with envy and kept thinking of a way to bring about her ruin. So she bought some sweets, put a sleeping potion into a little bottle, adorned herself and her daughter, and went to the castle just when the king had gone out to hunt and Sabedda lay sick in bed.

"Oh, you poor child," the lying stepmother said, "how happy I am to see you so well and alive. Look, I've brought some sweets and this refreshing wine that will do you good. Just try it one time."

Sabedda refused because she feared that her stepmother had something awful up her sleeve, but she did take some of the wine, and no sooner did she swallow some than she fell into a deep sleep. Then her stepmother quickly took off her nightgown and threw her into the cistern, which was in the garden and in which a large fish lived, and this fish swallowed poor Sabedda right away. The stepmother put Sabedda's nightgown on her ugly, one-eyed daughter and put her into the queen's bed. Then the duplicitous stepmother rushed home before the king returned from the hunt.

When the king entered his wife's room and saw the ugly, one-eyed figure lying in the bed, he had a fright and said, "What's happened to you?

"Oh," answered the false queen, "the sheep rammed me with its horns and knocked out one of my eyes."

Well, that terrible animal will no longer live," said the king, who summoned his cook and said to him, "Get your sharpest knives ready because I want you to cut the little sheep's throat tonight."

So the cook grabbed the sheep by the horns, dragged it out of the room, took it into the kitchen, and began to sharpen his knives. Meanwhile, the poor distressed sheep snuck out into the garden where the cistern was, and it began to weep bitter tears and groan:

Sabedda dear, Sabedda mine,
They're sharpening a knife
to cut my throat and take my life.*

When the cook wanted to fetch the sheep to cut its throat, he heard it moaning and groaning and was so horrified by what he heard that he quickly ran to the king and said, "Just think, your majesty, the sheep talks like a reasonable person."

"You're crazy," the king said, but he went with the cook to the cistern where the sheep was still standing and lamenting:

Sabedda dear, Sabedda mine,
They're sharpening a knife
to cut my throat and take my life.

---

* Sabedda, mia Sabedda,
  Pri mia mmolanu li cutedda,
  Pri tagghiari sta carni bedda.

When the king heard this, he sprung forth and cried, "If you can talk, then tell me why you're standing next to the cistern and calling my Sabedda. Otherwise, I'll cut off your head."

So the sheep told him how the stepmother had come and thrown poor Sabedda into the cistern, and that the woman who was lying in the queen's bed was really not the young queen but the stepmother's ugly daughter."

Immediately the king ordered his servants to catch the large fish. Once they had it, they opened it and poured warm oil down the fish's throat until it spit out Sabedda, who was well and alive and had become even more beautiful than she was before. At the same time, the magic that had caused her brother to turn into a sheep vanished, and he became a handsome young man who embraced his sister Sabedda full of joy.

Now the king had his dear wife bathed in precious sweet-smelling water and dressed in her royal garments. He had the ugly daughter cut into pieces, salted in a barrel, and had her head placed at the bottom. Then he sent the barrel to the stepmother and informed her that her daughter was sending her this barrel full of tuna fish. The wicked woman took off the top of the barrel and began to eat the fish. She had a cat that kept springing onto her lap and saying, "Give me something to eat too, and then later I'll also help you weep."

However, she kicked the cat off her and cried, "What? You think I should give you some of this beautiful tuna fish, which my daughter, the queen, has sent to me?"

Now, when she came to the bottom of the barrel and caught sight of the head, she realized that she had eaten her own daughter and began to scream loudly and hit her head against the wall until she sank dead to the ground. But the cat sang: "You didn't want to give me anything to eat, and now I won't help you weep," and it danced around the entire house.

The king and the young queen lived happy and content, and we still don't have a cent.

24

THE CLEVER SHOEMAKER

Once upon a time there was a shoemaker who was very poor and could not find work, and he and his wife almost died from hunger. One day he said to his wife, "My dear, I can't find any work here, so I'm going to set out for the plain of Mascalucia. Perhaps I'll have some luck there."

So he set out and wandered until he came to Mascalucia. No sooner did he begin to yell, "Who wants a shoemaker," than a window opened, and a woman asked him to sew a pair of shoes for her. When he was done, she asked, "How much do I owe you?"

"One tari."

"Here are ten grani, and may the Lord bless you."

The shoemaker began to cry out again, and soon another window opened, and he found some new work.

"How much do we owe you?"

"Three carlini."

"Here are twenty-five grani, and may the Lord bless you."

"Well," thought Master Giuseppe, "things are all right here. I don't think I'll return to my wife just yet. First I'll earn a nice little sum of money, and then I'll ride home on a donkey."

So he remained there many days, found as much work as he needed, and finally earned four gold ounces. Then he went to the marketplace, bought a good donkey for two ounces, and set out on his way back to Catania. As he was going through the forest, he saw four robbers coming at him from a distance. "Oh, now I'm lost," he thought. "They'll certainly take everything from me that I worked so hard to earn." However, he was sly and did not lose his courage. He took the five thalers that were left and stuck them under the donkey's tail. Soon the robbers came upon him and demanded his money.

"Oh, dear friends," he cried, "I'm a poor shoemaker and don't have any money. The only thing I own is this donkey."

But just at that moment the donkey lifted its tail, and the five thalers fell to the ground.

"Well, what is that then?" the robbers asked.

"Yes, my friends," the shoemaker answered, "this donkey is a gold donkey and brings me a good deal of money."

"Sell it to us," the robbers said. "We'll give you as much as you want."

At first the shoemaker refused, and then he pretended to be persuaded by them and sold them the donkey for fifty gold ounces.

"Listen to what I say," he told them. "Each one of you must ride him for one day and one night, one after the other. Otherwise you'll fight with each other over the gold that he produces."

The robbers were delighted and drove their donkey into the forest. Meanwhile Master Giuseppe laughed as he traveled home and rejoiced about the bargain that he had made. He bought a good midday meal, and he and his wife dined with pleasure. Finally, the very next day he bought a pretty vineyard.

Meanwhile the robbers had returned to their hometown with the donkey, and the captain of the robbers said, "I deserve the right to keep the donkey for the first night."

His companions agreed, and so the captain took the donkey to his house, called his wife, and ordered her to spread out a bed sheet in the stable so that the donkey could spend the night on it. She was puzzled by her husband's foolish idea, but he said, "What's it to you? Do what I say, and tomorrow morning we'll find treasures here."

Early the next morning the robber captain rushed to the stable, but instead of treasures he found something else, and realized that Master Giuseppe had tricked them.

"All right," he thought, "Master Giuseppe fooled me, but the others should experience just what I experienced."

When his first companion came to him and asked whether he had gotten a lot of thalers, the captain answered, "Oh brother, if you only knew what wonderful treasures I found! But I don't want to show them to you right now. I'll do it only when we can all show what we've gotten."

So the robber took the donkey with him, but things did not go any better for him than it had for the captain. In short, each one of the four robbers experienced the same thing. When the fourth night flew by and the robbers came together, they decided to attack the shoemaker in his own house and strangle him. They set out on their way and soon came to Master Giuseppe's house. However, he had already seen them coming from a distance and quickly thought of a new trick. He called his wife, took the skin of a sausage, filled it with blood, and tied it around her neck. Then he said to his wife, "When the robbers come, I'm going to tell them that I'll return the money to them, and I'll order you to rush and get the money. But I want you to hesitate a little as if you weren't going to obey me. I'll get mad and stick my knife into this sausage skin, and you'll fall to the ground as if you were dead. When you hear me playing the guitar, I want you to rise up and begin dancing."

It did not take long before the robbers entered the house and began heaping insults and accusing the shoemaker of tricking them.

"You mean, you didn't get any money?" the shoemaker asked in astonishment. "The poor beast probably lost its magic power because it had to change houses. Just calm down. We don't want to argue about something like this. I'll pay you back the fifty gold ounces right away. Agatha, run quickly into the next room and bring these gentlemen the fifty ounces."

"All right," she answered. "But first I must finish chopping the fish. I can't go right away."

"What? Do what I say when I say it!" the shoemaker yelled and pretended to be furious with his wife. "I'll show you!"

Upon saying this, he stabbed her in her neck so that she fell to the ground as if she were dead, and the blood streamed out of the sausage skin.

"Oh, Master Giuseppe, what have you done?" the robbers cried out. "Your poor wife didn't do anything to harm you."

"Oh, let's not waste any words about this," the shoemaker replied, and he took out his guitar and began to play. All at once his wife stood up and began to dance. The robbers stood there with their mouths wide open. Finally they said, "Master Giuseppe, keep the fifty ounces, but tell us how much you want for the guitar. You've got to sell it to us."

"Oh no, gentlemen, I can't do this," the shoemaker said. "Each time I have an argument with my wife, I murder her, and that's the way I cool off my anger. I've become accustomed to this, and if I do this again and don't have the guitar anymore, I won't be able to wake her up and bring her back to life."

But the robbers kept asking him until he finally sold the guitar to them for forty ounces of gold. The robbers were delighted and returned home with the guitar. Then the captain said, "I deserve to try out the guitar the first night."

When he went home, he called his wife and asked, "What's there to eat tonight?"

"Pasta," she said.

"Why didn't you bake any fish?" he screamed and stabbed her in her neck so that she fell down dead. Then he took the guitar and played it, but no matter how much he played, the dead woman did not awake again.

"Oh, that no-good shoemaker! That lousy scoundrel! He's tricked me a second time and I'll strangle him for this!"

But all his shouting could not help him. His wife was dead and remained dead. The next morning one of the other robbers came to fetch the guitar and asked, "Well, brother, how did things go?"

"Oh, wonderful. I killed my wife, and no sooner did I begin to play than she awoke and stood right up."

"Are you serious? Well, then I'm going to try it out this evening."

In short, the four robbers killed their wives, and later, after they came together on the fifth morning and exchanged their stories with each other, they swore they would murder the clever shoemaker. They set out and came to his house, but Master Giuseppe saw them coming from a distance and said to his wife, "Listen, Agatha, when the robbers come and ask where I am, tell them that I went into the vineyard. Then order the dog to call me and chase him out of the house."

Then Master Giuseppe went out a back door into the open and hid himself in a place near the house. Soon thereafter the robbers arrived and asked for him.

"Oh, gentlemen," his wife answered, "he just went into the vineyard. I'll have the dog call him right away." And she turned to the dog: "Go quickly into the vineyard and call your master. Tell him that four men are here to speak with him."

Upon saying this, she opened the door and chased him outside.

"Don't tell us that you're sending the dog to fetch your husband." the robbers said.

"Of course," she replied. "He understands everything, and he'll tell my husband everything that I told him."

After a short time the shoemaker entered and said, "Welcome, gentlemen. The dog told me that you wanted to speak with me."

"Yes, indeed," the robber captain said. "We've come to question you about the guitar. You're to blame for causing us to kill all four of our wives because none of us was able to bring his wife back to life."

"You probably didn't do things the right way," the shoemaker responded.

"Well, we'll forget about all this," the captain said, "but you must sell us your dog."

"Oh no, I can't do this. Just think how much he's worth."

However, the robbers kept asking until Master Giuseppe sold them the dog for forty ounces of gold. The robbers took the dog with them, and the robber captain told his companions that he deserved to have the right to use the animal first. So he took the dog home and said to his daughter, "I'm going to the tavern. When someone comes and wants to speak with me, I want you to set the dog loose and send him to me so that he can call me home."

When someone really came who wanted to speak with him, the daughter set the dog loose and said, "Go to the tavern and call father."

But instead, the dog ran back to the shoemaker.

Later, when the robber came home and did not see the dog anymore, he thought, "He must have returned to his former master." So he set out in the night and went to the shoemaker.

"Master Giuseppe, is the dog here?"

"Oh yes, the poor beast is very attached to me. He'll be like this until he gets accustomed to you."

So the captain took the dog home again and gave him to the second robber the next morning. But he did not tell him the truth about the dog, as the shoemaker had told him. In short, each robber wanted the dog to carry out a task, and each time the dog ran back to the shoemaker and the robbers were compelled to go fetch the dog. When they gathered together on the fifth morning, it became clear that Master Giuseppe had gotten the best of them again, and they decided to strangle him and not to accept anything more from him. So they went to him and began making violent accusations. Finally, they stuck him into a sack and intended to throw him into the sea. Master Giuseppe remained calm and did not resist at all.

As the robbers walked past a church, mass was just about to be held, and the robbers decided to hear the mass first because they were religious people.* So they left the sack outside and went to the church. Nearby a boy was looking after a large herd of pigs and was whistling a merry tune. When Master Giuseppe heard this, he began to shout in a loud voice: "I don't want to! I don't want to!"

"What don't you want to do?" the boy asked.

"Oh," replied the shoemaker, "I'm supposed to marry the king's daughter, and I don't want to."

---

* Divozianati.

"Oh," the swineherd sighed, "if only I could marry her!"

"Well, there's nothing easier than that," the sly shoemaker responded. "All you have to do is to get into this sack and let me out."

So the swineherd opened the sack and let the shoemaker out. Then he crawled inside himself, and the shoemaker drove the pigs along in great delight. When the robbers came out of the church, they took the sack on their backs and threw it into the sea where it was very deep. On their return home, however, Master Giuseppe came toward them with his herd of pigs, and they stared at him with open mouths.

"Oh, if you only knew how many pigs were in the sea!" he cried. "The deeper you go, the more you find. I got this nice herd and came back up to the shore."

"Are there still more there?"

"Oh, much more than you can bring back," the sly shoemaker said.

"Take us to the spot," they replied.

So the shoemaker led them to the beach and said, "First you all have to tie a rock around your necks. Otherwise, you won't be able to sink deep enough. I already caught all the pigs that were near the top."

Each one of the robbers tied a rock around his neck and jumped into the sea, but they all sank and drowned. On the other hand, Master Giuseppe happily drove his pigs back home and had enough for the rest of his life.

> The sounds of this tale ring from a shell,
> The words of this tale flow from a bowl!
> How beautiful that lady is
> Who told me to tell this tale!*

---

* Faula ntra conca, e faula ntrô bacili,
  Ch'è bedda sta Signura, chi mi l'ha fattu diri!

25

THE TWINS

Once upon a time there was a king who possessed a beautiful and large realm, but he did not have any children. Now a war with another king happened to erupt, and the king had to contend with him and lost the battle. Consequently, all his states were taken from him, and he had to flee from his realm with his wife. They wandered about for a long time until they came to a deserted beach near the sea. They decided to build a little hut there, and the king went fishing while the queen cooked the fish that he brought home, and this was the wretched way they lived with one another.

One day the king happened to catch a gold fish, that spoke to him.

"Listen to me," the fish said, "take me home with you and cut me into eight pieces. Give two to your wife, two to your horse, two to your dog, and bury two in your garden. This will bring you good fortune."

The king did just as the fish said. He took the fish home and cut it into eight pieces. Two he gave to his queen, two to his horse, two to his dog, and two he buried in the garden. Not long thereafter the queen appeared to be pregnant, and when her time came, she gave birth to two handsome boys, who looked so alike that nobody could tell them apart. On the same day, the horse brought two colts into the world, and the dog, two puppies. In the garden two swords grew, and they were made of gold and had magic powers. The two boys grew and flourished, and they became stronger and bigger with each passing day. They were so similar in appearance that their own mother and father could not tell who was who.

When they had become big strong young men, their father told them one day that he had once been a powerful king, but that he had been defeated by a more powerful king and had been robbed of his realm.

"Father," his sons said to him, "we want to set out into the world and regain all your states for you. Give us your blessing and let us depart."

The king and queen were very despondent and did not want to let their dear sons leave, but the brothers answered, "If you do not want to give your blessing, we shall have to leave without it because we are determined to depart."

So their parents gave their blessing, and each one of the brothers took a magic sword from the garden, mounted one of the horses, and took one of the dogs with them. Then they rode off. After they had ridden for some time, one of them said, "Dear brother, here is the spot where we should separate. You go in that direction, and I shall go in the other, and once we have achieved something, we'll meet back here at this spot."

The other brother agreed, and they went their separate ways. One of the brothers rode straight ahead until he came to a city that was decorated for some kind of event.

"Why is your city decorated in such a festive way?" he asked someone on the street, and the man answered, "Our king conquered the neighboring states of a king many years ago. Now he has a lovely daughter, and he has announced to all the knights that he is going to organize a tournament that will last three days, and whoever is the victor on each one of these days is to marry the princess. As a dowry he is going to give the victor all the neighboring states that he had one time conquered."

"What's the name of your king?" the young man asked.

The man gave him the name of the king, and the youth realized that it was the same king who had conquered his father's states. So he went first to a tavern and refreshed himself with food and drink. Then he mounted his horse, strapped on his magic sword, and rode to the tournament. Many noble knights had gathered there, but the unknown youth defeated all of them because no one could compete with his magic sword. The next day the unknown youth reappeared at the tournament and was victorious again, and on the third day he defeated everyone once more. Then the king spoke to him, "You were victorious on all three days, and now you shall marry my daughter. But tell me, who are you?"

All at once the young man identified himself and said, "I am the son of the king whom you defeated, and whose states you want to give away as your daughter's dowry. I have regained my father's states and am satisfied. So let's enjoy the wedding celebration."

Soon after this they held a splendid wedding, and the prince married the princess, who was more beautiful than the sun. Later he sent a carriage and beautiful clothes to his father, and invited him to return to his realm. In the meantime the prince enjoyed living with his young wife.

One day he decided to go hunting and said to his wife, "I want to go hunting today, and I'll be away for three days."

He took his gold sword, mounted his horse, and was accompanied by his dog. On the same day, however, his brother entered the same city from the other side, and since he looked just like his brother and had the same horse, dog, and sword, everyone thought he was the young king and greeted him in a most reverent way. He was puzzled about this and thought, "Perhaps my brother has already been here."

When he came to the castle, the servants led him up into his brother's quarters, and the princess rushed toward him and said, "My dear husband, you only rode off this morning and told me that you were going to stay away for three days."

"I changed my mind," the prince answered.

So the princess led him to the table for dinner, and in the evening he went with her into the bedroom. When she laid down, however, he took his double-bladed sword and placed it between himself and the princess, who was so frightened by this that she did not dare ask him why he had done it. He continued to do this for two more nights.

When three days had passed, the young husband returned from the hunt, and everyone was astonished when they saw the young king again. He went straight to the castle, and when he saw his brother standing in the castle courtyard, he rushed toward him, embraced him, and cried, "Dear brother, is that you? Now we can really enjoy ourselves."

Everyone was astounded, and he explained to the king and the princess how everything had come about, and his young wife snuggled up to him and said softly, "I've got to tell you that your bother spent three nights in your bed, but now I know why he always placed a double-edged sword between us."

After a some days had passed and the parents of the two brothers arrived, they traveled once again to their states, where the prince became the king and the beautiful princess, the queen. Later, the other brother married another princess, and so they remained rich and consoled, and we just sit here and continue to get old.*

---

* Iddi ristaru ricchi e cunsulati,
  E nui ristammu ccà sittati.

26

BEAUTIFUL INNOCENTA

Once upon a time there was a king and a queen who did not have a child, and would very much liked to have one. So the king made a promise that if he were blessed with a son, he would have a fountain built when the boy turned twelve, and he would let the fountain flow with oil for twelve hours so that anyone who needed oil could come and fetch some. Shortly thereafter the queen became pregnant, and when her hour came, she gave birth to a splendidly handsome boy. Just think how joyful his parents were!

The child grew and became handsomer with each day that passed. When he turned twelve, the king recalled his promise, had a beautiful fountain built in the castle courtyard, and announced throughout his realm that oil would flow for twenty-four hours. People could come and fetch as much oil as they wanted for nothing. So they came from far and wide and gathered around the fountain to get the oil. The prince stood on the balcony and took pleasure in watching the spectacle. Finally, when the oil had already stopped flowing, an old woman appeared with a small pitcher. When she saw that she would not be able to fill the pitcher, she took a sponge and carefully soaked up the oil that was left in the cracks. The prince stood at his window and watched, and when the pitcher was finally full, he took a stone and, in his arrogance, threw it at the small pitcher so that it broke, and the oil spilled out. Then the old woman called out in anger: "May you never marry until you have found the beautiful Innocenta!"

From that day on the prince thought of no one but the beautiful Innocenta and never enjoyed another peaceful day. When he became somewhat older, he went to his father and said, "Dear father, give me a horse and let me set out to look for the beautiful Innocenta."

"Oh, my son," the father cried in horror. "Are you crazy? Do you know how difficult it is to find the beautiful Innocenta? Do you know that her parents are ogres? Don't think about this anymore, my son, and stay here. You have everything you want, and you're our only son."

But the prince did not stop making his request. He kept asking the king to let him depart until his father finally gave him a horse, blessed him, and let him go.

The prince rode straight ahead for a long time until he eventually came to a wild region where there were no houses to be seen. In the distance he saw a light and went straight toward it. Soon he arrived at a cottage inhabited by a hermit, who was the first guardian of the beautiful Innocenta.

"Who's outside?" he asked in a deep voice.

"I'm a poor young man," the prince answered. "Please let me spend the night here. Tomorrow I'll continue on my way."

"What? Do you intend to kidnap the beautiful Innocenta? I'm going to eat you here and now."

"Don't eat me," the prince responded. "I have no idea who the beautiful Innocenta is. I just want to go hunting for my own pleasure."

So the hermit opened the door, gave him something to eat, and showed him to a bed. The next morning when the prince was about to say farewell, the hermit gave him a staff made of velvet and gold.

"Listen to my advice," he said. "Take this staff. It will be of use to you. My older brother lives a day's journey from here. You should spend the next night with him, and when you take leave from him, let him give you two loaves of bread that will also be of use to you. The day after you will travel to my oldest brother who will give you shelter. When you are sitting at the table with him, tear three hairs from his beard and keep them in a safe pace. They, too, will be of use to you."

The young man thanked the hermit and rode the entire day until he came to the second hermit in the evening. The prince knocked at the door, and the hermit said, "Who's there?"

"I'm a poor young man. Please let me rest here tonight, and tomorrow I'll continue on my way."

"What? Do you intend to kidnap the beautiful Innocenta?" the hermit growled. "I'm going to eat you here and now."

"Don't eat me," the prince responded. "I have no idea who the beautiful Innocenta is. I just want to go hunting for pleasure."

Then the hermit opened the door, gave him something to eat, and a bed for the night. When the prince was about to take his leave the next morning, he asked the hermit, "Please give me two loaves of bread so that I don't die of hunger in this desolate spot."

So the hermit gave him two loaves and bellowed, "Don't get any ideas of kidnapping the beautiful Innocenta or you'll be in for a lot of trouble."

"What concern is it of yours what happens to the beautiful Innocenta?" the prince said and rode off.

Toward evening he came to the third hermit who was ancient and had a long white beard. "Who's outside?" he growled with a deep voice.

The prince asked him for shelter for the night, but the hermit said, "Do you intend to kidnap the beautiful Innocenta? I'm going to eat you here and now!"

But the prince swore that he had no idea who the beautiful Innocenta was, and the hermit eventually let him enter. When they sat down to eat, the prince suddenly grabbed the hermit's beard and tore out three hairs.

"What do you think you're doing?" screamed the hermit. "Now I'm going to eat you."

"Why do you want to eat me?" the prince asked. "A fly became caught in your beard, and as I tried to get rid of the fly, there were three hairs that got caught in my fingers."

The old man settled down and then showed the prince to his bed. The next morning the young man mounted his horse and continued his journey. After he had ridden for some time, he came to some plains and saw a magnificent castle ahead of him. The door stood open, but a gigantic scissors stood in front and moved back and forth opening its blades up and down so that no one could get through. So the prince dismounted, took the staff made of velvet and gold, and stuck it between the scissors. While the scissors cut the staff in two, the prince slipped through the entrance. No sooner had he made his way into the castle than two roaring lions attacked him and wanted to eat him. He threw the two loaves of bread at them, and while they turned their attention to the bread, he rushed up the stairs. In the antechamber there was a big fly* who began to buzz loudly as soon as anyone broke into the castle so that the witch would hear and rush to the spot. But the prince

---

*Musca vana.

threw the three hairs from the hermit's beard so that the fly became wrapped up in them and no longer thought about buzzing. Finally, the prince entered a large hall in which he found the beautiful Innocenta sitting on a throne, and she was more beautiful than the sun.

"Oh, beautiful Innocenta," he said, "just look at how I've worked and suffered all because of you! Now you must follow me and become my wife."

"How's that possible?" she asked. "My parents have left the castle, but they will return very soon. When they find you here, they will eat you."

"You can take care of that," the prince said. "I've done so much for you. Now you must think of a way to flee this place."

"Good," answered the beautiful Innocenta. "I'll hide you in my room for now, and tonight we shall flee this place."

So she hid the prince in her room, and soon the ogre and his wife came and bellowed, "We smell human flesh! We smell human flesh!"

"Oh, stop it," cried their daughter. "How is it possible for a human to get here? Aren't I completely safe with the buzzing fly, the two lions, and the scissors that keep watch over me?"

Soon after, when the ogre and his wife went to bed, the beautiful Innocenta called the prince, spit on the floor one time, and fled with the young man. After a while the old witch woke up, and since her daughter was not to be seen, she cried out: "Beautiful Innocenta, come and lay down to sleep."

"Soon, I just have to finish sewing this stocking," said the saliva.

"How far are you?"

"I've sewn half a leg."

After an hour the witch called out again, "Beautiful Innocenta, come and lay down to sleep."

"Soon, I just have to finish sewing this stocking."

"How far are you?"

"I'm almost done."

Once again, after a short while, the witch called out, "Beautiful Innocenta, come and lay down to sleep."

"Soon, I must finish sewing the stocking."

"How far are you?"

"I'm sewing the heels."

In the meantime it was nearly day, and the witch cried out one more time. "Beautiful Innocenta, come and lay down to sleep."

Her saliva was already dry, and she no longer answered.

"Beautiful Innocenta, beautiful Innocenta!" the witch cried out, but beautiful Innocenta had long since made her getaway over the mountains.

The witch woke the ogre and cried out, "Our daughter has fled. Come, we've got to follow her."

In order to catch up with the beautiful Innocenta, the ogre and his wife changed themselves into red and white clouds and soon had overtaken the two refugees.

"Look behind you and tell me what you see," the beautiful Innocenta said to the prince.

"I see a red and white cloud," the prince answered.

"Well, I'll become a church, and you'll become the sexton," the beautiful Innocenta said, and she was immediately turned into a church, and the prince into a sexton.

Meanwhile, the ogre and his wife reassumed their natural forms, approached the sexton, and asked him, "Have a man and a woman come riding by here?"

"It's not time yet for mass," he said and pretended as though he did not understand them.

"Have a man and a woman come by here?"

"The priest hasn't arrived yet."

"Have a man and a woman come riding by here?"

"The goblet hasn't been brought yet."

"Have a man and a woman come by here?"

"The host has been forgotten."

"Have a man and a woman come by here?"

"The book for the mass cannot be found."

Well, the ogre and the witch finally lost their patience and returned home grumbling all the way. However, the witch could not settle down and said, "I've got to catch up with them, and if you refuse to come with me, I'm going alone."

So she transformed herself into a white cloud and flew after them.

"Look behind you and tell me what you see," said beautiful Innocenta.

"I see a white cloud,"

"Then I'll become a garden, and you become the gardener."

So she became a garden, and the prince, a gardener. When the witch came, she asked him, "Have a man and a woman come by here?"

"The fennel isn't ripe yet."

"Have a man and a woman come by here?"

"I can't give you any lettuce yet."

"Have a man and a woman come by here?"

"Why are you looking for lettuce at this time of the year?"

"Are you mocking me?" the witch yelled at the gardener and wanted to attack him, but just then the beautiful Innocenta cried out, "You become a rosebush, and I'll become a rose."

Suddenly the prince became a rosebush with a wonderfully beautiful rose budding on it. The witch knew for sure that the rose was her daughter and wanted to pick it, but the rosebush stuck her with its thorns so that she became scratched all over. Still, she kept trying to pick the rose and stuck out her hand so that the beautiful Innocenta cried out again, "You become a fountain, and I'll be the eel in it."

All of a sudden the bush disappeared, and instead there was a fountain standing there, filled with clear water and an eel that was playing in it. The witch wanted to catch the eel, but just as she thought she had the eel in her fingers, it would slip through them.

"Beautiful Innocenta, beautiful Innocenta," she called. "Come with me or else you'll regret everything."

However, no matter how often she cried out to her daughter, the beautiful Innocenta would not listen to her. Finally the witch yelled, "May the prince forget you with the first kiss that his mother gives him!"

Then the witch returned to her castle.

In the meantime, the beautiful Innocenta and the prince continued on their way, and when they approached the city where his parents were living, he said to her, "Beautiful Innocenta, it's not proper at this time to enter my father's castle like this. Stay here until I go and announce your arrival to my father. Tomorrow I'll return with a splendid coach and large entourage, and I'll lead you in triumph to the castle."

"Oh, no," she said. "Don't leave me here. When your mother kisses you, you'll forget me."

"Don't worry," he answered. "I won't kiss my mother, and I'll return tomorrow."

So he led her to one of his father's peasants and left her in a farmhouse. When he arrived at the castle, his parents were full of joy to see their son again. However, he said to his mother, "Dear mother, I'm afraid you can't kiss me, otherwise I'll forget my dear bride. You see, I've found the beautiful Innocenta, and tomorrow I want to drive out with a large entourage and bring her here."

In the evening, however, after he had laid down to sleep, the queen could not resist her desire to kiss her son and thought, "I'll be able to remind him about the beautiful Innocenta." So she went into his room and kissed him, and right away he forgot the beautiful Innocenta. When he awoke, he had no idea who Innocenta was.

"My dear son," his mother said to him, "don't you want to set out and fetch the beautiful Innocenta?"

"Who is the beautiful Innocenta? I don't have any idea who she is, and I don't want to know," the prince replied.

So he stayed with his parents and led a splendid life. After some time had passed, he decided to marry another woman, and their wedding was to be celebrated soon.

The farmer with whom the beautiful Innocenta remained used to go to the city every now and then. When he came home one day, Innocenta asked him what news there was in the city. "The prince has chosen a bride for himself, and the wedding is to be celebrated in the near future."

"Do me a favor," the beautiful Innocenta said. "Buy me seven rolls of sugar and honey, and seven rolls of almond dough."

After the farmer brought her the sugar, honey, and dough, she formed two beautiful doves out of these things and cast a magic spell. Then she gave the doves to the farmer and said, "Take these to the royal castle, and have them placed secretly in the prince's room."

The farmer did exactly as she wished, and when the prince went into his room, the doves were sitting there.

"Oh, how pretty these doves are," he said and as he approached them, one of the doves began to sing, "Kirr, kirr, do you remember how I fled with you in the night and spit on the floor so that my saliva would answer for me instead of myself?"

"Yes."

"Kirr, kirr, do you remember how my parents followed us, and I changed myself into a church and you into a sexton? Do you remember how they asked whether a man and woman came by and you answered that the priest had not come, and that the goblet and the host had not arrived yet, and that the book for mass could not be found?"

"Yes."

"Kirr, kirr, do you remember how my mother overtook us, and I changed myself into a garden and you into a gardener? Do you remember how she asked you whether a man and a woman had come by, and you spoke instead of fennel and lettuce?"

"Yes."

"Kirr, kirr, do you remember how you became a rosebush, and I a rose, and how my mother wanted to pick me, and how you scratched her with your thorns?"

"Yes."

"Kirr, kirr, do you remember how you became a fountain, and I became an eel in it, and how I slipped through my mother's fingers?"

"Yes."

"Kirr, kirr, do you remember how my mother cried out to me, 'beautiful Innocenta, come with me, otherwise you'll regret everything,' and I did not listen to her? Instead I left my mother and father to follow you. Do you remember then how my mother cursed me by saying that the prince will forget me with the first kiss that his mother gives him?"

"Yes."

"Kirr, kirr, do you remember how you left me in the farmhouse, and promised to come back to me?"

When she spoke about the farmhouse, the prince remembered everything that had happened and rushed to the king and said, "Dear father, send my bride back to her home, for I already have a bride, my beautiful Innocenta, the one for whom I have suffered a great deal."

Then he got into a magnificent coach and took splendid clothes with him as well as a large entourage and drove to the farmhouse to fetch the beautiful Innocenta.

"Didn't I tell you that you shouldn't leave me here?" she said.

"My mother kissed me while I was sleeping," he answered. "That's why I forgot you. But now all our suffering has come to an end, and I've come to take you to my castle."

So she put on the beautiful clothes and sat down next to him in the magnificent coach and rode to the royal castle in honor. The king and queen were very happy about their son's beautiful bride and arranged a wonderful wedding. So they finally became man and wife, and now the story is done.

27

THE WICKED SCHOOLMASTER AND
THE WANDERING PRINCESS

Once upon a time there was a king and a queen who had just one daughter, and they loved her very much. They sent her to a teacher, who looked after other children in his school as well. However, the teacher was a wicked man and often hit the poor children.

Every day he would say to them, "Children be still and quiet until I return." Then he went into his room and only came out again after many hours had passed. As a result, the children became curious, and one day they said, "Let's crawl to the door and look through the keyhole."

But the princess was afraid and did not want to do what the others had decided to do.

"If we all go there, you must come with us as well," they insisted and continued to push her until she decided to go along. So they crept up to the door and looked through the keyhole and saw that the teacher was occupied with a dead person, but they could not see exactly what he was doing because he approached the door very quickly. They all ran back to their places, but the princess lost a shoe on the way and had to return to her place with one missing. When the schoolmaster entered with the shoe, she pulled her foot beneath her skirt so he could not see it.

"Which one of you has lost a shoe?" he asked.

All of the other children showed their feet and cried out: "Not me!"

The poor little princess, however, refused to show her foot, and the teacher said, "Well then, you were the one who was looking through the keyhole. Just you wait. Your punishment will come."

At noon when the other children went home, the servant came to fetch the princess, but the teacher said, "Tell your majesty that the girl would like to eat with me today. She'll come home this evening."

The princess wept, but she had to remain there. When all the children left, the teacher beat the poor child and mistreated her in a terrible way. Finally, he placed a curse on her. "Seven years, seven months, and seven days you shall spend in your bed, and when you are eventually cured, a cloud will come and carry you to the top of Mount Calvary."*

The poor child went home and became sick, so sick that she had to go to bed. She remained sick for many years, and there was not a single doctor who could help her. When the seven years and seven months had passed, however, she became completely healthy and turned into a astonishingly beautiful young woman.

Then, one day, a chambermaid said to her, "It's such a beautiful, sunny day. Come out on to the terrace.† I shall comb your hair."

At first the princess refused, but the chambermaid persuaded her to climb out onto the terrace. When they were on top, the chambermaid took down her beautiful braids and wanted to comb her hair, but she noticed that she had forgotten the ribbons for her hair and said, "I just have to go and fetch the ribbons. I'll return right away."

"Oh, stay with me," the princess said. "It doesn't matter. You can comb my hair without the ribbons."

"No, no," the chambermaid responded. "I want to make you look pretty. I'll be back in a moment."

As she rushed down the stairs, a cloud came by, sank down to the terrace, and swept the princess away to Mount Calvary. When the chambermaid returned to the terrace, she saw that her young mistress had disappeared and she began to yammer. "Oh, if only I hadn't left!" Then she ran to the queen and told her what had happened. The entire castle was in an uproar, and everyone searched for the princess all over, but she was nowhere to be found. Her parents were deeply distressed, and her mother said, "My poor child is certainly cursed."

Let's leave the parents now and see what happened to the princess.

The cloud carried her to the top of Mount Calvary and set her down there. It was such a terribly steep mountain that no one had ever managed to climb it. Because she did not want to remain there, she

---

* Munti Calvàriu.

† Lastrino.

placed herself in the hands of our dear Lord and began to climb down the mountain. The thorns and stones ripped her clothes and wounded her tender arms and legs. Finally, however, she reached the foot of the mountain. She wandered until she came to a large magnificent castle, which she entered and went through all the rooms. She did not see a single human soul, but she could not help but notice the most beautiful treasures and a table covered with delicious food. When she reached the last room, she saw a handsome young man lying on the ground. He seemed to be dead, and next to him was a note that read: "If a maiden rubs me for seven years, seven months, and seven days with the grass from Mt. Calvary, I shall return to life, and she shall become my wife."

Then the princess thought: "I'm indeed a poor maiden. I can't find my way back to my parents. I don't have anything to do, so I might as well do a good deed."

So she made the strenuous climb back up Mt. Calvary without worrying about the thorns that ripped her tender arms and legs. Once she was on top, she cut the grass and made many bundles, which she threw down the mountain. Then she climbed down and reached the bottom more dead than alive. After she had somewhat recovered, she began to carry the bundles of grass into the castle and set herself to work rubbing the young man, day and night without sleeping or resting. But once a day she got up to eat something from the delicious food on the table.

This was how seven years and seven months passed. When there were only three days left of the seven, she became so tired that she could barely continue. All at once she heard someone offering a slave for sale on the street and thought, "I could buy this slave and let her rub a little while I rest for a few hours." So she bought the slave who was as black and ugly as one's debts,* and she commanded her to rub the handsome young man while she rested. When she laid down, however, she was so tired that she slept for three days without waking, and when she awoke, the seven years, seven months, and seven days were over. The handsome young man had awakened, regarded the ugly black slave as his savior, and said to her, "You have rescued me. So you shall be my wife." When the princess now appeared, he asked, "Who is this beautiful maiden?"

"She's my kitchen maid," the slave said.

Therefore, the poor princess had to go to the kitchen and do the most demeaning kind of work. Meanwhile, the entire castle became alive with servants and foresters and the entire entourage of a king, for the

---

*Brutta comu i debiti.

handsome young man was a prince who had been under a magic spell. Now he celebrated a splendid wedding with the black slave, and the princess had to work in the kitchen.

However, once the king's marshal saw her, he found her so beautiful and good that he developed a great fondness for her. One day, when he had to go on a journey, he called her and said, "I must travel to Rome. Would you like me to bring you anything?"

"Bring me a knife and a stone of patience."

The marshal left, and while he was in Rome, he searched for a long time until he found a stone of patience, which he brought back to her with a knife. Now, of course, he became curious about why the princess wanted these things. So he crept after her and saw that she went into her room and closed the door. When he looked through the keyhole, he saw that she placed the stone of patience and the knife on a table, and she began to complain: "Oh stone of patience, listen to what has happened in my life." Then she told her entire life history beginning with the first day of school. As she told her story, the stone began to swell, and she said, "Oh stone of patience, if you are swelling when you hear about my sufferings, just think how I must feel."

When the marshal heard all this, he rushed to the prince and asked him to come with him and witness this marvelous event. So the prince went with him and looked through the keyhole and heard the princess tell how she had rubbed the handsome young man for so many years and had gone to fetch the grass on top of Mount Calvary. In the meantime the stone became even more swollen, and finally, when the princess told how she had been betrayed by the deceitful slave after all her efforts and work, the stone burst with a powerful bang.

"Oh, stone of patience," she cried, "if you burst upon hearing the story of my life, then I no longer wish to live." As she said this, she grabbed the knife and wanted to kill herself, but the prince knocked down the door, took her by the arm, and said, "You and no other shall become my wife, and the lying slave will pronounce her own sentence."

So he went to the slave and said, "Today my cousin is coming to visit. I want you to give her a good reception."

When the cousin arrived, it was none other than the princess who had meanwhile dressed herself in costly garments so that the slave would not recognize her. After they sat down at the table, the prince asked the slave, "What does a maiden deserve who has betrayed her mistress?"

The slave was distracted and answered, "The best thing to do would be to put her into a barrel of boiling oil and to let her be dragged by a horse through the entire city."

"You've spoken your own sentence," the prince said, "and I want the sentence carried out now."

So she was put into a barrel of boiling oil and dragged through the entire city. Meanwhile, the prince married the beautiful princess, who informed her parents about her wedding. And then they all lived happily and content, but we were left without a cent.

28

THE FOUR PRINCESSES

Once upon a time there was a king who had four beautiful daughters. One day he summoned a fortuneteller who was to tell him the fate of the princesses.

"Before the youngest princess turns fourteen," the fortuneteller said, "a cloud will come and carry off the four sisters."

As a result, the king had his daughters locked up in the castle, and they were not allowed to go even into the garden. Since the cloud never appeared, however, he finally came to the conclusion that the fortuneteller had made a mistake, and one day, when the princesses had a great yearning to go into the garden, he allowed them to do so. Unfortunately, there were only a few days left before the youngest princess would complete her fourteenth year. No sooner did the princesses enter the garden than a large cloud sank down and whisked away all four of them. Now the king was very sad, and he issued a proclamation announcing throughout his kingdom that whoever brought back his daughters would be able to choose one of them for his wife and could succeed him as king.

Three brothers heard about the proclamation, sons of a neighboring king, and they set out to search for the four princesses. They kept traveling straight ahead because they did not know where the princesses were staying. One day they encountered an old woman who asked them, "My handsome lads, where are you heading?"

"We've set out to find the four princesses who were carried away by a cloud," the youngest answered.

"Oh, you poor boys!" cried the old woman. "You'll have to put up with many dangers and difficulties. After you have traveled for a long time, you'll come to a cistern, and you'll have to climb down into it. But at the bottom is a dragon with seven heads, and this monster guards the princesses. You will have to kill it to rescue them."

The princes thanked the friendly old woman for the information and continued their journey. After they had wandered for many days, they finally came to the cistern in which the dragon was living.

"Let me go down first," the eldest brother said, "and when I ring this bell, pull me up quickly."

So they tied a rope around his body and let him down into the cistern, and he held the little bell in his hand. It was so very dark and eery in the cistern that he soon lost his courage and rang the bell. His brothers pulled him up at once, and the second had the rope tied around his body and wanted to try his luck. But he did not go much further than the eldest. He, too, lost his courage and gave the signal to have himself pulled up. Now it was the youngest's turn. He had the rope tied around him like his brothers and took the little bell with him. However, because he had more courage than the other two, he landed successfully at the bottom of the cistern. Then he entered a large space where the princesses were chained to the wall, and in the middle stood the dragon with seven heads, who looked fierce and horrible. The prince pulled out his sword and began to fight the dragon. Whenever he became exhausted, he looked at the youngest princess who inspired him so that he regained his strength and finally managed to cut off the seven heads of the dragon. The princesses were full of joy, and the prince undid their chains and led them to the place where his brothers were supposed to pull him up. Yet no matter how often he rang the bell, no one responded or pulled the rope up because his brothers had become impatient and had abandoned him.

"What shall we do now?" the prince asked the princesses.

They didn't know how to get out of their dilemma either. Finally the youngest princess said, "Every day an eagle comes and flies down into the cistern. If we ask the bird in a friendly way, perhaps it will carry us above with its wings."

So they waited patiently until the eagle came flying down into the cistern, and they asked the bird whether it would carry them on its wings.

"I'll gladly do this," the eagle replied, "but you must feed me until I'm full."

"That can easily be done," responded the prince. "Right here we have the dragon lying on the ground."

Upon saying this he cut the dragon into tiny pieces and gave them to the eagle to eat. The bird ate until it was full and carried the eldest princess to the top of the cistern. When he returned, he ate another piece of the dragon and carried the second princess up to the spot where there was daylight. Then he took the third and finally the fourth as well.

Only the prince was left, but the eagle had eaten the entire dragon and said, "Unless you give me something to eat, I won't carry you up."

"Where do you expect me to find something in this desolate spot?" the prince replied to the eagle. "Once we get to the top, I'll give you what you want."

But the eagle would not be moved by the prince's plea and said, "Cut some of your flesh from your arms and legs, and give it to me. Then I'll be satisfied."

"I have nothing to lose because I'll be dead if I don't do what the bird asks," the prince thought. "I might as well try this last way to save myself."

So he cut some flesh from his arms and legs and offered it to the eagle. After the bird devoured the flesh, it carried him to the top. When the princesses saw how bloody he was, they were horrified. They immediately dressed his wounds and took care of him until he was healthy again. Then the prince led the princesses to their father and chose the youngest for his wife. Afterward they celebrated a splendid wedding, and when the king died, the prince received the crown and lived happily and content, but we did not receive a cent.

29

ZAFARANA

Once upon a time there was a merchant who had three daughters. They were all very beautiful, but the youngest was the most beautiful of all. When he went on his business trips, he always asked his daughters what he could bring back to them.

One day he had to take another trip, so he went to his daughters and said, "Dear children, I must travel to France. What should I bring back to you?"

The two eldest chose beautiful clothes and jewelry, but the youngest, Zafarana, said, "Dear father, just greet the son of the King of France for me."

When the merchant had ended all his business in France, he asked for permission to see the king's son and gave him his daughter's greetings. Then the prince replied: "I want to marry your daughter Zafarana."

The merchant was very happy about this and took the prince on his ship and returned home. When they arrived at the strait of Messina, however, they heard a threatening voice:

"Do not touch Zafarana! She is mine!"

The father became so frightened by this that he changed his mind and was unwilling to give his youngest daughter to the prince. So the merchant had him marry his oldest daughter.

After some time had passed, the merchant had to travel again and asked his daughters what he should bring back to them. The second daughter asked for some beautiful jewelry, but Zafarana said, "Dear father, just greet the son of the King of Portugal for me."

When her father had finished all his business, he asked permission to see the prince and conveyed Zafarana's greetings. In reply, the prince said, "I want to marry your daughter, Zafarana."

So they boarded the merchant's ship and set sail for Messina. However, when they entered the strait, they heard the same voice, which was even more threatening: "Do not touch Zafarana! She is mine!"

Now the father was very distressed and thought, "There must be some magic spell on my daughter. Who knows what lies ahead for her." So he did not want to give his youngest daughter to the prince. Instead, he gave him the middle daughter.

Now Zafarana lived alone with her father who could not forget the threatening voice. Moreover, he could not think at all of traveling again because he was afraid to leave her alone. However, finally he could not put off his business any longer, so he called together all his servants and said, "I have to take a trip, and I am placing you in charge of my daughter. Do everything that she wishes and keep her out of danger."

The servants promised to do his bidding, and he departed with a heavy heart. But Zafarana had everything that she desired, and the servants did whatever she wanted. One day she felt a desire to drive out somewhere and take a walk. So she went to the coachman and asked him to take a drive into the woods. Once she was there, the coach stopped, and she got out and told the coachman, "I want to walk by myself a while. Wait here, and I'll return soon."

Then she began to climb a hill. When she reached the top, a cloud sank down and took her away. At first the coachman waited a while, but when his mistress did not reappear, he followed the way she went up the hill. But no matter how much he called and searched, he could not find a trace of her. Soon it became dark, and there was nothing he could do except to return to Messina.

"Oh," he thought, "what am I going to say after the master returns?"

When the coachman returned home, the chambermaid came running and called out, "Why did you stay out so late? It's already pitch black. What's the matter? Where's our mistress?"

Now the coachman explained that Zafarana had disappeared, and all the servants began to moan and groan. They set out in search of the maiden, but it was all in vain. When the father returned from his journey, his servants met him with such sad faces that he became very anxious and asked right away: "Where is my daughter?"

Then they had to tell him how she had disappeared. The unfortunate father could not console himself at all and kept on saying, "I knew it. There's a magic spell on my daughter!"

In the meantime Zafarana was carried by the cloud through the air and set down in a beautiful castle. A very old man lived there, and she had to serve him. He was, however, an enchanted prince. Zafarana served him faithfully, and the old man was always friendly to her. One day he called her to him: "Zafarana, come into the garden with me, and clean the lice from my hair."

When they were sitting together the old man said, "I have some news to tell you. Your oldest sister has given birth to a beautiful baby boy."

"Oh," Zafarana said, "would you do me a favor and let me make a short visit to my sister?"

"No," the old man answered. "If you go and visit your sister, you certainly won't return."

But Zafarana kept asking and promised for sure that she would return so that the old man finally consented. He gave her the most beautiful clothes and a beautiful coach in which she was to travel to her sister. Before her trip he took her into a room in which there were three chairs—the first was made of gold; the second, silver; the third, lead.

"Look," he said to Zafarana, "you may go, but you are not allowed to tell anyone where you live. And as soon as you hear my voice, you must return right away. Then you are to come into this room. If I am sitting on the golden chair, it is good for you. If I am sitting on the silver chair, it will be neither good nor bad for you. If I am sitting on the lead chair, it will be unfortunate for you."

Now Zafarana departed and traveled to her oldest sister, who was very happy to see Zafarana again, especially because she had been absent for such a long time. But no matter how much people asked her questions, she told them nothing about her life. After she had many conversations with her sister, she suddenly heard the voice of the old man calling to her. So she embraced her sister on the spot, rushed out, and traveled back to the castle. As she entered the room with the chairs, the old man was sitting on the gold one. "Thank God," she thought. "That's a good sign."

Some weeks passed by, and the old man called her to him once more and said, "Zafarana, come into the garden and clean the lice from my hair."

When they were sitting in the garden together, the old man said, "I've got some more news for you. Your middle sister has given birth to a beautiful baby girl."

"Oh," Zafarana cried, "dear master, let me go to her so that I can see my little niece."

The old man did not want to consent, but he finally yielded. Her sister was very happy to see her again when she arrived, and they had many delightful conversations. All of a sudden Zafarana heard the old man calling to her. She pretended not to hear his voice and remained seated. After a while the old man called again: "Zafarana!" She became scared, embraced her sister, and returned to the castle. When she entered the room, the old man was seated in the silver chair. "Now," she thought, "even if it doesn't mean anything good, at least it doesn't mean anything bad."

Once again, some weeks passed, and the old man called her into the garden, and when they were sitting together, he said, "Zafarana, I've got some more news for you. I'd prefer not to tell it, for you'll certainly want to leave again, and that will be your misfortune."

"Then you shouldn't have told me," said Zafarana. "You've already told me too much, now you must finish what you began to say."

"Your father has died," the old man said.

Zafarana began to weep and said, "I was unable to see my father once more while he was still alive, and I want at least to see him dead."

The old man did not want to let her go. "You'll see. It will be your misfortune!" he said.

But Zafarana wept such bitter tears and kept asking for such a long time that he finally consented. Then he had a beautiful mourning dress made for her and sent her to her father's house. She went up the stairs and entered the room where her father was lying on a bed, and candles were burning all around him. Zafarana threw herself on top of him, wept bitterly, and kept crying out: "Father, dear father!"

When the old man called, she heard him, but she did not pay attention because of her great suffering. He called a second time, and once again she did not obey. When he called a third time, she had to obey and returned weeping to the castle.

As she entered the room, the old man was sitting on the lead chair, and he gave her such a strict and serious look without saying a word that she became very frightened. They sat down together at a table and had their evening meal, but the old man did not say a word. He kept staring at her with the same look. When she went to bed and midnight arrived, the old man called, "Zafarana, get up. Open the window and see what the weather is like."

She obeyed and saw the sky was overcast, and it had started to rain. When she told this to the old man, he said, "Good. Now go back to sleep."

After a half an hour had passed, he called again: "Zafarana, get up and see what the weather is like."

"Oh," she said, "let me sleep. You've never called me so much before."

It did not help. She had to get up and see what the weather was like. She saw that it was raining more heavily, and it was thundering and lightning. She told the old man, and he said, "Good. Go back to sleep."

After half an hour he called her a third time: "Zafarana, get up and see what the weather is like."

"Why are you continually waking me up?" Zafarana asked. "You usually don't do this."

However, she had to obey, got up, and looked out the window. She saw such a storm and such bad weather that she quickly closed the window out of fright.

"I believe the world's falling apart," she said. "I've never seen such weather like this in my entire life."

"Good," the old man answered. "Get dressed and go. You can't stay here any longer."

Zafarana began to moan and said, "I've served you faithfully for a long time. You couldn't be so cruel now as to throw me out!"

But the old man kept saying, "You can't stay here any longer. I told you so. I told you it would be your misfortune."

He gave her a bundle of clothes and three pig bristles and said, "Keep them in a safe place. They'll be of use to you."

Then Zafarana had to go out in the dark of night into the terrible storm. At first she managed to make some progress, but as the weather became more and more awful, she crouched down behind a barn door and waited for daybreak. When dawn came, she stood up and wandered into the open with a heavy heart. Soon she came upon a cottage, and a peasant was sitting in front of it. She approached him and said, "My good man, would you please do me a great favor?"

"What would you like?" asked the peasant.

"Give me your clothes," Zafarana answered, "and I'll give you my clothes and everything that I have in my bundle."

The peasant did not want to do this, for he saw that Zafarana's clothes were much more beautiful than his simple garment. But Zafarana kept asking until he agreed to exchange clothes in his cottage and give his to Zafarana, who went into the cottage and soon came back out disguised as a peasant.

Now she wandered farther until she came to a large beautiful city where she went straight to the king's castle and walked back and forth in front of it. The king's personal coachman stood there, and when he saw the handsome young man, he said to him: "Where do you come from, my handsome young man?"

Zafarana answered, "I'm a stranger here, and I'm looking for some work because I'm poor and must find a way to earn money."

The coachman said, "We need to hire a stable boy for the king's horses. If you will accept the job, I can manage to get it for you."

Zafarana agreed and entered the service of the king. She combed and groomed the horses and was always diligent and orderly, but the king had a daughter who was stubborn, and everything had to be done according to her will. When she saw the young stableboy, she fell in love with him, went to her father, and said, "Dear father, there's a young man in the stable who was hired as stable boy. He looks too fine for such coarse work. I want him to work as a servant in the castle."

The king did just what his daughter demanded right away. He had Zafarana summoned, made a beautiful uniform for her, and she had to work as a servant in the castle. After some time passed, the princess went to her father again and said, "Dear father, none of my servants please me. I want the young man to become my personal page, and no one else."

Once again the king fulfilled her wish.

Now the princess fell more and more in love with Zafarana while she worked as her personal servant. One day the princess called her page and said to him, "Listen, I like you very much and want to marry you. Today I'll ask my father for his consent, and he'll certainly give it to me, for he never refuses me anything."

"Oh, princess," Zafarana answered very frightened. "Don't do this. You deserve a great, rich king, not a poor young man like me."

But no matter what she said, the princess kept insisting, and because Zafarana always responded with the same answer, the princess finally went to the king fully enraged and said, "The young page demanded something inappropriate from me, and because of this he must die."

Now Zafarana was placed in chains and was to die in three days. Finally, as she was being led to the gallows, she thought about the three pig's bristles that the old man had given to her, and when she came to the square where the gallows stood, she asked, "Please grant me one last request, and give me a pail with glowing coals."

Her request was granted, and when the pail was brought to her, she threw the three pig's bristles into it, and they burned. Just as this happened, a cloud of dust whirled in this distance, and a handsome, rich prince approached with his entire entourage. It was none other than the old man who had been released from the magic spell.

"Stop!" he called from a distance. "Stop!"

After he arrived at the square, he asked, "Why is this young man going to be hung?"

Then the king told him how the page had insulted his daughter and had to die because of it.

"All right," the prince responded, "But if I can prove that he never insulted your daughter, she must die in place of the page."

"I swear it on my royal honor!" the king said.

When they returned to the castle, the prince had Zafarana sent to a room where she had to put on royal clothes that belonged to women. Then they all recognized that she was indeed a young woman, and the princess had to die in her place. But the strange prince took Zafarana back to his realm where he became king and she became princess. They continued to live happy and content, but we were left empty-handed.

30

Peasant Truthful

Once upon a time there was a king who had a goat, a lamb, a ram, and a sheep. Because he loved all the animals, he wanted to put them in charge of someone totally trustworthy. Now the king had a peasant whom he simply called Peasant Truthful* because this man had never told a lie. So the king summoned him to his court and placed the animals in his care. Every Saturday the peasant had to come to the city and give the king a report about the animals. When the peasant appeared before the king, he always took off his cap and said, "Good morning, your majesty."†

"Good morning, Peasant Truthful. How's the goat?"

"It's white and mischievous."

---

* Massaru verità.

† "Bon giornu, Riali Maestà!"
  "Bon gironu, Massaru Verità;
  Comu è la crapa?"
  "Janca e ladra!"
  "Comu è l'agneddu?"
  "Jancu e beddu!"
  "Comu è lu muntuni?"
  "Beddu a vidiri!"
  "Comu è lu crastu?"
  "Beddu a guardari!"

"How's my lamb?"

"It's white and beautiful."

"How's my ram?"

"Beautiful to look at."

"How's my sheep?"

"Beautiful to watch."

After they had spoken to one another this way, the peasant would go back to his mountain, and the king believed everything he said. However, among the king's ministers, there was one who was very jealous of the favor the king showed to the peasant, and one day he said to the king, "Is the old peasant really incapable of telling a lie? I'm willing to bet that he'll lie to you next Saturday."

"If my peasant tells a lie," the king cried, "I'm willing to lose my head."

So they made a bet, and whoever lost was to lose his head. However, the more the minister thought about it, the more difficult it became for him to find some means to get the peasant to tell a lie by Saturday, that is, within three days. He thought in vain the entire day, and when it became evening and the first day was gone, he went home in a bad mood. When his wife saw him in such a terrible mood, she said, "What's bothering you and making you so miserable?"

"Leave me in peace!" he responded. "Why do I have to tell you!"

But she continued to ask in a friendly way so that he finally told her.

"Oh," she said, "it's nothing more than that? I'll take care of everything for you."

The next morning she got dressed in her most beautiful clothes, put on her best jewelry, and placed a diamond star on her forehead. Then she took a seat in her coach and traveled to the mountain where Peasant Truthful had led the four animals out to pasture. When she appeared before the peasant, he stood still as if he had been turned to stone, for she was incredibly beautiful.

"Oh, dear peasant," she said, "would you please do me a favor?"

"Noble lady," the peasant answered, "I'll do whatever you order."

"Look," she said, "I am pregnant and have an irresistible desire for roasted liver from a sheep, and if you don't give it to me, I'll have to die."

"Noble lady," the peasant said, "demand what you want from me, but I can't grant you this wish. The sheep belongs to the king, and I can't kill it."

"Oh, how unfortunate I am!" she cried. "I'll surely die if you don't satisfy my desire. Oh, dear peasant, please don't refuse me! The king wouldn't have to know a thing. You can tell him that the sheep fell off a cliff."

"No, I can't say that," the peasant resisted, "and I can't give you the liver."

The woman began to moan and groan even more. She pretended that she was about to die, and since she was so extraordinarily beautiful, the peasant's heart was finally moved by her pleas. He slaughtered the sheep, roasted the liver, and brought it to her. Then the woman ate it full of joy, took leave of the peasant, and departed. Now the peasant became despondent because he did not know what to say to the king. In his embarrassment he took a stick, planted it in the ground, and placed his small jacket on top of it. Then he took some steps toward it and began: "Good morning, your majesty!" However, when he came to the last question the king usually asked about the sheep, he always remained stuck and could not find an answer. He tried it with lies: "The sheep has been stolen," or "the sheep fell over a cliff," but the lies stuck in his throat. He placed the stick in another place on the ground and hung his jacket on top of it again, but nothing came to his mind. He could not sleep the entire night. Finally, the next morning he thought of an appropriate answer. "Yes," he thought, "that will work." He took his stick and jacket and set out to visit the king's castle, for it was Saturday. Along the way he stopped from time to time, set up the stick with the jacket as if it were the king, and held a conversation. Each time he did this, he liked his answer more.

When he entered the castle, the king sat in the throne room with his entire court, for the bet was to be decided on that day. Then Peasant Truthful took off his cap and began as usual.

"Good morning, your majesty."*

"Good morning, Peasant Truthful. How is my goat?"

---

* "Bon giornu, Riali Maestà!"
 "Bon giornu, Massaru Verità!"
 "Comu è la crapa?"
 "Janca e ladra!"
 "Comu è l'agneddu?"
 "Janca e beddu!"
 "Comu è lu muntuni?"
 "Beddu a vidiri!"
 "Comu è lu crastu?"
 "Riali Maestà!
 Ju ci dicu la verità.
 Vinni na donna di autu munti,
 Janca e bedda, cu na stidda in frunti
 Tàntu di sciamma a lu cori mi misi
 Chi pri l'amuri soi lu crastu uccisi."

"It's white and mischievous."
"How is my lamb?"
"It's white and beautiful."
"How is my ram?"
"Beautiful to see."
"How is my sheep?"
"My lord and king
I scorn the lie . . .
Up in the mountain far away
a woman appeared like a star ablaze
Her beauty struck me as did her gaze
that pierced my heart and made me a wreck—
as for the sheep I broke its neck."

Everyone at the court applauded the peasant, and the king gave him a rich reward. The minister, however, had to pay for his jealousy with his head.

31

About Joseph, Who Set Out to Seek His Fortune

Once upon a time there was a peasant and his wife, and they had just one son called Joseph. These people were poor and led a wretched existence. One day, Joseph went to his mother and said, "Dear mother, give me some clothes and your blessing, for I want to set out and seek my fortune."

"Oh, my son," his mother began to weep and said, "you want to leave us? I have enough troubles already, but when you also go away, my only child, there'll be nothing left for me to do but die."

"Mother," Joseph insisted, "I want to set out to seek my fortune."

Finally his parents yielded. They packed his clothes into a knapsack, added some bread and onions, and let him depart with heavy hearts.

After Joseph had wandered about for some time, he became hungry. He sat down behind a door to eat some of the bread and the onions. While he was eating, a fine gentleman came riding by on horseback and asked him who he was.

"Oh," responded Joseph, "I'm just a poor boy and have set out to seek my fortune."

"If you come with me and serve me faithfully," the gentleman said, "you'll have a good life."

Joseph was satisfied and decided to go along with the stranger, who took him to a magnificent castle that contained a great deal of treasures.

"This is where I live," the gentleman said to Joseph, and he had him take off his peasant clothes and gave him an elegant suit. "You are to live here with me and enjoy your life. You may take and use as much money as you want. But once a year you must do something important for me."

"I'll do whatever you order," Joseph replied, and he lived with the strange gentleman in splendor and joy. When the year was almost over, Joseph had a great longing to see his parents. So he went to his master and said, "Please let me go for a few days so that I can visit my parents."

At first his master did not want to let him depart because he thought Joseph would not return, but when Joseph promised to be back within a few days, he let him go.

When Joseph arrived in his hometown, people on the street wondered, "Isn't that the son of old Joseph?"*

Others thought differently and remarked, "That's a fine gentleman. Joseph was only a peasant."

Finally Joseph reached the house of his parents, and when he entered, only his mother was there. He greeted her, and she bowed before the fine gentleman. Then he said to her: "Isn't old Joseph at home?"

"Oh yes," his mother said, "I'll go and call him right away," and she went into the garden and said to her husband. "A strange man has come to our house, and he's asking for you."

The old peasant went into the room, took off his cap, and said, "What may I do for you?"

Then Joseph began to laugh and said, "Don't you recognize me? I'm Joseph, your son."

There was great joy in the house, and Joseph had to tell them everything that had happened to him, and he immediately gave them a great deal of money so that they could live in comfort.

"Unfortunately, I must leave right away and return to my master," he announced.

His mother began to weep and asked, "Oh, my dear son, stay with me."

But Joseph said, "I promised my master that I would return."

So they let him depart and Joseph returned to his master.

After a few days had passed, the strange man said, "Joseph, today you must do me that service for which I hired you."

And he led him into a room that had hunter's clothes laid out in it, and Joseph had to put them on. Then the two of them mounted their horses. There was also a third horse loaded with many empty sacks that

---

* Zio Peppe.

Joseph had to lead by the reins. They rode for many hours until they came to some plains with a mountain that soared into the sky. This mountain was so steep that no human could climb it. They dismounted at the foot of the mountain and refreshed themselves with food and drink. Then Joseph's master ordered him to kill the third horse and take off its skin. Joseph did this, and then they lay the skin in the sun to let it dry.

"Now we can rest for a while," the master said.

Soon, however, he called Joseph again, gave him a sharp little knife, and said, "I'm going to sew you in the skin along with all the empty sacks. Then crows will come and carry you to the top of the mountain. Once you're there, you are to cut yourself out of the skin with this knife, and I'll call up to you and tell you what you're to do next."

Joseph was ready to do anything, and his master sewed him into the skin. Right after the crows came, lifted him, and carried him to the top of the mountain where they set him down. Then Joseph cut himself out of the skin with the knife and looked around. The entire peak was covered with diamonds.

"What should I do now?" he asked his master.

"Fill all the sacks with diamonds and throw them down to me," his master yelled.

When Joseph had filled all the sacks and had thrown them down to his master, he called, "What should I do now?"

"Live well," his master responded, "and find some way to get down from there."

Upon saying this, he loaded the sacks onto Joseph's horse and rode away, laughing as he went.

Joseph stood there and did not see any way he could descend the mountain. He stamped his feet in rage, and all of a sudden he heard a noise like knocking on wood. He leaned over, and yes, he was right. He was standing on a wooden door with a lock. He managed to open the door and thought, "At least the wild birds can't eat me here." When he slipped inside, he saw some stairs which he descended carefully, for it was completely dark. Finally he came to a bright hall. As he was standing there and looking around, a door opened and a giant came out.

"How dare you enter my palace!" the giant said in a deep voice.

At first Joseph was terrified, but he soon summoned his courage and replied cheerfully, "Oh, dear uncle, is it you? How happy I am to see you!"

"Are you really my nephew?" asked the giant who was somewhat dumb.

"Certainly," Joseph said, "and I want to stay with you."

The giant was satisfied, and so Joseph lived with him and had a good life.

But soon he noticed that the giant was overcome by some terrible sickness every day at a certain hour that caused him to suffer a great deal.

"Dear uncle," Joseph asked, "where does this sickness come from? Can I help you get better?"

"Oh, dear nephew," the giant answered, "it's possible to cure me, but how could someone like you succeed in doing it?"

"Just tell me, uncle," Joseph insisted. "Perhaps I can help you."

"All right," the giant said. "Every day four fairies come and bathe in the pond in my garden, and as long as they are in the water, I am overcome by this sickness."

"How can I save you from the fairies?" Joseph asked.

"Before they climb into the water," the giant said, "they take off their blouses and leave them on the stone fence. You must hide yourself there, and while they are in the water, you must grab the blouse of the fairy queen* so she cannot fly away, and without her the others will not return."

So Joseph hid himself behind the stone fence. Soon he heard a rustling in the air, and four fairies appeared. They took off their blouses and climbed into the water. Joseph stuck out his hand and took the blouse of the fairy queen. At that very same moment the fairies jumped out of the water with a cry, took their blouses, and flew away. But the fairy queen could not fly away without her blouse. Then the giant stepped forward and put her into chains. Every morning he brought her a slice of bread and some water and asked her, "If you marry my nephew, I'll set you free."

But the fairy always answered, "No, I refuse."

"Then you'll stay in chains," declared the giant.

After a while he brought her a little lamp, placed it next to her head, and said, "If you don't marry my nephew, you will live only as long as there is oil left in this lamp."

"All right," said the fairy, "I'll marry him!"

So the chains were taken off, there was a beautiful wedding, and Joseph was very happy.

The next day the giant said to him: "You can no longer stay with me. Take your wife and go home to your parents. Here is your wife's blouse. No matter what, do not give it back to her unless someone shows you a

---

* Capo-fata.

snuffbox that looks like this one." And he gave him a gold snuffbox and a magic wand and told him to leave.

So Joseph took his wife and set out on his way. The journey was long, and soon they were tired.

"I wish I were home already," Joseph said, and because he had the magic wand in his hand, they found themselves at his home right after he had spoken those words. Then he wished for a beautiful house with coaches and horses, and servants and beautiful clothes for him and his wife. Afterward he went to his old parents. They were very glad to see him again, and Joseph said, "Come with me to my palace. I want to introduce you to my wife."

They went with him and stayed there. Now Joseph led a glorious life, held great parties, and was the richest and most distinguished man in the entire country. As for the blouse, he gave it to his mother for safe-keeping. He also showed her the gold snuffbox, and she had to swear to him that she would not give up the blouse unless someone showed her the same kind of snuffbox, and he always carried his box with him. Meanwhile, his wife remained discontent and kept thinking of ways to get the gold snuffbox, for she missed the other fairies and wanted to return to them.

Now one evening Joseph threw another great ball. A gentleman stepped up to Joseph's wife and asked her to dance.

"I'll be glad to dance with you," the fairy said, "but when we form lines, you must dance near my husband and try to take away the gold snuffbox that he's carrying with him."

The gentleman promised this, and since Joseph did not suspect anything, he was not on his guard. The gentleman succeeded in taking away the snuffbox without being observed, and he gave it to the fairy right away. She was very happy about this and immediately sent her chambermaid to her mother-in-law. The fairy had told the chambermaid to say, "Here is the gold snuffbox. Give me my mistress's blouse in exchange."

When the old woman saw the snuffbox, she innocently gave the blouse to the chambermaid, who took it to the fairy right away. No sooner did the fairy put on the blouse than she disappeared, and with her the beautiful castle vanished along with the servants, coaches, and horses. Joseph sat on a stone on the roadside in his old peasant clothes. He was very depressed for he had loved his wife very much. When he returned to his parents' house he could not console himself, and one day he said, "Mother, give me your blessing. I want to set out to seek my wife."

His mother wept bitter tears and did not want to let him depart, but Joseph insisted, and so his parents finally had to consent. Now Joseph went straight to the place where the strange gentleman had found him and sat down behind the same door. It was not long before the stranger came riding by and asked him again who he was and what his name was. He did not recognize Joseph because he thought that he had long been dead. Joseph answered that his name was Franco. Then the gentleman hired him, and everything went like the first time. After he had lived one year in splendor, he had to accompany his master to the plains where he was sewn into the horse skin and carried by the crows to the top of the mountain of diamonds. However, instead of filling the sacks full of diamonds, Joseph grabbed large stones and began throwing them at his master. Then the gentleman recognized him and yelled, "Oh, it's you! This time it's you who's cheated me!"

But because Joseph kept throwing even more stones, the gentleman had to clear out and ran from the spot as fast as he could. Meanwhile Joseph opened the wooden door, climbed down the stairs, and went to the giant.

"What, my nephew," the giant asked in astonishment, "you're here again?"

Then Joseph told the giant what had happened to him.

"Didn't I tell you that you should keep the blouse in safekeeping?" the giant said. "What do you want from me?"

"I want to search for my wife," Joseph replied, "and you must help me."

"Are you totally crazy?" the giant exclaimed. "You'll never ever be able to find your wife again. Another giant has captured her, and you'll never be able to kill him."

However, Joseph continued to ask for his help until the giant said, "I can't help you anymore, but I'll show you the right direction and give you some bread so that you won't die of hunger."

So the giant showed him the way, and Joseph set out to search for his wife. After he had wandered for a long time, he became hungry and sat down on a rock and began to eat some bread. As he was eating, some crumbs fell on the ground and a bunch of ants suddenly appeared and began pecking at the crumbs.

"Poor little insects! You're all so hungry," thought Joseph, and he broke a large piece of bread into pieces and spread them on the ground. Then the king of the ants came and said, "As thanks for the way you have so kindly fed my ants, I am giving you this ant leg. Keep it safe, for it will be of use to you."

To be sure, Joseph thought that such an ant leg would not be much use to him, but since he did not want to insult the king of the ants, he took the leg, wrapped it in a piece of paper, and stuck it into his pocket.

As he continued on his way, he saw an eagle nailed to a tree with an arrow.

"Oh, this poor bird!" he thought, and he pulled the arrow out.

"Thanks a lot," the eagle cried. "Because you were kind enough to save me, I want to give you something. Pull out a feather from my wing. It will be of use to you."

Joseph pulled out the feather and stuck it with the ant leg. After a short while he saw a lion, who was limping and groaning in a miserable way.

"Poor beast!" Joseph thought, "he probably has a thorn in his foot." And Joseph leaned over and carefully pulled the thorn out.

"Because you have been so kind to help me," the lion said, "I want you to have a hair from my beard as thanks. Yank it out, for it will certainly be of use to you."

Joseph took the hair and put it with the other things. After he wandered for a while, he became tired and almost lost heart, for he still had very far to go. Then he remembered the eagle's feather and thought, "I can at least try it one time." He took the feather in his hand and said, "I'm a man and want to become an eagle."*

No sooner than he said these words, he became an eagle and flew through the air until he landed at the giant's castle. Once there he said, "I'm an eagle and want to become a man." As soon as he said this, he was restored to his natural shape. Now he took the ant's leg out and said, "I'm a man and want to become an ant." Then he became transformed into an ant and crawled through a crack in the wall of the palace. He wandered though many rooms until he came to a large hall where he saw his wife, who was tied with heavy chains along with many other fairies who were all chained. Then he said, "I'm an ant and want to become a man." All of a sudden he stood before his wife in his true shape.

When she saw him, she was very happy but also scared.

"Oh, when the giant finds you here, he'll kill you!" she cried.

"Let that be my concern," Joseph said. "Just tell me how I can free you."

"Oh," his wife said, "even if I tell you, what good will it do? You can't free me."

"Just tell me," Joseph insisted.

Then his wife responded: "First you must kill the dragon with the seven heads that lives in the mountains behind the castle. If you manage

---

* Cristianu sugnu e acula diventu.

to cut off his seventh head, you must split it in two. A raven will fly out, and you must grab hold of it and kill it. Then you must cut out the egg in its body. If you hit the giant right in the middle of his forehead with this egg, he will die. But this is much too difficult for you. You'll never succeed in doing it."

All of a sudden they heard heavy footsteps, and his wife anxiously cried out, "Oh Joseph, the giant is coming!"

Joseph grabbed his ant leg right away, spoke the magic words, and immediately became an ant. Now the giant entered the hall and growled in a deep voice: "I smell human flesh!"

But the fairy said, "How could a human being come to us. You've locked us up so securely."

Upon hearing this the giant became calm. Meanwhile Joseph crawled through a crack into the open and said, "I'm an ant and want to become a man." Then, as a man, he took the feather in his hand, transformed himself into an eagle, and flew with quick beats of his wings to the foot of the mountain where the dragon was living. There he saw a shepherd, who was sitting on the path and looked distressed. Joseph turned himself into a man again, stepped toward the shepherd, and asked him what was wrong.

"Oh," the shepherd said. "I had such a large herd of sheep, and the dragon has eaten so many that I only have a small herd left. But I don't dare drive them on to the meadow because the dragon will eat them."

"If you hire me to serve you," Joseph said, "I can perhaps help you. Give me four sheep and let me drive them on to the meadow."

At first the shepherd did not want to hire him, but Joseph kept encouraging him until the shepherd finally gave him four sheep. Then Joseph began climbing the mountain, and soon he caught sight of the dragon, lured by the smell of the sheep. Immediately Joseph took the lion's hair in his hand and said, "I'm a man and want to become a lion," and he was transformed into a fierce lion so large and strong that there was none his equal. He attacked the dragon, and after a long battle, he succeeded in biting off two heads, but he became so exhausted he could not fight anymore. Fortunately the dragon was also just as exhausted so that it crawled into its cave. Then Joseph assumed his human shape again, gathered his four sheep, which had eaten as much as they wanted, and returned to the shepherd quite pleased with himself. The shepherd was astonished to see Joseph and his four sheep alive again and asked what had happened to him. But Joseph declared, "What's that to you? I've brought back your sheep just as healthy as they were before. Tomorrow I want eight."

The next morning Joseph drove eight sheep to the meadow. The shepherd was curious and quietly followed him. Then he watched as the dragon appeared. Joseph grabbed the lion's hair, said the magic words, and was transformed immediately into a fierce lion, and fought the dragon. On this day he succeeded in biting off four heads, but he became so exhausted that he could not fight anymore, and the dragon had also lost its strength.

"Yes," the dragon said, "if I had a glass from the water of life, I'd show you the power of the king of the dragons!"

"And I," responded Joseph, "if I had a good soup of wine and bread, I'd show you the power of the king of the lions."

When the shepherd heard this, he rushed to his hut, quickly cooked a soup of bread and wine, and took it to the lion. No sooner did the beast eat the soup than all his former strength returned to him. He began to fight once more and bit the seventh head off the dragon. Now he said, "I'm a lion and want to become a man," and he split the seventh head, whereupon a raven flew out and into the air. But Joseph was on top of everything: "I'm a man and want to become an eagle," and as an eagle he flew after the raven and killed it. Then he took on his human shape again, cut the egg from the raven's body, and began traveling home once again with the shepherd and his sheep. The shepherd wanted to keep him in his employ and promised him anything he desired if he would only stay on with him. But Joseph answered: "I can't stay with you. I'm glad that I have freed you from the dragon, and I thank you for your quick help."

Joseph flew as an eagle to the giant's castle and crawled through the crack into the hall as an ant. "I'm an ant and want to become a man," he said and told his wife about everything he had accomplished and that he had brought the egg.

"The giant's sleeping in the next room," she said. "Now's the time to kill him."

Joseph sneaked into the room next door, aimed directly at the forehead of the giant, and killed him. Then all the fairies were freed from their chains, and his wife embraced him. Afterward she showed him all the treasures that had been gathered there. They took as much as they could carry and traveled home again to Joseph's parents. Once there, they built a house much more beautiful than the first and lived in splendor and joy until their happy end.

32

THE WASTEFUL GIOVANNINU

Once upon a time there was a rich young man named Giovanninu. He had great treasures and wealth, but he did not want to work and attend to his business. Instead, he lived a life of luxury and pleasure, went to all the parties, and gambled and drank away his money. His faithful servant Peppe kept saying to him, "Oh, master, pay attention! You can't continue living like this. If you always give away your money without earning any, you'll soon run out of it."

However, Giovanninu always answered, "It will be a long time before I run out of money. Just let me take care of things."

So he lived from one day to the next, went to each and every party, and gambled away his money.

"Master, be careful," warned the faithful Peppe. But his master did not heed his warnings until one day, all the treasures were used up, and he did not even have enough for Peppe to buy food for the midday meal. Giovanninu began to sell all the silverware and beautiful furniture in the house, but he took the money and used it to return to his former life style.

He did this until he had sold everything and was completely poor and stripped of everything he had.*

"Oh master, I warned you," the poor Peppe said and wept bitter tears.

---

* Ristau poviru e pacciu.

"You were right," Giovanninu said. "There's nothing left for us to do but to seek our fortune. Why don't you head off in that direction, and I'll go in this one, and we'll see whether we can find our fortunes."

So they separated, and Giovanninu wandered forth and had to beg along the way. After he had traveled for a long time, he came one day to a region that he did not know. In front of him stood a magnificent palace, and since the sun was shining so brightly, he sat down on the threshold to warm himself a bit. While he was sitting there, a lovely little white sheep came out of the palace, sat down next to him, and let him pet it. Indeed, he was very happy to have the cute little animal next to him. All of a sudden the sheep opened its mouth and said, "Do you want to go up into the palace with me, handsome lad? You see, I'm an enchanted princess, and if you do everything I tell you to do, you can rescue me from this magic spell."

"Tell me what I have to do," Giovanninu said, "and I'll set you free."

"Come up into the palace," the sheep said. "You'll find some good food and wine and beautiful clothes. There's also a good bed ready for you. If you can survive everything that happens to you each night without making a sound, you'll be able to save me."

Once again Giovanninu promised he would free her from the spell. The enchanted princess led him into the palace, where he ate and drank to his heart's content and then laid down to bed.

Soon he fell asleep and was completely relaxed. When it turned midnight, however, he was wakened by a great noise. The door sprang open, and in marched a long line of people, each one carrying a burning candle.

"Get up and come with us," they said to Giovanninu.

However, he did not answer them and remained quiet. Then they tore him out of the bed and dragged him into the middle of the room, formed a circle, and danced around him. In the process they kicked and hit him and treated him in an awful way, but he withstood everything and did not utter a sound. When morning arrived, they left him half dead on the ground and disappeared. Then the little white sheep entered, dressed his wounds, and brought him food and drink so that he could recover. This is what happened every night for the next two weeks.

One morning, however, a maiden entered his room instead of the little white sheep, and she was so beautiful, it was as if God had created her.*

---

* The customary expression is: as if his mother had made her, çomu la fici so matri.

"I'm the little white sheep," she said, "and you have freed me from the magic spell. I'm not going away. I'm just returning to my parents. I can't take you with me yet, but in eight days I'll come again. I'll come three days in a row, each time at noon, and you must wait for me at the palace gate. Make sure that I don't find you asleep, otherwise you'll regret it!"

Giovanninu promised to keep on his guard, and the beautiful princess drove off. When she returned home, her parents rejoiced to see their daughter once more because they had lost her many years ago. Then she said to them, "Giovanninu rescued me, and I want him to become my husband."

When eight days had passed, she climbed on a gorgeous horse, took a large retinue of people with her, and rode to the palace. Giovanninu had been sitting on the threshold and waiting for her, but in the palace there were still many other enchanted maidens, who had been filled with jealousy against the beautiful princess because she was the first one to be freed from the magic spell. They cast a magic spell on poor Giovanninu, and at the very moment that the princess appeared in the distance, he suddenly felt very tired and fell into a deep sleep. When the princess arrived and found him asleep, she became very despondent, climbed off her horse, and cried out: "Giovanninu! Giovanninu! Wake up."

But he did not hear her because he been enchanted by magic. When she realized that she wouldn't be able to wake him, she took a piece of paper and wrote on it: "Look out for yourself! I only have two days left." She stuck the note into his pocket and rode off. When he finally woke up and saw that the sun was setting, he became very frightened and thought to himself, "I'm going to be sorry for this! I'm sure the princess came and found me asleep." When he then put his hand into his pocket and found the note, he became even sadder and lamented, "Oh, how unlucky I am! How could I fall asleep?"

The next day he sat down again on the threshold at the right time and thought,

"Today I'm definitely going to remain awake." But things did not go any better for him than the first time. At the very moment that the princess appeared in the distance, he was overcome by a deep sleep. Because she found him asleep a second time, she was even more despondent and got off her horse and cried out, "Giovanninu! Giovanninu! Wake up!"

When he did not wake up, she took a piece of paper and wrote on it: "Now I'll be coming only one more time. If you are asleep tomorrow, you'll regret it!"

She stuck this note into his pocket, mounted her horse, and rode off. When Giovanninu woke up and found the note, he groaned very loudly and said, "How's this possible? Something strange is going on here—I fall asleep at noon each day."

On the third day he did not sit down. Instead, he walked up and down in front of the palace, but nothing helped him. As soon as the princess appeared in the distance, he was overcome by the magic sleep. When the princess found him asleep again, she cried out, "Well, because you didn't want to be blessed by fortune, you won't have any! If you want to regain me, you'll have to wander a long time before you find me." Once again she put a note in his pocket, mounted her horse, and rode off. Just imagine Giovanninu's sorrow when he awoke and found the note. "How unlucky I am! How shall I ever find her?" he moaned.

There was nothing left for him to do but grab his walking staff once again and wander into the wide world, and since he had nothing but the clothes on his back, he had to beg. Giovanninu traveled for a long, long time, and his clothes became tattered, but he did not find the beautiful princess. One day, as he was lying along the road worn out and weak and could go no further, an eagle flew by and asked him, "Handsome lad, why are you so sad and lying on the ground?"

"Oh," answered Giovanninu, "I'm so weak that I can't go any farther."

"Get on my back," the eagle said, "I'll carry you a good part of the way."

So Giovanninu climbed on the back of the eagle, who flew off with him into the air and soared like the wind. After they had flown for some time, the eagle suddenly cried out, "Meat!"

"What should I do now?" thought Giovanninu. "If I don't give the eagle any meat, the bird will drop me."

Since he had no meat with him, he cut off his left hand and gave it to the eagle. But after a short time passed, the eagle cried out again, "Meat!" Then Giovanninu cut off his left arm and gave it to the eagle, and since the bird continued to demand more, he had to slice off his left foot and left leg. Finally, the eagle swooped down to the ground and said, "Get off my back and continue on your way."

"How can I continue wandering in this condition?" Giovanninu complained.

When the eagle saw him so crippled, it asked, "Why did you do that?"

"You kept demanding meat, and I had no other meat to give you except my own flesh."

The eagle was moved by this and said, "Don't worry. I'm going to heal you."

Upon saying this he brought forth poor Giovanninu's arm and leg,

"I know that you've been wandering in search of the beautiful princess, so listen to my advice. If you travel for another two days, you'll come to a small cottage and find a wise old woman who will help you."

So Giovanninu set out on his way again and wandered two days. On the evening of the second day he came to a cottage just as the eagle said he would. He knocked on the door and an ancient woman came and asked him what he wanted.

"I'm a poor young man," answered Giovanninu. "Please take pity on me and let me rest here tonight."

"Come in, my son," the old woman said as she opened the door. She invited him in and gave him something to eat and drink. "What has brought you to this desolate region?"

Giovanninu told her everything that had happened and afterward he said, "Please tell me how I can find the beautiful princess again."

"Just sleep for now," replied the old woman. "Early tomorrow morning I'll tell you what you're to do."

So Giovanninu laid down and slept peacefully until morning. When he awoke, the old woman gave him something more to eat and said, "The princess is living in the nearby city, and you are to continue wandering until you get there. Here is a magic wand. When you're finally in the city, ask someone where the king's palace is, and during the night, use the wand to create a palace, much more beautiful than the king's, right across from it. Now you will make up for whatever you've had to tolerate because of the princess."

Upon saying this, the old woman gave him the magic wand, and Giovanninu thanked her very much and wandered off. After he traveled for some time, he finally came to the city where the princess was living. He asked for directions to the royal castle and took note of exactly where it was standing. During the night he crept back to the spot with his magic wand and cried out: "Listen to my command!"

"What's your command?" the wand asked.

So Giovanninu wished for a fully furnished palace. In addition he asked for coaches, servants, and horses. All at once a magnificent castle stood before his eyes, more beautiful than any other castle in the world. Servants appeared and washed and dressed Giovanninu in costly garments. He became such a handsome young man that no one recognized him. When the princess saw the magnificent palace the next day, she was astonished and said, "Is there something wrong with my eyes, or has such a beautiful palace really arisen over night?"

While she was still thinking about this, Giovanninu appeared at the window, but she did not recognize him. Since he was such a handsome young man, however, she fell passionately in love with him and said, "This man is to become my husband and no other."

She tried to make his acquaintance, but he pretended not to notice her. The more indifferent he was toward her, the more passionate her love for him became. So she sewed twelve shirts made from the finest cloth, placed them on a silver platter, covered them with a gorgeous embroidered scarf, called her servant, and sent them to Giovanninu. The servant was to say: "The princess who is living across from you sends her greetings and requests that you make good use of them out of love for her."*

When the servant took this message to Giovanninu, he replied, "Very good. I wanted to buy dust rags for the kitchen today, the scarf you can take to the church, and tell your mistress that I am very grateful for the gifts."

The servant returned to the princess very distressed.

"Oh, your majesty," he said, "this man must be much richer than you are. Just think—he had the shirts taken into the kitchen to be used as dust rags for the kettle."

So the princess became very sad, and had a gold candelabra, which was more beautiful than anyone had ever seen, sent to Giovanninu with the message: "The princess sends her greetings. May you use this candelabra as a light next to your bed out of love for her."

However, when the servant went to Giovanninu and took him the message, the young man responded again, "Good. The candelabra comes just at the right time. I wanted to buy a lamp for the kitchen today. Bring the candelabra into the kitchen, and tell your mistress that I am very grateful."

The servant took this reply to his mistress, which caused the princess to become even sadder. She then sent her faithful servant to Giovanninu once more and told him to say: "The princess has fallen passionately in love with you and wants to ask you whether you will honor her by becoming her husband."

When Giovanninu heard this, he answered, "If the princess wants to become my wife, I must see her carried through the city in a coffin like a dead woman with priests and music until she is brought beneath my window."

When the princess heard this, she had herself placed into a coffin and carried through the entire city. The priests accompanied her with

---

* Mi voi struditi pi l'amuri soi.

burning candles, and all the people ran after the procession. When she came beneath the window where Giovanninu was standing, he spit and cried out in a loud voice: "How can you let yourself be put to shame just because of a man? Now I've repaid you for everything that I had to suffer because of you!"

All at once the princess recognized him. She jumped out of the coffin, ran to him, and fell down at his feet.

"Giovanninu, my dear Giovanninu, forgive me! Oh, you've made me suffer very much!"

"And I suffered for you very much," answered Giovanninu. "That's why I wanted you to suffer because of me."

They embraced each other, and there was great joy in the entire land. For three days there were festivities, and then they were married. When the old king died, Giovanninu succeeded him. And so they lived happy and content, but we've been left without one cent.

33

THE BANISHED QUEEN AND HER TWO ABANDONED CHILDREN

Once upon a time there was a woman who had three daughters. They were all very beautiful, but they were poor and had to earn their living by spinning. When the moon shone brightly in the evening, they would sit by their little window and spin. Across the way was the royal castle, and when the king went up and down the stairs, he always had to walk by the girls.*

One time the oldest daughter said, "If I could have the king as my husband, I would bake four loaves of bread and feed an entire regiment, and there would even be some bread left over."†

Then the second daughter said, "If I could have the king as my husband, I would fill an entire regiment with one glass of wine, and there would even be some wine left over."

Finally, the youngest daughter announced, "If I could have the king as my husband, I would bear him two children, a boy with a gold apple in his hand, and a girl with a gold star on her forehead."

---

* There is another variant where this story takes place during the times when kings listened at the doors of their subjects to discover what they were saying, and the king had listened at the door of these girls.

† In the variant this maiden declares that she would provide garments for an entire army with one piece of cloth, and there would be some cloth left over.

They repeated these words each time the king came by, and one time the king heard it and ordered the three sisters to appear before him up in his castle.

"Who are you?" he asked them. "And what are you doing at your window each evening as I come by?"

They answered, "We're poor girls and have to earn our living by spinning. So we sit at our little window each evening and spin. In order to pass the time away, we chat with one another."

"What did you say last evening as I went by?" he asked the oldest.

"Your majesty," she responded, "I said that if I could have the king as my husband, I would bake four loaves of bread and feed an entire regiment, and there would even be some bread left over."

Then the king asked the second sister, "What did you say?"

"Your majesty," she responded, "I said that if I got the king as my husband, I would fill an entire regiment with one glass of wine, and there would even be some wine left over."

At last he asked the youngest sister, "What did you say?"

She was ashamed and did not want to answer. However, she finally had to tell him: "Your majesty, I said that if I got the king as my husband, I would bear him two children, a boy with a gold apple in his hand and a girl with a gold star on her forehead."

After the king heard all this, he said, "You will be my bride."

He ordered beautiful clothes to be made for her, and she became his wife. The two sisters also moved into the castle and lived there in joy and splendor.

Now, after some months had passed, a war broke out and the king had to go off to the battlefield. He called the two sisters to him and said, "I shall expect you to look after my wife while I am gone. When it's time for her to give birth, take good care of her."

But the two sisters were jealous of the youngest sister and her good fortune. When the young queen was about to give birth, they pretended to take care of her, and when their sister really gave birth to two children, a boy with a gold apple in his hand, and a girl with a gold star on her forehead, they placed them in a crate and threw it into the water. In their place the sisters put two puppies next to the young queen.

When the king returned home from the war and wanted to see his children, the sisters said to him, "The young queen has given birth to two puppies."

The king became angry and ordered his servants to build a shed in the courtyard at the foot of the stairs. The queen was to live in it day and night with bread and water. Next to the shed stood a sentinel who forced anyone who went up or down the stairs to spit into the face of the queen.

In the meantime the crate with the poor children was dragged from the water by an old fisherman. When he opened it and saw the two beautiful children, he brought them to his house, and his wife suckled them. The children remained there and became more beautiful and larger as each year passed. After they became older, however, they had an argument with the sons of the fisherman, who had called them bastards. That was when they learned they were not the children of the old couple, and so they said, "Give us your blessing. We want to go and search for our parents."

They wandered into the world, and after a while they met a friendly old man who asked them, "Where are you traveling, and why are you so alone?"

They told him how they had left their home to seek their parents. Then the old man gave them a magic wand and said, "Whatever kind of treasures you wish, this wand will help you obtain them."

They continued wandering until they came to the city ruled by their father and wished for a magnificent house across from the royal castle. No sooner had they made their wish than a splendid palace stood before them. The next morning the two jealous sisters went to the window and could not stop gazing in astonishment at the beautiful palace that had arisen over night. While they were talking about it, they saw the king's two children, and the aunts immediately recognized them by the gold star and apple. They were terrified and called to a poor woman, to whom they used to give alms every Friday, and said to her: "Go over to that house. Some rich people are living there. They will certainly give you something. When the young maiden gives you something, you're to say to her, 'noble lady, you are beautiful, but your brother is more handsome than you are beautiful. If you get some of the dancing water, that will change.'"

Indeed, the terrible aunts thought, the brother will set out to get the dancing water for her, and he will die when he tries to do it. Then we'll also get rid of her in no time. So the poor woman went into the palace and said to the chambermaid, "Tell your mistress that a poor beggar woman is here and is asking for alms."

The maiden herself came, and the poor woman said, "Noble lady, you are beautiful, but your brother is more handsome than you are beautiful. If you get some of the dancing water, that will change."

When the maiden heard this, she felt such a longing for the dancing water that she became very melancholy, and when her brother came home, she told him what the beggar woman had said and asked him to fetch the dancing water for her.

"But dear sister," her brother responded, "you don't know what dangers are involved here. I'll gladly go to fetch it for you, but you'll see, I won't return."

"Oh, I'm sure you'll return," his sister said, and because he loved her so much, he could not refuse her request and prepared himself for the journey. Then he gave her a ring and said, "As long as this ring remains clear and white, I'll return. But if the ring becomes misty, that will be a sign that I cannot return."

Upon saying this he embraced his sister, mounted his most splendid steed, and set out on his way. He had to travel for many days until he came to a dense forest. When it became evening, he could not find his way out. He wandered about and thought, "By morning the wild animals will have eaten me." Suddenly he saw a light in the distance, and as he approached it he saw a small hut. He knocked on the door, and an old hermit opened it.

"Oh, my son," the old man said, "what are you doing in this wild place so alone?"

"Father," the young man answered him, "I've been searching for the dancing water."

"Oh, my son," the old man said, "renounce your foolish quest. There have been many princes, kings, and dukes who have passed by here in search of the dancing water, and none has ever returned."

The young man, however, did not let himself be scared off, for he loved his sister very much.

"Well, if you insist on going ahead," the hermit said, "then go with God. To be sure I can't help you, but my older brother lives about a day's journey farther into the woods. You should seek him out. Perhaps he can advise you what to do."

The next morning the young man continued his travels until it was late at night. He saw a light in the distance and it was the little hut inhabited by the second hermit. The young man knocked on the door, and the hermit opened and asked him what he wanted. When he heard that the young man had set out in search of the dancing water, he tried to warn him even more seriously than his brother had done. But the young man would not abandon his quest, and so the hermit said, "I can't give you any advice, but my oldest brother lives a day's journey farther in the forest, and perhaps he'll be able to help you."

The next morning the young man rode off again, and toward evening he came to the third hermit, who was ancient.

"My son," the hermit asked, "what are you doing in this miserable place?"

When he heard why the young man had set out on his travels, he became horrified and said, "My son, let me warn you. Don't do this. So many have met their ruin in pursuit of the dancing water. How can you possibly succeed?"

Since the young man would not be deterred, the hermit said, "All right, if you insist, may God bless you. Do you see the mountain over there? You must first climb it. But since it is inhabited by wild animals, you must fill your knapsack with meat and throw it to them so they will let you pass. On top of the mountain there is a magnificent castle. Go inside and through all the rooms. Be careful not to touch any of the glorious treasures that you will see there. In the last room there are numerous cups filled with water. Do not touch any of them until you see the water move. Then grab one of the cups and flee as fast as you can."

The old man now gave him his blessing and let him depart.

Meanwhile, the young man bought some oxen, which he had slaughtered and chopped into pieces. He filled his knapsack with the meat and headed for the mountain. When he began to climb the mountain, wild animals sprung up from all sides, but he threw large pieces of meat to them, and they allowed him to pass. Thanks to his luck, he reached the peak of the mountain, got off his horse, and entered the castle, where he saw so much glistening treasure and wealth that he was practically blinded by it all. But he thought about the hermit's warning and did not touch a thing. Indeed, he did not even turn around but strode through all the rooms until he came to the chamber where he found the cups with the dancing water. He waited for the water to gush, and then he grabbed a cup and fled as fast as he could. Along his way home, he stopped to visit the hermits who were happy to see him again so healthy, and finally he returned to his sister, who was glad that he had returned. After he gave her the cup, he placed it in the window and enjoyed watching the gushing water.

When the two aunts saw that their nephew had returned safe and sound, they were terribly frightened and called the beggar woman again.

"When you go over to the house next Friday, we want you to tell the young lady, 'your brother is handsome, but you are now much more beautiful. If you fetch the talking bird, that will change.'"

The woman went to the maiden and did what the sisters had ordered her to do. When the young man came home, he found his sister so sad again that he asked whether he could do something for her that she would like.

"Oh, dear brother," she answered, "you fetched the dancing water for me. Now you must also go and fetch the talking bird!"

"Dear sister," he said, "I'll gladly do this for you, but this time you won't see me again. That's for sure."

But the sister was convinced that he would return, so the young man mounted his horse again and rode until he came to the first hermit.

"Father," he said, "you helped me find the dancing water. Now please help me fetch the talking bird."

"My son," the hermit replied, "you succeeded the first time, but be careful. You will not succeed the second time."

The young man refused to heed his warning and moved on to the second hermit, and then the third, who said to him: "My son, if you insist on trying your luck no matter what, then go with God. Make sure that you have enough meat to throw to the wild animals. When you are in the castle, go through all the rooms, but make sure that you don't touch anything. When you reach the chamber with a great number of birds, wait until the birds begin to speak. Then grab one of them and flee as fast as you can. But make sure that you don't touch the bird unless it speaks."

The young man went up the mountain loaded with meat and was fortunate to be able to pass through the wild animals. He dismounted in front of the castle and went through the rooms. There were even more beautiful things, than before, but he went by them without touching them. When he entered the chamber with the birds, however, he forgot the hermit's warning and grabbed a bird that was not speaking. All of a sudden he was turned into stone, and his horse as well.

Meanwhile, his sister looked at his ring every day and was happy that it remained so clear and bright. Yet one morning, the ring was totally misty. She began to weep and said, "I'm going to set out to save my brother." So she wandered forth for many days until she reached the first hermit in the forest. She knocked on his door, and the old man opened it. When he saw a woman standing there, he said, "Oh my daughter, what are you doing in this wilderness so alone?"

"Father," she answered, "I've set out in search of my brother."

"Yes, daughter," the wise man spoke. "We warned your brother enough times, but he did not want to listen to us."

Then he directed her to the second hermit, and he sent her to the third.

"Oh, daughter," the third hermit said to her. "How can you save your brother? You're just a weak maiden. Do you know the dangers awaiting you?"

She would not let herself be dissuaded, and the wise man told her how to protect herself against the wild animals and continued: "When you enter the castle, go through all the rooms but make sure that you don't touch anything. There is a magnificent bed in the innermost room. The sorceress will be sleeping on it. Beneath the bed are her diamond slippers. Be careful not to touch them. Instead, approach the bed quietly without looking around, stick your hand beneath the pillow without waking the sorceress, and pull out the gold can which is hidden there. Take the salve that is in the can and rub your brother with it. Once you do this, he will come back to life."

The maiden set out on her way, loaded with meat, and she bravely passed through the wild animals while throwing them the meat. Then she strode through the rooms without touching anything. When she reached the room where the sorceress was sleeping, she approached the bed quietly, stuck her hand cautiously beneath the pillow, and pulled out the gold can. Immediately thereafter she rushed through the rooms without making a sound, rubbed her brother with the salve as well as all the other princes and brave men who had been turned to stone, and they were all brought back to life. After this she went down the stairs and rubbed the horses, and once all the men were gathered, they mounted their horses and fled as fast as they could. The brother made sure, however, to take the talking bird with him. When they had all descended the mountain, the sorceress awoke and screamed: "I've been betrayed! I've been betrayed!" But her power was gone, and she could no longer harm anyone. The sister and brother rode to the three hermits and thanked them for their help. Then they returned to their beautiful house and placed the bird next to the cup in the window.

One day the king noticed the wonderful objects and invited the sister and brother to a meal in his castle. When they were climbing the stairs, they passed their mother and lowered their eyes. Although the sentinel told them that the king had ordered everyone to spit into the face of the woman, they did not do it. After the meal, the king said, "You have a cup with dancing water and a talking bird in your window. Might I be able to see them one time?"

The sister and brother sent a servant to their house to fetch the bird and cup and set them on the table. All of a sudden the bird began to speak: "Dear water, I know a beautiful story. Should I tell it to you?"

"Please do," answered the water.

Then the bird told the entire history of the sister and brother, how they had been thrown into the water, and what had happened to them afterward. When the two aunts heard this, they became pale, for the king recognized his children, and there was great joy in the castle. Now his poor wife, the queen, was bathed and given beautiful clothes. Meanwhile the king ordered the two evil sisters be put in a barrel with boiling oil. The barrel was then tied to the tail of a horse that was driven through the entire city.

34

THE PIOUS CHILD

Once upon a time there was a pious God-fearing peasant, who found a poor little child in a field.

"Oh, you innocent little creature!" he cried. "What kind of a vile mother would abandon you to this fate? I'm going to raise you as my own."

So he picked up the child and began caring for him, and after that day, things began to go very well for him. His fruit trees flourished, the grain harvest and wine were good, and the peasant led a comfortable life. The child grew and became a pious young boy, but he was naive and didn't know anything about our savior and the saints. One time, while he was playing with clay, he formed big and small balls and made them into a rosary. The beads were just right. Nothing was missing, not even a gloria patri. When the peasant saw this, he was astonished and decided to take the boy to the city of Catania.

"Do you want to come with me?" he asked one morning. "I'm riding to Catania."

"Whatever you want, master," he replied and went with the peasant to the city.

When they approached the dome, the peasant said, "Why don't you go into the church for a while until I finish my business."

The boy went into the church and saw all the gold and silk robes, the embroidered covers for the altar, and the numerous flowers and candles, and he was very amazed because he had never seen anything like it. Finally he came to the altar where the crucifix was standing, knelt down on the steps to the altar, and spoke to the crucifix: "Little brother, why have you been nailed to this wood? Did you do something bad?"

The crucifix nodded his head.

"Oh, poor little brother, you should never do that again because now you know how much you must suffer for it."

And the Lord nodded his head once more.

This conversation went on for a long time, and he talked with the crucifix until mass was completed and the sacristan wanted to close the church door. When he caught sight of the little peasant boy, he asked him to get up and leave the church.

"No," the boy answered. "I'm staying here. Otherwise, this poor man will be completely alone. First you nailed him to this wood, and now you've abandoned him to his fate. Isn't it true, little brother, you'd like me to stay with you?"

And the Lord nodded his head. When the sacristan heard and saw this, he became frightened and ran and told the priest everything he had just witnessed.

"He must certainly be a holy soul," the priest remarked. "Let the boy stay there and take him a plate of macaroni and some wine."

When the sacristan took the macaroni and wine to the boy he said, "Set it down. I'll eat soon." Then he turned to the crucifix and said, "Little brother, you must be hungry. Who knows how long it's been since you've had something to eat. Have a little macaroni."

Then the boy climbed onto the altar and gave the Lord some macaroni, and the Lord ate it. Then the boy said, "Little brother, you must also be thirsty. Drink a little of my wine," and he gave the Lord some wine to drink, and the Lord drank. Soon after he had shared all his food and wine with the Lord, the boy fell down dead, and his soul flew to heaven and praised God.

The priest had concealed himself behind the altar, and when he saw the transfigured body of the boy, he spread the news throughout the city that there was a saint in the dome, and he had the boy placed in a gold coffin. The people came and saw the boy's transfigured body and prayed to him. When the peasant came, he recognized the little boy he had raised, and he thanked the Lord for having brought the boy to him. Then he went home, and everything he undertook was so successful that he became a rich man. To be sure, he used the money to do many good things for the poor, and he led a holy life until he died and went to Paradise.

May our lives be just like his.

35

KATERINA'S FATE

Once upon a time there was a merchant who had such an enormous treasure that he was richer than any king in the world. In the grand hall where he granted audiences, there were three marvelous chairs. One was made of silver, the second of gold, the third of diamonds. Aside from his wealth, this merchant had a daughter, his only child, named Katerina, and she was more beautiful than the sun.

One day as Katerina sat in her room, the door suddenly sprang open by itself, and a beautiful tall lady entered. She held a wheel in her hands.

"Katerina," she said, "when would you prefer to enjoy your life, during your youth or during your old age?"

Katerina looked at her in astonishment and could not compose herself. The beautiful lady asked once more: "When would you prefer to enjoy your life, during your youth or during your old age?"

Now Katerina thought, "If I say in my youth, then I'll have to suffer in my old age. Therefore, I'd prefer to enjoy my life during my old age, and I'll place myself in God's hands during my youth." So she answered, "During my old age!"

"Let it be as you wish," the beautiful lady said, spun her wheel one time, and disappeared. This tall, beautiful lady was none other than Katerina's Fate.*

---

* Sorte.

A few days later her father suddenly received news that several of his ships had sunk in a storm. A few more days passed, and he learned that more of his ships had capsized. To make a long story short, within a month he lost his entire fortune and had to sell everything that he had. Yet even this money was soon lost and he finally was completely poor and miserable. Eventually he became sick from all the sorrow and died.

As a result, Katerina was completely alone in the world without a cent to her name, and without anyone who might take care of her. So she thought, "I'll go to another city and look for some employment." Soon she set out and wandered until she came to another city. As she walked through the streets, she saw a lady standing at a window who asked her, "Where are you going so alone, beautiful maiden?"

"Oh, noble lady, I'm a poor maiden and would like to find a position so that I can earn a living. Could you use me?"

The lady hired her as her servant, and Katerina was very loyal to her. After some days had passed, the woman said to Katerina one evening, "I must go out tonight and shall lock the door."

"Good," Katerina said, and when her mistress was gone, she took her work, sat down, and began sewing. Suddenly the door flew open and her Fate entered.

"So!" she cried. "Here you are sitting, Katerina, and you think I should leave you in peace!?"

Upon saying these words Fate ran to all the closets, took out all the clothes and linen that belonged to Katerina's mistress, and ripped them to shreds.

"Woe is me!" Katerina thought. "When my mistress returns and finds everything in this condition, she'll certainly kill me."

In her fear she ran through the door and fled, but her Fate gathered together all the torn and destroyed things, made them whole again, and restored everything to its proper place. When the mistress returned home, she called for Katerina, but the girl was nowhere to be found.

"Did she steal anything from me?" the woman thought, but when she checked, there was nothing missing. She was very surprised, but Katerina did not return. Rather the girl continued to travel until she came to another city. As she went through the streets, another lady was standing at a window, and she asked Katerina, "Where are you going so alone, pretty girl?"

"Oh, noble lady, I'm a poor woman, and I'm looking for some employment to earn my living. Could you use me?"

The woman did indeed employ her, and Katerina served her and thought she would finally have some peace. However it lasted only a few days until, one evening while her mistress was out, her Fate reappeared and addressed her with some harsh words: "So, here you sit! Did you really think you could escape me?"

As she said this, her Fate ripped and destroyed everything in sight so that poor Katerina fled, fearing for her life.

To make a long story short, Katerina led this horrible existence for the next seven years. She ran from one city to the next and tried to find a job in each place. But, after a few days her Fate would appear, tear and destroy the things that belonged to her mistress, and the poor maiden had to flee. When she left the house, however, her Fate would restore things to their previous order.

After seven years her Fate finally seemed to become tired of persecuting the unfortunate Katerina. One day Katerina came to a city and saw a lady standing at a window who asked her: "Where are you going so alone, you beautiful maiden!"

"Oh, noble lady, I'm a poor maiden and am looking for some employment to earn a living. Could you use me?"

"I'd very much like to employ you," the woman answered, "but you must do something for me every day, and I don't know whether you have the strength to do it."

"Tell me what it is," Katerina said, "and I'll do it if I can."

"Do you see that big mountain over there?" the lady said. "Well, every morning you must carry a large board with freshly baked bread to the top of it, and you must cry out in a loud voice: 'Oh Fate of my mistress! Oh Fate of my mistress! Oh Fate of my mistress!' three times. Then my Fate will appear and take the bread."

"I'll gladly do this," Katerina said, and the lady hired her.

Now Katerina worked many years for this woman, and every morning she took the tray with the freshly baked bread to the top of the mountain, and after she cried out, "Oh, Fate of my mistress" three times, a beautiful, tall woman appeared and took the bread. However, Katerina often wept when she thought about how she had been so rich and was now working as a poor maid.

One day her mistress said to her, "Katerina, why do you weep so much?"

Then Katerina told her how badly things had gone for her, and her mistress said, "Do you know what, Katerina? Tomorrow, when you take the bread to the top of the mountain, ask my Fate if it could possibly convince your Fate to leave you in peace. Perhaps this will help."

This advice pleased poor Katerina. The next morning, when she took the bread to the Fate of her mistress, she told the beautiful lady about her misery and said, "Oh, Fate of my mistress, please ask my Fate not to persecute me anymore."

"Oh, you poor girl," the Fate replied. "Your Fate is wrapped in seven covers. Therefore, she can't even hear you. When you come tomorrow, I shall lead you to her."

After Katerina returned home, the Fate of her mistress went to the girl's Fate and said, "Dear sister, why don't you stop making poor Katerina suffer so much? Let her enjoy some happy days again."

"Bring her to me tomorrow," Katerina's Fate replied. "I want to give her something that should help her out of her misery."

The next morning, when Katerina took the bread to the top of the mountain, the Fate of her mistress led her to her own Fate, who was wrapped in seven covers. Her Fate gave her a skein of silk and said, "Keep it in a safe place. It will be of use to you."

Then Katerina went home and told her mistress, "My Fate gave me a skein of silk as a gift. What should I do with it? It's not worth much money."

"Well," her mistress said, "I would keep it in a safe place. It might do you some good."

After some time had passed, it so happened that the young king was to marry and wanted to have some royal garments made for himself. When the tailor was to make a beautiful suit, he could not find silk of the same color. The king sent out messengers throughout the realm who spread the word that whoever had a certain kind of silk was to bring it to the court and would be well paid for it.

"Katerina," her mistress said, "your skein of silk is this color. Take it to the king so that he will give you a beautiful gift."

So Katerina put on her best clothes and went to the court, and when she came before the king, she was so beautiful that the king could not take his eyes off her.

"Your majesty," Katerina said, "I've brought you a skein of silk of the color that you could not find."

"Do you know what, your majesty," one of his ministers cried out, "let us give the maiden the weight of the silk in gold."

The king agreed, and a scale was brought. The silk was placed on one side, and on the other, gold. Now just think what happened. No matter how many pieces of gold the king placed on the scale, the silk was always heavier. The king ordered a larger scale to be brought, and all his treasures were placed on one side, but the silk still weighed more. Finally, the king took his gold crown from his head and placed it on top of all the other treasures, and just look: now the side with the gold came down and weighed just as much as the silk.

"Where did you get this silk?" the king asked.

"Your majesty," Katerina responded, "I received it from my mistress as a gift."

"No, that's not possible," the king said, "and if you don't tell me the truth, I'll have your head chopped off."

Then Katerina told everything that had happened to her since the time she had been a rich girl. Meanwhile there was a wise woman who was living at the court, and she said, "Katerina, you have suffered too long. You will now see happier times, and because it was only after the gold crown brought about a balance on the scale, this is a sign that you will become a queen."

"If she is to become a queen," the king declared, "then I shall be the one who makes her one, for Katerina and no one else shall become my wife."

And this is indeed what happened. The king informed his bride that he did not want to marry her anymore, and he married the beautiful Katerina instead. So, after Katerina had suffered so much in her youth, she enjoyed bliss and happiness in her old age, and she remained happy and content, but we still can't pay the rent.

36

GODFATHER DEATH

Once upon a time there was a man who had just one son. In those times many people did not have their children baptized while they were young. Rather, they waited until they were somewhat older. So, when this child reached the age of seven, he still had not been baptized.

When our dear Lord saw this from heaven, he was annoyed and called Saint John to him and said, "Listen to me, Saint John, I want you to go to this village and tell this man that I want to know why he hasn't had his son baptized yet."

So Saint John went to the earth and knocked on the door of this man's house.

"Who's there?" the man asked.

"It's me, Saint John."

"What do you want from me?" the man asked.

"Our dear Lord has sent me," the saint said, "and he wants to know why you haven't had your son baptized yet."

"Well, it's because I haven't found a good godfather," the man replied.

"If that's the case," Saint John said, "I'll be glad to be your child's godfather."

"I want to thank you," the man said, "but this cannot be. If you become my child's godfather, then you'll have only one wish, and that would be to take him to Paradise as soon as possible, and I don't want that."

So Saint John had to return to heaven without accomplishing anything.

Next, the dear Lord sent Saint Peter to the earth to warn the man, but things did not turn out any better for him. The man gave Saint Peter the same answers as he gave to Saint John and did not want Saint Peter as the godfather.

Then the dear Lord thought, "What does he have in mind? He certainly wants his son to have immortality. Well, I can only send Death to him now."

So the dear Lord sent Death to the man to ask him why he had not had his son baptized. When Death arrived on earth, he knocked on the man's door.

"Who's there?" asked the man.

"Our dear Lord has sent me," Death answered, "to ask you why your child has not been baptized yet."

"Tell the dear Lord," he replied, "that I haven't found the right godfather."

"Don't you want me to be the godfather?"* Death asked.

"Who are you?"

"I am Death."

"Yes," the man declared. "I'd very much like you to be the godfather of my child, and we can let him be baptized right away."

Soon thereafter the child was baptized. Then after several months had passed, Death reappeared to the man, who gave him a friendly reception and wanted to offer him all kinds of good food. But Death said, "Don't go to so much trouble. I've only come to fetch you."

"What?" the man exclaimed. "I especially chose you so that you would protect me, my wife, and my son."

"That's not possible," Death answered. "The scythe cuts all the grass that it finds on its way. I can't protect you."

Then Death took the man into a dark cellar in which there were a lot of lamps burning on the walls.

"You see the lamps?" he asked. "They are the lamps of life. Each person has this kind of lamp, and when it goes out, he must die."

"Which is my light?" the man asked.

Then Death showed him a little lamp in which there was very little oil left, and when it ran out, the man fell down dead.

Did Death also have the son die? Of course. Death cannot protect anyone. When the son's time came, he too had to die.

---

* This should actually be godmother because death is a female in Sicily.

37

Beautiful Anna

Once there were three sisters who were all very beautiful, but the youngest was the most beautiful among them, and she was called Anna. The three girls had neither father nor mother, and they made a living through their handicraft. The first spun and made reels of yarn. The second did the weaving, and the youngest sewed shirts and other clothes.

One day, as they were sitting and working in front of the door to their house, the prince came riding by on his way to the hunt. When he saw the three beautiful girls, he cried out, "What a beauty she is, the maiden who's spinning! What a beauty she is, the maiden who's weaving! But the maiden who's sewing will be the end of me!"*

The two older sisters became jealous when they heard that the prince preferred their sister to them, and the eldest said, "Tomorrow I shall do the sewing, and Anna will spin."

When the prince came by again the next morning, however, he said, "What a beauty she is, the maiden who's sewing! What a beauty she is, the maiden who's weaving! But the maiden who's spinning will be the end of me!"

The sisters became even more jealous, and on the third morning Anna had to weave. But the prince said, "What a beauty she is, the

---

* Ch'è bedda, chidda chi 'ncanna, ch'è bedda chidda chi tessi, chidda chi çusi muriri mi fa.

185

maiden who's sewing! What a beauty she is, the maiden who's spinning! But the maiden who's weaving will be the end of me!"

As a result of all this the sisters could not stand Anna any longer and began to plan how they might cause her ruin. Eventually they decided to lead her to a wild, desolate region where they would leave her so that she would not be able to find her way home. So the oldest sister said to Anna, "Come with me, Anna. We've got some dirty clothes, and we'll have to wash them in a little brook."

Anna agreed to follow her, and so the two of them wandered off. When they came to a wild desolate spot, the sister said, "Oh Anna, I've forgotten to bring some soap with me. Wait for me here a while, and I'll go fetch it."

So beautiful Anna sat down and waited for her sister. She waited and waited, but nobody came. Then she began to shed bitter tears and thought, "She left me here alone intentionally so that I would die. Well, I won't return to my sisters. Instead, I'm going to set out and seek my fortune in the wide world."*

So she set out and wandered until she finally came to a large beautiful house. She knocked on the door and a woman opened and asked her what she wanted.

"Oh, my good woman," the beautiful Anna asked, "please let me rest here tonight. I'm a poor maiden and am completely alone in the world."

"Oh, you poor child," the woman cried. "How did you manage to wind up here? If my husband finds you, he'll eat you. However, I feel sorry for you and shall hide you. Perhaps I'll be able to soften him up."

So the woman hid the beautiful Anna, and soon her husband came home and muttered, "I smell some human flesh! I smell some human flesh!"

"Oh, what are you talking about?" his wife responded. "You're always smelling human flesh. That's what comes from your having already eaten so many humans. Just think, today a maiden came by here, and she was more beautiful than the sun. I believe that if you had seen her, you would have let her live."

As she now saw that she had softened her husband, she brought beautiful Anna from her hiding place, and she was so beautiful that the ogre immediately became very fond of her and did not want to eat her.

"Stay with us, beautiful maiden," he said, "and you will have a good life."

* Pri circari a me vintura.

So beautiful Anna stayed with the ogre and his wife and was just like their own child.

When some time had passed, the ogre died and soon after his wife as well. The beautiful Anna remained alone in the large house, and all its treasures belonged to her. One day when she was standing on the balcony, her eldest sister happened to pass by and recognized Anna and asked her how she was.

"I'm doing fine," Anna answered, but she did not invite her sister to come up.

"If I had known that I was going to meet you here, I would have brought you a present," the sister said.

"Thanks," Anna answered. "I don't need anything, nor do I want presents from anyone."

Her eldest sister continued on her way home and said to the second sister, "Just think, I saw our sister Anna, and she's become even more beautiful than she was. She's wearing elegant clothes and lives in a large house."

The hearts of both the sisters became filled with jealousy, and they began thinking how they might be able to bring about Anna's ruin. So they took some grapes* and poisoned them. The next day the eldest sister made her way to the beautiful Anna's house, who was sitting and working on the terrace. When her sister saw her, she went up and called to her in a friendly way: "Oh, dear little sister, how nice it is to see you again. And how beautiful you've become! Look, I've brought you some beautiful grapes. Do me a favor and eat them."

"I thank you," Anna replied. "You see that my garden is full of grapes. I don't need yours."

The sister kept insisting until Anna took a grape and put it into her mouth. As soon as she did, she fell down, and the grape stuck in her throat. Her sister left her lying on the terrace and went home pleased with what she had done.

Now it just so happened one day that the prince went hunting and passed by this house. He saw a beautiful bird on the terrace and he shot it, and the bird fell onto the floor of the terrace. So the prince climbed the stairs and wandered through all the rooms, but there wasn't a human soul to be found. When he came to the terrace, an astonishingly beautiful maiden was lying there, and when he looked at her more closely, he saw beautiful Anna. Then he began to weep and kissed her and said,

* Un grappu ri curniola.

187

"How beautiful this little nose is! How beautiful this little mouth! But I'll die just by looking at her tender little neck."*

As he bent over and touched her throat, the grape sprung out of her mouth, and beautiful Anna opened her eyes and came to life. The prince was overjoyed and said, "You shall become my wife!"

But the prince had an evil mother who was living with him, and he could not bring the beautiful Anna to his castle. Instead, he left her in her house, and every day, when he went hunting, he came and visited her. After a year Anna gave birth to a son, and since he was as handsome as the sun, she named him Sunny. The next year she gave birth to a daughter as beautiful as the moon, and she called her Luna. The children grew fast and became even more beautiful, but their mother was not allowed to go to the royal castle. However, the prince came every day and visited her. Then one day he became sick—so sick that he had to remain in bed for many days and could not visit Anna. He cried out loud: "Oh my son, Sunny! Oh my daughter, Luna! What is my wife Anna doing so alone?"†

His mother overheard all this and called her son's faithful servant and said to him, "If you don't tell me right now what the prince is talking about, I'll have your head chopped off."

The servant confessed that Anna was the wife of the prince and Sunny and Luna were his children.

"Very well," the queen said. "Then go immediately to Donna Anna and tell her: 'Your husband has confessed everything to his mother, and she wishes to see her little grandchildren.' Then take the children, murder them, and bring their hearts and tongues to me as proof that you have carried out my command."

So the servant went sadly to beautiful Anna and told her that the prince had sent him to fetch his children, and she put on their very best clothes and gave them to the servant. He took them away, but even though he was supposed to murder them, he took pity on the innocent children. Indeed, he let them live and took them to his own mother. As for the queen, he brought her the hearts and tongues from two billy goats.

The next morning the queen sent the servant to Anna once more with orders to bring her to the castle. The beautiful Anna had three dresses adorned with little bells, one dress with silver bells, the second

---

* Ch'è beddu stu nasuzzu, ch'è bedda sta vucuzza, e stu codduzza muriri mi fa.

† Figghiu miu suli, figghia mia luna, comu fa Donn' Anna sula?

with gold, and the third with diamonds. She put on all three, one on top of the other, and went this way to the castle. There was an enormous fire burning in the courtyard, and on top of it was a kettle with boiling oil. Next to the fire stood the old queen, who ordered the servants to throw Anna into the boiling oil. When Anna heard this, she threw off all her three dresses, which began to ring with their little bells. The sound was so lovely and loud that the prince heard it in his room. He jumped out of bed and saw that the servants were about to grab hold of beautiful Anna and throw her into the boiling oil.

"Stop!" he yelled as he ran to free beautiful Anna from their hands. Then he ordered the evil queen to be thrown into the oil in place of Anna. As he now embraced her full of joy, Anna asked, "Where are my dear children? You summoned them to the castle yesterday?"

"I didn't order our children to be brought here," the prince replied. "It was certainly my evil mother who did this. Oh my children, my dear children!"

All at once the servant came, threw himself at the prince's feet, and confessed everything to him. Then he told the prince that the children were safe and sound with his mother. When the children were fetched, their parents embraced them full of joy. Afterward there were three days of celebrations, and the prince became king and beautiful Anna queen. They remained happy and content, but we still can't pay the rent.

38

THE DRAGON SLAYER

Once upon a time there was a brother and a sister. They had neither father nor mother and loved each other with all their hearts. They were very poor and only had two goats, which the sister drove to the meadow every day. One day one of the goats escaped, and she had to run after it. She ran and ran until it became night, and she found herself in a desolate place and could no longer make her way back home. The goat kept running ahead of her, and when it came to a house, it stopped at the door and laid down on the threshold. The girl found the goat and thought, "It's pitch dark, and I can't find my way home. I might as well stay here until it becomes day."

When it began to dawn, she heard a powerful voice in the house that roared, "I smell human flesh!" and all at once a giant came out the door. He was so terrible to look at that the girl became frightened.

"What are you doing here?"

The girl told the giant how she had to run after the goat and had arrived at the house in the dark of the night.

"Good," said the giant. "Come into my house and serve me."

"Oh, no," answered the girl, "you'll certainly eat me."

"Don't worry," he answered. "if you serve me loyally, I won't harm you."

So the girl remained with the giant, served him well, and had a good life with him. Meanwhile, because her brother had not been able to find his little sister, he became sad and continued to miss her very much.

Now one day while he was moping about and looking after the one goat that had remained, the animal escaped. He ran after it over hill and valley until he came to an unknown place and could not find his way back home. The goat ran ahead of him, and when it came to a house, it stopped at the door and laid down. The boy thought, "It's so dark now that I won't be able to find my way back. I might as well remain here until it becomes day."

Now this was the house of the giant in which his sister was staying. The next morning she opened the door and saw a handsome boy lying there. When she took a closer look, she recognized her brother and embraced him with joy, but also with great fear, for she was scared that the giant might kill him.

"Dear brother," she said. "I must hide you, for the giant, my master, will soon wake up and might eat you."

So she hid him in the cellar. When the giant woke up, he roared, "I smell human flesh!"

"Oh, what are you saying?" she answered. "Nobody's here."

He continued to roar: "I tell you, I smell human flesh!"

Then she summoned her courage and said, "I must tell you that my brother's here. As you spared my life, so must you spare his."

The giant promised to do this as long as the brother worked for him as a servant. So now the sister and brother both lived with the giant, served him, and led a good life.

When they became older, they wanted to depart and be with human beings again, but the giant would not let them go. So one day the brother said to the sister, "I can't hold out any longer in this desolate spot. We can't stay here forever. Besides, we can never be sure that he won't do something to us. Who knows whether the giant won't decide one beautiful day to eat us. So try to find out from him how we can get rid of him. Then I'll kill him, and we can get away from here."

His sister agreed with his proposal, went to the giant, and said to him, "Do you want me to clean the lice from your head?"

The giant said "yes," and when they were together, she began to speak: "Why don't you tell me what one would have to do to get rid of you? Of course, I hope it will never happen."

"Well, my dear child," the giant answered, "there's only one way to kill me. Do you see all those rusty swords hanging in my room? The middle one is a magic sword. Whoever wields it can never be defeated, and if it is cleaned so that it shines, this sword can cut off my head. Whoever kills me will be a lucky man because he will find an ointment in my head. Any wound that is rubbed with this ointment will heal right away."

"Oh, stop now!" the maiden cried. "I don't want to hear these stories any longer. May you live a long life."

However, she secretly went to her brother and told him everything the giant had said. The brother waited a few days and began to clean all the swords in the giant's room so that they became bright and shiny.

"What are you doing there?" the giant asked.

"I'm cleaning your swords. Just look how rusty they are," the young man answered.

When he cleaned the magic sword, it glistened so brightly that he never saw anything like it before in his life. One evening when the giant slept, the young man crept into his room and cut off the giant's head with the magic sword. Then he collected the ointment in the giant's head and kept it in a little box. Afterward he and his sister dug a grave for the giant and put him inside. Finally, they took all the treasures that had been stored in the hut and moved to the nearest city, where they bought a pretty house and continued to enjoy living together.

One day, however, the brother said, "Dear sister, I can't stay with you any longer, for I want to see the world and try my luck."

She wept and did not want to let him depart, but he would not let himself be deterred from setting out into the world. He took some beautiful armor, fastened the magic sword onto his belt, and stuck the little box of ointment in a pocket. Then he mounted a beautiful steed and rode away.

He traveled for a good deal of time and finally came to a large beautiful city that was completely decked in black, and all the people wore black clothes. So he asked an innkeeper what all this meant.

"Oh," he answered, "the city is plagued by a dragon with seven heads. It lives on top of that mountain over there, and each year we have to bring him a virtuous virgin. Otherwise, he would devastate the entire city. This year the king's daughter lost the lottery, and today she must be led to the mountain. The king has proclaimed that any knight who kills the dragon can have his daughter for his wife, but nobody wants to try because the dragon is much too terrifying."

"I want to try my fortune," the young man thought. "After all, I have the magic sword."

So he mounted his horse again, fastened the magic sword, stuck the box with the ointment into a pocket, and rode toward the mountain. When he came near the dragon's cave, the monster crawled out because it had smelled human flesh. Then the young man pulled out his magic sword, fought with the dragon, and cut off some of the heads. But, the dragon wounded him on his leg, and also wounded the horse. The young man retreated a bit, took out the little box, and rubbed his wounds and the horse's wounds with the ointment. All at once the two of them were fresh and well again so that he could wield his sword and finally kill the dragon. Then he cut out the seven tongues from the seven heads, wrapped them in a scarf, and returned to the inn.

In the meantime the princess prepared herself for the difficult march to the mountain, and although she wept bitter tears, she finally had to bid farewell to her parents and begin climbing the mountain. One of her father's slaves accompanied her. When they came to the top of the mountain, they saw the dragon lying in his blood. The princess thanked God from the bottom of her heart that she did not have to die, but the slave thought he would make use of this situation. He placed his sword against her breast and said, "If you don't swear me that you'll tell your father I've killed the dragon, I'll take your life."

Struck by fear, she promised him what he wanted, and he took the seven heads that had been cut off as proof that he had killed he dragon. When the princess returned safe and sound from the mountain and said the slave had killed the dragon, there was great joy in the entire land, and the king said to the slave, "You have rescued my daughter and shall have her for your wife."

So a great celebration was arranged. Everyone in the country was happy, but the princess was sad, for she did not want to marry the slave. When the true conqueror of the dragon heard that the slave was to marry the princess, he quickly had a splendid garment made for himself, took the seven tongues in his pocket, went to the castle, and had himself announced to the king.

"Your majesty," he said. "I've heard that a slave has performed a heroic deed and has killed the dragon. Please tell me how everything happened."

"My slave accompanied my daughter to the top of the mountain," the king responded. "Fortunately he had the strength to defeat the dragon and to cut off its seven heads. As proof he brought the seven heads with him."

"May I see the seven heads just once?" the young man asked.

So the king gave the order to fetch the seven heads of the dragon and to show them to the unknown young man.

"Yes, they are certainly powerful heads," the young man said. "I wonder how large the tongues are?"

Upon saying this, he opened the jaws of each one of the heads, but there were no tongues inside. The king and his ministers were very astonished and said, "How's that possible? Did the monster not have any tongues?"

All at once the youth pulled his scarf out with the seven tongues and placed a tongue in each one of the jaws of the dragon's heads, and what do you know, they fit perfectly.

"Isn't it true, your majesty," he said, "that the conqueror of the dragon must be the one who cut out the tongues before the heads were brought to you? I am the one who fought the dragon and defeated him. The slave is a miserable liar."

The king summoned his daughter and asked her once more whether the slave really had killed the dragon. She fell on her knees and said, "Oh no, dear father, he didn't do it. Instead he threatened to kill me if I told you the truth."

The king became very happy and said, "Look, this handsome young man is your rescuer, and he is the one whom you shall have for your husband."

And that's what happened. The deceitful slave was led to the gallows and hung. The unknown youth married the beautiful princess and had his sister join them. Then they all lived happy and content, and we still can't pay the rent.

39

SAINT JAMES OF GALICIA

Once upon a time there was a king and queen who did not have any children and would have liked to have a son or a daughter. At one time the queen turned to Saint James of Galicia* and said, "Oh Saint James, if you will grant me a son, I swear to you that he will make a pilgrimage to you when he becomes eighteen years old."

Soon thereafter the queen became pregnant through God's grace and through the saint, and when her time arrived, she gave birth to a baby who was so beautiful it was as if God had made him. The boy grew rapidly from one day to the next and became bigger and more handsome. When he was twelve years old, the king died, and the queen remained alone with her son whom she loved like her own eyes. Many years passed, and soon the prince was to turn eighteen, but when the queen thought that she would have to separate from him very soon and send him by himself on the pilgrimage, she became very sad and wept the entire day.

One day the prince asked her, "Mother, why do you sob the entire day?"

"It's nothing, my son," she answered. "I only have some worries."

---

* In Sicilian the name San Japicu is used. It is a very old form for Saint James. Compare *La venutadi lu re Japicu a Cantania* of 1287 in the book *Cronache Ciciliane*, ed. V. di Giovani (Bologna, 1865), p. 165.

"What are you worried about?" he responded. "Are you concerned that your estates in Chiana* are not doing well? Let me go there so I can see everything and report back to you."

The queen agreed, and the prince set out on the road to the estates that belonged to his mother in Chiana. He found that everything was in the best condition and returned to his mother.

"Dear mother," he said, "be happy and forget your worries. Everything is in order on your estates. The animals are flourishing, the fields have been plowed, and the wheat will soon be ripe."

"Good, my son," she replied, but she did not become happy, and the next day she began to sob and weep again. So the prince said to her, "Mother, if you don't tell me why you are so troubled, I'm going to set out and wander throughout the world."

"Oh, my dear son," she answered, "I'm troubled because you must separate from me. Before you were born, I yearned so much to have a child that I promised Saint James of Galicia that if he granted me a son, I would send you on a pilgrimage to him when you turned eighteen. This is why I am troubled. You will have to wander off alone and spend many years away from me. You see, it will take a whole year just to journey to the saint."

"If that's all it is, dear mother," the son said, "don't be so worried. Only the dead don't return. If I stay alive, I'll soon come back to you."

So he consoled his mother, and when he turned eighteen, he took his leave from the queen and said, "Farewell, dear mother, and God willing, we shall see each other again."

The queen wept bitterly and embraced him with many tears. Then she gave him three apples and said, "My son, take these three apples, and pay attention to my words. You are not to take this long journey all by yourself. If another young man joins you and wants to travel with you, take him into a tavern and invite him to eat with you. After the meal you are to cut an apple in two parts, one small and one large. Ask the young man to take one of the pieces. If he takes the larger half, you are to separate from him because he won't be a true friend. If he takes the smaller piece, regard him as your brother and share everything you have with him."

Upon saying these words, she embraced her son again and blessed him, and the prince wandered off. He traveled for quite a long time without meeting anyone, but one day he saw a young man who came

---

* This is Piana, the plain of Catania.

along his way. This fellow stopped and asked him, "Where are you going, handsome lad?"

"I'm taking a pilgrimage to Saint James of Galicia. When my mother was younger and could not have any children, she swore to him that if he would grant her a son, this son would take a pilgrimage to the saint when he turned eighteen. So the saint granted her a son, namely me, and because I'm now eighteen, I'm making the pilgrimage to Lizia."

"I've got to go there too," the other fellow said. "My mother had exactly the same experience as yours. So if we both must make the same journey, we might as well travel together."

So they continued their trip together, but the prince was suspicious of his companion and thought, "I had better make the test with the apple."

At one point they came to a tavern, and the prince said, "I'm hungry. Let's get something to eat here."

The other agreed, and they went inside and ate together. After they had eaten, the prince took out an apple, cut in two uneven parts, and asked his companion to choose one of them. When he took the larger piece, the prince thought, "You're not a true friend," and in order to separate from him, he pretended to be sick and had to stay in a bed there. Then the other fellow said, "I can't wait for you because I have a long trip ahead of me. So I bid you farewell."

"Farewell," replied the prince, and he was happy to get rid of him.

Later, when the prince continued his journey, he thought, "Oh, if only God would lead a true friend to me so that I would not have to travel alone!"

Soon afterward another young man joined him and asked, "Where are you traveling to, handsome lad?"

So the prince told him how his mother had taken an oath to send him on a pilgrimage to Saint James of Galicia, and that he was making this journey.

"I must also travel there," the young man said. "My mother took the very same oath."

"Then we can journey there together!" the prince exclaimed, and they continued their trip together.

When they rode up to the next tavern, the prince said, "I'm hungry. Let's stop here and get something to eat."

So they entered and ate with one another, and after the meal the prince cut the second apple into two uneven pieces and handed them to his companion, who took the larger piece. "You're not a true friend," thought the prince, and once again, in order to separate from his companion, he pretended to be sick and let the other continue the journey alone. Later, however, he set out again with a sad heart and thought, "Oh God, let me find a true friend who will be like a friend to me on this journey." While he was praying to God, he suddenly saw a young man coming his way. He was such a handsome fellow and looked so friendly that he took a liking to him right away and thought, "If only this were the true friend!"

The young man joined him and asked, "Where are you traveling to, handsome lad?"

So the prince told him about the oath his mother made and why he had to make this holy pilgrimage.

"I must also go there!" the young man cried out. "My mother made the very same oath."

"Well then, we can travel together," the prince said, and so they continued their journey together.

The young man was so friendly and polite that the prince wished more and more that this fellow might finally show himself to be the true friend. Just as they were riding by a tavern, the prince said, "I'm hungry. Let's go inside and eat something together."

So they entered and ordered something to eat. After the meal the prince cut the last apple into two uneven parts and asked his companion to take one. Now just think, the companion took the smaller piece, and the prince was happy that he had found a true friend.

"My handsome fellow," the prince said, "we must regard one another as brothers. What's mine is also yours, and what's yours is mine. And this is how we should travel together until we come to the saint. And if one of us should die along the way, the other must carry the dead one to the final destination. Let's swear on this!"

Both of them swore this oath, and they regarded each other as brothers and continued on their way. Since it took an entire year to reach the saint, just imagine how much the two had to wander. One day, as they were tired and exhausted and had come to a large beautiful city, they said, "Let's stay here a few days and rest, and later we can continue on our way."

So they rented a small house and lived in it. Across from them stood the royal castle. One morning, when the king went onto the balcony and saw the two handsome young men across from him, he thought, "Well, these two young men are very handsome! One is even more handsome than the other, and I think I'll give him my daughter for his wife."

As it turned out, the prince was more handsome than his companion.

To accomplish his purpose, the king invited both young men for dinner. When they came to the castle, he received them in a friendly way and called his daughter to his side. She was more beautiful than the sun and the moon. Later, before they went to bed, the king slipped the prince's traveling companion a poison drink so he fell down dead in his room. Indeed, the king thought, "When the friend dies, the other will be glad to stay here and no longer think about his pilgrimage. Rather, he will marry my daughter."

The next morning, when the prince awoke, he asked, "Where is my friend?"

"He died suddenly last night and is to be buried right away," the servants replied.

"If my friend is dead, I can't stay here any longer," he responded. "I've got to leave as soon as possible."

"But why don't you stay here?" the king asked. "I want to give you my daughter for your wife."

"No," the prince said. "I can't stay here. But I would appreciate it if you would do me a favor. Give me a horse and let me depart in peace. After I have completed my pilgrimage, I'll return and marry your daughter."

So the king gave him a horse, and the prince mounted it. He carried his dead friend on the saddle in front of him, and gradually he finished the journey. But, his companion was not dead. Rather, he lay in a deep sleep. When the prince came to Saint James of Galicia, he got off his horse and took his friend in his arms like a child and carried him into the church. Then he laid the dead man on the steps of the altar before the saint and prayed: "Oh Saint James of Galicia, look—I've fulfilled my oath and have come to you with my friend! I'm now leaving him in your hands. If you bring him back to life, we shall praise your mercy. If he does not return to life, he at least fulfilled his oath."

Just imagine—as the prince was still praying, his dead friend rose up and was alive again and well! So the two young men thanked the saint, gave him great presents, and set out on their way back home.

When they came to the city where the king lived, they rented the little house again that stood across from the royal castle. The king was very happy that the handsome prince was there again and had become even more handsome. He organized great festivities and ordered a splendid wedding to be celebrated. Thus the prince married the beautiful princess. After the wedding they remained a few months more with her father, but then the prince said, "My mother is waiting anxiously at home for me. Therefore, I can't stay here any longer. I need to set out with my wife and my friend to return to my mother."

The king agreed, and they prepared for the journey. However, the king still had a deep hatred for the poor, unfortunate young man, whom he had one time tried to poison, but who had returned alive to his castle.

Now he wanted to harm him again, and so he sent him on an urgent mission over land on the day of the departure.

"Go quickly," said the king. "Your friend will certainly wait for you before he departs."

So the young man rushed off to carry out the king's mission without saying goodbye. Meanwhile, the king said to the prince, "You must hurry and depart. Otherwise you will not reach your first destination before evening."

"I can't leave without my friend," the prince answered.

But the king said, "Just set out on your way. He'll be back in less than an hour and will catch up to you soon with his fast horse."

The prince let himself be convinced, took his leave from his father-in-law, and departed with his wife. The poor friend needed many hours to carry out the king's mission, and when he finally returned, the king said to him, "Your friend is already far away from here. You'd better see how you can best catch up with him."

So the poor young man had to leave the palace and was not even given a horse. He began to run, and he ran day and night until he caught up with the prince. But due to the great stress, he developed a terrible case of leprosy so that he looked sick and miserable. Nevertheless, the prince received him in a friendly way and cared for him like a brother.

Finally they reached home where the queen had been waiting very anxiously and embraced him full of joy. The prince immediately had a bed set up for his sick friend and called together all the doctors of the city and land, but none of them could help him. Since the prince's friend did not get better, the prince turned to Saint James of Galicia and said, "Oh Saint James, you brought my friend back from the dead. Please help him one more time, and let him be cured from this wicked leprosy."

As he was praying, a servant entered the room and said, "There is a strange doctor outside who wants to cure the poor young man."

Well, this doctor was none other than Saint James of Galicia, who had heard the prince's prayer and had come to help his friend. You must also know that the prince's wife had already given birth to a little girl, who was a beautiful, lovely child.

When the saint stepped toward the sick man's bed, he examined him and said to the prince, "Do you really want to cure your friend? At any price?"

"At any price," the prince responded. "Just tell me how I can help him."

"This evening you are to take your child," the saint said, "and cut open all her veins. Then you are to rub her blood into the wounds of your friend, and this is how he will be cured."

Of course the prince was shocked and scared when he heard that he had to kill his little daughter, but he said, "I promised my friend to treat him like a brother, and if there is no other means, I shall have to sacrifice my child."

When it became evening, they took the little child and cut open her veins and rubbed her blood into the wounds of the sick man. All at once he was healed from the wicked leprosy, but the little child became completely white and weak and looked like she was dead. So they placed her in her cradle, and her poor parents were very despondent because they thought that they had lost their child.

The next morning the saint came and asked after the sick man.

"He's well and healthy," the prince answered.

"And where did you put your little daughter?" asked the saint.

"She's lying in her cradle and is dead," the father spoke in a sad voice.

"But just look and see how she's doing," the saint said, and when they went over to the cradle, the child was sitting in it and was once again lively and healthy. Then the saint said, "I am Saint James of Galicia and have come to help you because I saw how true your friendship was. Continue to love one another, and if things should go badly, call upon me, and I shall come and help you."

Upon saying these words he blessed them and disappeared right before their eyes. Meanwhile, they led pious lives and did much good for the poor and remained happy and content, while we still can't even pay the rent.

40

THE HERMIT

Once upon a time there was a pious hermit who lived on top of a high mountain. He fed himself on grass and roots and spent the entire day doing atonement with his forehead always touching the ground. Now one day a company of rich people from the city made an excursion to the very same mountain for pleasure. They ate and drank, and everyone spent a delightful day there. In the evening one of the men called his servant and said to him, "Collect all the spoons and forks that we brought with us. We want to get ready for our return trip."

So the servant collected all the silverware, but instead of packing everything, he stuck one of the silver serving spoons into his pocket. The hermit saw all this but said nothing, and the entire party rode off toward home. Along the way it occurred the gentleman to count the silverware, and it became apparent that the silver serving spoon was missing.

"What's this?" he asked the servant. "Did you perhaps forget the spoon? Let's return and look for it."

When they returned to the same place where they had been eating, a poor pilgrim had appeared in the meantime and was collecting crumbs and bones and eating them to still his hunger.

"I'm sure you're the one who stole the spoon," said the man who was missing the spoon.

"Oh, my dear gentleman," the pilgrim implored. "I've taken nothing but the bones and the crumbs. You may search me, and you'll see that I have certainly not taken your spoon."

"Nothing there! But it could only have been you. No one else has been here other than you!"

All at once they beat him and abused him. They tied him to the tail of a horse and dragged him with them. The hermit saw all this, and his heart began to grumble about God's justice. "What's this?" he thought. "Is this the way things are to happen on earth? Is that thief of a servant to go unpunished while the innocent pilgrim is mistreated in such an awful way? God is unjust to tolerate such things. Therefore, I'm no longer going to do atonement. Instead, I'll return to the world and enjoy my life."

Said, done. The hermit left the mountain and no longer did atonement. Rather he set out to enjoy his life. As he wandered about, he met a strong handsome young man who asked him, "Where are you traveling to?"

The hermit indicated the city to which he was traveling.

"I'm going there too. Why don't we travel together?"

So they continued wandering together. The trip was long, and they soon became tired. All at once a mule driver came the same way.

"Hey, good friend," the young man called out, "would you permit us to ride your mules for a while? We're very tired and weak."

"I'd be glad to," answered the mule driver, "You can ride the mules as far as our paths are heading in the same direction."

So they each sat on a mule and rode along with the mule driver. The young man had noticed that there was a bunch of gold in the back sack of the mule driver, and he began taking the coins out and throwing them on the road without the mule driver noticing it. The hermit saw all this and felt in his heart, "What? This poor man has shown us some kindness, and now my companion's doing this wicked thing!" However, since the young man was so strong, he was afraid to say anything. After they had traveled a good distance, the mule driver said, "Now, my friends, our ways part, and I really can't take you with me any farther."

They got off the mules, thanked him, and continued traveling by foot, but the hermit said, "How could you be so unfair to the poor man and throw away his money after he was so good to us?"

"Be quiet!" the young man answered. "Mind your own business and not mine!"

In the evening they came to an inn, and when the innkeeper's wife came to them, they said, "Good woman, could you give us shelter for the night? Unfortunately, we don't have any money to pay you."

"Oh, don't even speak about it," the innkeeper's wife said, and she kindly took them in and gave them something good to eat and drink. Then she showed them to a room in which there was a bed for each one of them. There was also a cradle in this room, and the woman's small child was sleeping in it. The next morning, as they prepared to continue their journey, the young man went over to the cradle and strangled the poor little child.

"Oh, you villain!" exclaimed the hermit. "That good woman showed us many kind favors, and yet you've murdered her child!"

"Be quiet!" the young man responded. "Mind your own business!"

So they continued wandering, and the hermit walked silently next to the young man. All of a sudden the young man changed into a beautiful shining angel and said to the hermit, "Listen to me, you simple human being, you who have dared to grumble about God's justice! I am an angel sent by God to open your eyes. That innocent pilgrim whom you saw being abused murdered his father on that very same spot many years ago, and that's why God sent him this punishment. Know that God forgives quickly, but he hesitates to punish. The money, which I threw on the road, did not belong to the mule driver. He had stolen it from someone else. After he discovers he has lost the money, he will perhaps contemplate his life and regret his sin. The woman's child might have become a robber or murderer if he had lived. The mother is, however, pious, and she had prayed every day to God, 'Oh, Lord, if my child will not lead a holy life, then I would prefer you take him to you as long as he is innocent.' Indeed, God heard her prayer. So now you see that God's justice has greater vision and sees further than human beings. Therefore, return to your hermitage and do atonement for your grumbling and see whether you may be forgiven."

As soon as the angel had spoken these words, he flew up to heaven. Meanwhile, the hermit returned to his mountain and became even more committed to doing atonement than before, and he died as a saint.

41

THE PRINCE'S TWO CHILDREN
FROM MONTELEONE

Once upon a time there was a prince, the prince of Monteleone,* who lived with his wife in a glorious castle. He was enormously rich and had everything his heart desired. However, he and his wife were always sad because they did not have any children.

"Oh," she often thought, "who will inherit our treasures one day?"

Finally, after many long years had passed, the princess was going to have a child. The prince had a tower without windows built in a desolate region, and he had it lavishly furnished with costly furniture. The princess was, however, no longer to be seen. When her time came, she gave birth to a son and a daughter. The prince had the babies quietly baptized, hired a nurse, and had her locked in the tower with the children. There the children thrived. They grew bigger each day† and became more and more beautiful. When they were older, their father sent them a clergyman, who taught them to read and write and everything else appropriate for a good education.

After some years passed the princess became sick and died. Soon thereafter the prince became very sick, and because he felt that his end was near, he summoned the clergyman and said, "I feel that I shall have

---

* Principi did Muntiliuni. (Monteleone in Calabria)

† Criscìanu un jornu pi dui.

to die. I am going to put you in charge of my children. You shall be their guardian and in charge of my entire fortune. But do not let them leave the tower until there is a good opportunity for them to marry."

The clergyman promised the prince he would care for the children as though they were his own, and soon the prince passed away. Then the clergyman locked all the treasures in the castle, moved to be with the children in the tower, released the nurse after she promised not to tell anyone about the children, and lived alone with them in their solitary dwelling. Meanwhile, the children became more beautiful from day to day and were hard-working students. When they read about foreign countries and cities in their books, the boy was astounded and wanted to know how the world was made. The older he became, the more he desired to set out and see the world. Since he had now become a handsome young man, he went one day to the clergyman and said, "Uncle, let me out of the tower, for I want to get to know the world."

At first the clergyman did not want to allow him to depart, but the young prince insisted so much that the clergyman finally had to consent. So he had a magnificent ship built for the young man's journey, hired a crew, and filled the ship with valuable treasures. When the prince took leave of his sister, he gave her a ring with a precious stone and said, "As long as this stone is clear, then I am well and alive and shall return to you. However, if the stone becomes misty, then I'll be dead and won't be able to return." Upon saying this, he embraced her, boarded the ship, and sailed away. Everything seemed beautiful to him, the sky, the sun, the stars, the flowers, the sea. Everything was unfamiliar to him and everything made him happy.

After he had traveled a while he arrived at a beautiful city ruled by a king. When he sailed into the harbor, he ordered the guns of the ship to be fired. The king heard the firing, became curious, and went to the harbor, and once he saw the beautiful ship, he wanted to board it. As soon as he was on the ship, he was very well received by the young prince, and the king took such a great liking to the handsome and noble young man that he took him on land and invited him into his castle, where he gave him great honors and made him one of his steady companions. Indeed, he took him everywhere—to the theater, to the balls— but there were many among his ministers who were jealous over the favor shown to the young man, for there is no lack of jealous people in the world.

One day when the king was holding court, the young prince told the king about his sister, how beautiful she was, and that no man had ever laid eyes on her. Indeed, he boasted about her great virtue. One of the ministers shrugged his shoulders and said that his sister would lose her virtue with the first attempt on it, and he bet that he could succeed in tempting her. One word led to the next, and finally the minister and the young man made the bet. Whoever lost the bet would be hung. Now the minister boarded a ship, and after he had searched for the place called Monteleone for a long time, he finally found it. But when he inquired about the daughter of the dead prince, everyone laughed in his face, for they believed that the prince and princess had died without children. No matter where he asked, he could not obtain any news about her. So he became very scared and began to fear for his life.

As he meandered through the streets in a terrible mood, a poor woman asked for alms. He rejected her harshly, and she asked why he was so ill-tempered. Finally, he told her about the bet he had made and that he could not find the princess of Monteleone.

"If someone could only help me," he cried, "I'd give a rich reward."

The woman was none other than the nurse of the two children. Because the minister had promised such a rich reward, she let herself be bribed and said, "Come tomorrow to this same place, and I shall help you."

The next morning the duplicitous woman made her way to the tower and knocked on the door. By chance the clergyman had gone to the city, and the maiden was all alone in the house. When the nurse saw the maiden, she said, "Dear child, I'm your former nurse, and I've come to visit you."

The maiden let her enter, and the old woman strode through the room and inspected everything in great detail. When she went into the maiden's bedroom, she said to her: "Come my dear child, I want to dress you in some pretty clothes."

The maiden had a birthmark on her shoulder with three gold hairs woven together with a thread. She was also wearing her brother's ring that was sewn to a corset. As the old woman began dressing her, she noticed the exact form of the birthmark and stole the ring without being observed. Then she departed and returned quickly to the minister and told him everything that she had noticed and gave him the ring.

Now the minister returned in a great hurry to his country, appeared before the king, and said, "I've won the bet." He described the inside of the house and said, "The princess has a birthmark with three gold hairs on her shoulder, and they are woven together with a thread. Finally, she gave me this ring."

When the young prince heard this, he could not contradict the minister, but he became furious and enraged with his innocent sister.

"All right," he said. "I'm prepared to die, and I only ask for an eight-day delay."

The king, who was very sad about the fate of his favorite, granted the delay, and so the young prince called his faithful servant Franz to him and said, "You've served me faithfully up to now. So I'd like you to fulfill my last command. Rush to my unworthy sister, kill her, and bring me a little bottle of her blood so that I can drink it. Then I'll be happy to die."

The servant was very distressed by this mission, but he had to obey and thus traveled to Monteleone. When the young princess saw him and noticed how sad he was, she asked him why.

"Oh," Franz replied. "I must kill you, for you've committed a great sin. On account of you my poor master must die."

"What have I done?" asked the poor maiden.

"What? Didn't you receive the king's minister and even let him have the ring that your brother gave you?"

It was only then that she noticed that the ring was gone, and she immediately suspected the nurse who had helped her get dressed a few days before. So she threw herself at the clergyman's feet and cried, "Dear uncle, let me depart. I must go and save my brother."

"Oh child," the clergyman responded, "you'll never succeed!"

But she kept asking until he finally consented.

"Now, dear uncle," she continued. "You must fetch the most beautiful pearls and jewels that belonged to my mother."

The clergyman went to the castle, filled a chest with the most precious stones and valuable pearls, and the maiden set off with Franz to the king's city.

"Now you must rent me a room in an inn," she said. "Then kill some chickens, take my brother a bottle of their blood, and tell him that you've carried out his command."

Franz did everything that his mistress ordered, and after the young prince drank the blood, Franz returned to the inn. Then he accompanied the princess to the best goldsmith of the city, and she said to him, "Master, I want you to make a sandal out of these pearls and jewels within three days, and I want it to be as precious as you can possibly make it."

The master immediately hired a group of apprentices, who had to work day and night but within three days the precious sandal was finished.

Soon, the eight days had passed, and the poor young prince was to be led to the gallows. Now his sister had a small platform constructed along the way her brother would be led to his death. She sat down on it, and in front of it lay a silver tea tray with the sandal. As the procession that accompanied her brother came by, she waited until the king appeared in his coach and called out, "Your majesty, I beg for justice and your protection!"

"What is your wish?" asked the king.

"One of your ministers stole a sandal from me, which belongs to the one that you see on this tea tray. That man over there is the thief."

She pointed to the minister who was responsible for the execution that her brother was about to suffer.

"What!" the minister exclaimed. "How can I have stolen your sandal? If I see you one more time, then I shall have seen you only two times in my life."*

"Oh you miserable creature!" the princess cried. "If you don't recognize me now, how can you boast that you've already enjoyed my favor? I am the sister of this unfortunate young man sentenced to death because of your slander."

When the king heard all this, he ordered the young prince to be freed right away. But the minister was seized and hung on the gallows intended for the prince. Then the king led the sister and brother to his castle, and since the maiden was so beautiful, he took her for his bride. Soon afterward the sister and brother sent for their treasures, and the clergyman was also invited to live with them. They lived happy and content, but we were left without a cent.

---

* Si vi vidu n'autra vota, v'aju vidutu dui voti.

42

THE CLEVER FARMER

Once upon a time there was a king who had gone hunting. All at once he saw a farmer working in a field.

"How much do you earn in a day?" the king asked him.

"Your majesty," he replied. "I earn four carlini per day."

"What do you do with the four carlini?" the king continued to ask.

"I eat the first. The second I use to earn interest. The third I give back, and the fourth I throw away."*

The king continued riding, but after some time passed, he decided that the farmer's answer was strange, and he turned back and asked him, "Tell me, did you mean to say that you eat the first carlino, earn interest with the second, give the third away, and throw the fourth away?"

"With the first carlino," he answered, "I nourish myself. With the second I nourish my children, who must take care of me when I get old. With the third I nourish my father and give him back what he did for me, and with the fourth I nourish my wife, and so I regard that as throwing it away because I don't gain anything from it."

"Yes," said the king. "You're right. But promise me that you won't tell anyone what you've just told me, not before you have seen my face one hundred times."

---

* Unu m'u manciu; unu lu scuntu; unu lu ristituisciu e unu lu jettu.

The farmer promised to do this, and the king rode happily toward home. When he was sitting down to dinner with his ministers, he said, "I want you to listen to a riddle. A farmer earns four carlini a day. He eats the first. He earns interest with the second. He gives the third away, and the fourth he throws away. What's the meaning of this?"

No one could solve the riddle. Finally, one of his minsters remembered that the king had spoken with a farmer on the day before, and decided to seek out the farmer and get him to tell him the answer to the riddle. When he came to the farmer, he asked him for the solution to the riddle, but the farmer answered, "I can't tell you because I promised the king not to tell anyone until I had seen his face one hundred times."

"Oh," responded the minister, "I can certainly show you the king's face," and he pulled a hundred thalers out of his purse and gave them to the farmer. On each and every one of the thalers the king's face could be seen. Once the farmer looked at each one of the thalers, he said, "Now I've seen the king's face one hundred times. So I can tell you the answer to the riddle," and he told the minister.

The minister was delighted and went to the king and said, "Your majesty, I have found the solution to the riddle. Here's the answer." And he told it to him.

"Only the farmer himself could have told you this!" the king cried, and he had the farmer summoned and took him to task.

"Didn't you promise me not to tell the answer to the riddle until you saw my face one hundred times?"

"Your majesty," the farmer answered, "your minister showed me your picture one hundred times."

Upon saying this he showed the king the sack with the money that the minister had given him. Then the king was pleased with the clever farmer and gave him a generous gift so that he became a rich man for the rest of his life.

NOTES

These notes are based on material that I have gathered from the following works:

Aarne, Antti and Stith Thompson. *The Types of the Folktale A Classification and a Bibliography*. 2nd rev. ed. FF Communications No. 3. Helsinki: Suomalainen Tiedeakatemia,1961.

Gonzenach, Laura. *Sicilianische Märchen*, 2 vols. Leipzig: W. Engelmann, 1870. The notes were prepared by Reinhold Köhler and are in the second volume.

Gonzenbach, Laura. *Fiabe Siciliane*, ed. Luisa Rubini. Rome: Donzelli, 1999. The notes were written by Luisan Rubini, who has also provided source material in her book, *Fiabe e mercanti in Sicilia*. Florence: Olschki, 1998.

Zipes, Jack. *The Great Fairy Tale Tradition: From Straparola and Basile to the Brothers Grimm*. New York: Norton, 2001.

Luisa Rubini's notes are by far the most revealing about parallels to other folk-tale collections in Italy, and she has also provided exhaustive historical material. I have generally kept the references to various tales and collections in the original language. In the cases in which the tales and collections are well known and accessible in English, I have provided English translations and sources. Whenever the name of a folklorist, collector, or scholar is recorded in the notes without mention of the work, the work can be found listed in the bibliography which follows the notes.

Each tale title is accompanied with the German title and designated number in Gonzenbach's original compilation. The titles are followed by the tale-type classification in Aarne/Thompson's work as a helpful reference.

1. *The Clever Maiden—Von dem klugen Mädchen, Nr. 17*
Tale Type AaTh 884—The Forsaken Fiancée: Service as Menial,
AaTh 884 B*—Girl Dressed as a Man Deceives the King,
and AaTh 1273*—Numskull Bales out the Stream.

This story is more a humorous anecdote or Schwank than a fairy tale. Moreover, it has an unusual "feminist" tendency, for the brother with seven daughters turns out to be more fortunate than his brother with seven sons, thanks to the cleverness of his youngest daughter. Giambattista Basile published an early version of this tale, "The Plot of Garlic" ["La serva d'agulie"] in *Cunto de li cunti* (1634–1636). It was recorded by Vincenzo della Sala and published in the journal *Giambattista Basile: Archivio de letteratura popolare I* (1883): 2–3. Evidently a popular tale told in the region of Campana, "The Two Merchants" reflects on family rivalries and class differences that existed in the countryside from the sixteenth to the twentieth century. Most interesting is the valorous role played by the youngest daughter of a family blessed with too many daughters.

Vittorio Imbriani also published an important tale, related as "Fanta Ghiro, Persona bella" in *La Novellaja Fiorentina* (1877) that is related to "The Clever Maiden." Imbriani's nineteenth-century Florentine tale is similar in some respects to the lengthy tale "Belle-Belle ou Le Chevalier Fortuné" (1698) by Mme d'Aulnoy in *Contes Nouveaux ou les Fées à la mode*. It concerns the third and youngest daughter of a sick king whose realm is under attack. Her name, Fanta-Ghiro, means valorous young girl, according to Imbriani, and she disguises herself as a young knight to save her father's kingdom. When she meets her enemy, a handsome young king, he suspects that she is a woman and falls in love with her. He tries to set traps for her and prove that Fanta-Ghiro is truly a female, but she cannot be caught. Indeed, she wins the battle of wits and prevents the young king from possessing her father's realm. However, in the end, the young king pursues her, declares his love for her, makes peace with her father, and marries the brave and cunning heroine.

2. The Robber with a Witch's Head—*Vom Räuber, der einen Hexenkopf hatte, Nr. 22*
Tale Type AaTh 621—The Louse Skin, AaTh 311—Rescue by the Sister, and AaTh 302—The Ogre's [Devil's] Heart in the Egg.
This story has a major important literary source in Giambattista Basile's "Lo polece" in *Lo cunto de li cunti* (1634–1636). As is often the case, it is the youngest sister who rescues her older sister or sisters from a robber or ogre. There are also three variants of this tale in Giuseppe Pitrè, *Fiabe, novelle e racconti popolari siciliani* (1875).

3. The Clever Farmer's Daughter—*Die kluge Bauerntochter, Nr. 1*
Tale Type AaTh 1533—The Wise Carving of the Fowl,
AaTh 875—The Clever Peasant Girl,
and AaTh 875—A Girl's Riddling Answer Betrays a Theft.
This story is part of the tradition of exempla that can be traced to the medieval period in Europe. These exemplars were often used in church services as stories to instruct the people and became a vital part of the oral tradition. Two versions of this tale can be found in Giovanni Gobi's *Scala Coeli* (c. 1350) and Franco Sachetti's *Il Trecentonovelle* (fourteenth century). Pitrè published three versions, "Lu cuntu du lu 'nnimimu" and "La panza chi parra" in *Fiabe, novelle e racconti popolari siciliani* (1875) and "Lu Re e la figghia di lu mercanti" in *Fiabe e Leggende popolari siciliani* (1888), and Domenico Comparetti, one version, "La Ragazza astuta" in *Novelline popolari italiane* (1875).

4. The Count and His Sister—*Vom Grafen und seiner Schwester, Nr. 56*
Tale Type AaTh 1419 E—Underground Passage to Paramour's House,
and AaTh 926—Judgment of Solomon.
This story can be traced back to the late Middle Ages and is found in the anonymous *Seven Wise Men* of the thirteenth century among other works. The traditional plot concerns adultery, not virginity. Generally speaking, it is not a brother who guards the chastity of his sister and is deceived. Rather, it is a husband who is deceived by an adulterous wife, who manages to meet her lover through an underground passage. This theme is common in many of *The Lais of Marie de France* from the late twelfth century. Variants of "The Count and His Sister" were widespread in India, Turkey, Greece, and

Italy. Giuseppe Pitrè published a version similar to Gonzenbach's story with the title "La Soru di lu Conti" in *Fiabe, novelle e racconti popolari siciliani* (1875).

5. *Clever Peppe—Die Geschichte vom klugen Peppe, Nr. 82*
Tale Type AaTh 1538—The Youth Cheated in Selling Oxen.
This story, which is more a funny anecdote (*fabliau/Schwank*) about a buffoon than a fairy tale, can be found in most countries of Europe, but it is not particularly popular. In the Italian tradition, Rachel Busk published a version, "Ass or Pig" in *The Folk-Lore of Rome* (1874), and Giuseppe Pitrè included a variant, "Lu scarparu e li monaci" in *Fiabe, novelle e racconti popolari siciliani* (1875).

6. *Maria, the Evil Stepmother, and the Seven Robbers—Maria,*
die böse Stiefmutter und die sieben Räuber, Nr. 2
Tale Type AaTh 327—Hansel and Gretel, and AaTh 709—Snow White
The beginning of this story is similar to the beginning of the Hansel and Gretel tale type. Here Maria is abandoned by her father, who is compelled to do this by the evil stepmother. Thereafter, the tale resembles "Snow White." Of course, there are major differences with the traditional Grimms' tale. Instead of dwarfs, there are robbers who take care of Maria, and she is sent into a death-like sleep by a magic ring, not an apple. Finally, though Maria is rescued by a king, the stepmother is never punished. Giuseppe Pitrè published another Sicilian variant, "La 'Nfanti Margarita" in *Fiabe, novelle e racconti popolari siciliani* (1875). There are other versions in Glinski, Bodenstedt, Arnason, Maurer, Hahn, Wolf, and Schneller. In Gonzenbach's collection, there are two other similar tales, "Maruzzedda," Nr. 60, and "Beautiful Anna," Nr. 87.

7. *Bensurdatu—Die Geschichte von Bensurdatu, Nr. 62*
Tale Type AaTh 301—A Quest for a Vanished Princess
This story is a mixture of many tale types, but the frame is derived from the plot of the vanished princess and is similar to "The Abbot Who Rescued the Princess," Nr. 35; "The Courageous Prince and His Many Adventures," Nr. 38; "Fata Morgana," Nr. 36; "Armaiinu," Nr. 63; "The Four Princesses," Nr. 78. See note 35 in *Beautiful Angiola*.

8. *The Rooster Who Wanted to Become Pope—Von dem Hahn,*
der Papst werden wollte, Nr. 66
Tale Type AaTh 20 D*—Cock and Other Animals Journey to Rome
to Become Pope, AaTh 130—The Animals in Night Quarters,
and AaTh 210—Cock, Hen, Duck, Pin, and Needle on a Journey.
This story not only mocks the rooster's vanity, but also makes fun of his illiteracy and those of his companions. The tale is a pastiche of different fables that can be found in the works of the Brothers Grimm, Korn, Vernaleken, Haltrich, Waldau, Grundtvig, and Campbell.

9. *The Brave Prince—Vom tapferen Königssohn, Nr. 26*
Tale Type AaTh 590—The Prince and the Arm Bands,
and AaTh 314—The Youth Transformed to a Horse.
This tale is similar to Gonzenbach's "Paperarello," Nr. 30. For background material see note 30 in *Beautiful Angiola*.

10. *The Innkeeper's Beautiful Daughter—Von der schönen Wirthstochter, Nr. 24*
Tale Type AaTh 706—The Maiden without Hands.
The major literary sources for this tale are Ser Giovanni Fiorentino, "Dionigia and the King of England" ["Dionigia e il re d'Inghilterra,"] in *Il Pecorone* (1554); Giambattista Basile, "The Maiden without Hands" ["La Penta Mano-Mozza"], in *Lo cunto de li cunti* (1634–1636); Jacob and Wilhelm Grimm, "The Maiden without Hands" ["Das Mädchen ohne Hände"] in *Kinder-und Hausmärchen* (1857).

The mutilation of women, especially daughters, to preserve their virginity or to keep a religious vow has been a common theme in the East and West and can be traced back to antiquity. The fairy tales that involve a maiden who has her hands cut off or cripples herself in some way because of a father who betrays her or wants to sleep with her are related to the fairy tales about incest. Here the plot generally concerns a father who threatens his daughter sexually or makes a bargain with a mysterious power that seeks to attain control over her. She has her hands cut off and runs away. After meeting a prince in a chance encounter, often in his garden as she is seeking something to eat, she weds him, but her jealous mother-in-law or the demonic power from whom she has escaped, interferes with her life when she gives birth to a son and her husband is far away fighting a war or taking care of some urgent business. She is forced to flee with her son into a forest, where she miraculously recovers her hands in a solitary spot. Her husband returns from his journey and learns how he has been deceived. He pursues his wife and is reunited with her and his son.

There were numerous medieval tales in Europe based on the fifteenth-century legends and chapbooks, *La belle Hélène de Constantinople* and the legends about the powerful King Offa of the eight century and that may have influenced Giovanni Fiorentino's "Dionigia and the King of England" and Basile's "The Maiden without Hands." In France, Philippe de Rémi wrote an important verse romance, *La Manekine* (c. 1270), which may have been influenced by French folk tales with the motif of the persecuted woman in Brittany. The plot of De Rémi's verse romance is highly significant because it combines motifs that can be found in all the literary tales about incestuous and traitorous fathers: After ten years of marriage the king and queen of Hungary have a daughter whom they name Joie. Soon thereafter, however, the queen becomes sick, and before she dies, she makes her husband promise that he will not marry unless he finds a woman who looks just like her. Once she is dead, the nobles of Hungary search for a beautiful woman to match the dead queen. Years pass, but they cannot find one until a nobleman realizes that Joie has flowered into the spitting image of her mother. The nobles of Hungary want the king to marry his daughter, but he at first refuses until he eventually falls in love with Joie and explains to her that he must marry her to follow his dead wife's wish. However, Joie cuts off her left hand and throws it into the river. According to the law of the land, the king was not allowed to marry a woman who was missing a part of her body. Furious, the king commands that she be burned at the stake, but when he departs for a distant castle, his steward takes pity on Joie and puts her in a small boat and sets her out to sea. She arrives in Scotland, where she is taken to the young king's court. Though she is missing a hand and keeps quiet about her past, the king is taken by her beauty and desires to wed her. In contrast, his mother is jealous of her and threatens her. When the king becomes aware of this, he takes Joie under his protection and marries her. His mother retreats to her own castle in the country. When Joie becomes pregnant, the king wants to win some glory in a tournament in France, and he departs. Joie gives birth to a handsome son named John, and his steward sends a messenger to France to inform the king about the happy news. However, the queen mother intercepts the message and changes it to read that the queen had given birth to a monstrous creature. When the king reads this message, he writes back that his steward should preserve their lives. Once again, however, the queen mother intercepts the message and exchanges it for one that instructs the steward to have Joie and her son burned at the stake. But the steward burns two wooden statues instead and sets Joie out to sea with her son in a ship without masthead and sail. Somehow the ship manages to make its way to the Tiber River and lands in Rome where a kindly senator takes care of Joie and her son. When the King of Scotland returns home from France, he learns about his mother's treachery and has her buried in a wall alive. Then he sets off in search of his wife and son, and after seven years of wandering, he is reunited with them in Rome. In the meantime, Joie's father, the King of Hungary, has arrived in Rome to beg pardon from the pope for his sin that has been weighing on his conscience. While he is there, Joie miraculously finds her left hand in a fountain and is happily reunited with her father. Finally, the pope prays that Joie's left hand be reattached, and lo and behold, this is what occurs.

In Italy, *La Manekine* became very popular in the fourteenth and fifteenth centuries. Joie was called Olivia and the King of Hungary was Emperor Giuliano. There were verse and prose editions with the title *La Rapresentazione di Santa Uliva*, and chapbooks in the nineteenth century with the titles *Istoria dela Regina Oliva* and *Istoria piazevole della Regina Oliva*. By the nineteenth century there was a similar story, *Stella e Mattabruna*, which had become just as popular in Italy. This tale concerned the stepdaughter of the empress of France, who wants to have Stella killed while the emperor goes off to war. Instead, the hired henchman cuts off her hands, and she is later found in a forest by the Duke of Burgundy, who marries her.

Many nineteenth-century variants can be found in the collections of Pröhle, Schneller, Zingerle, Nerucci, and Pitrè, among others.

11. *The Beautiful Maiden with the Seven Veils—Die Schöne mit den sieben Schleiern, Nr 13*

Tale Type AaTh 408—The Three Oranges, and AaTh 313 C—Forgotten Fiancée. This story may have originated in Italy and was widespread mainly in southern Europe and the Orient. The most significant literary source is Giambattista Basile's "Le tre cetra" in *Lo cunto de li cunti* (1634–1636). This tale served as the basis for Carlo Gozzi's popular play *L'amore delle tre melarance* (1761). Many nineteenth-century variants can be found in the collections of Hahn, Wolf, Simrock, Schott, Zingerle, and Nerucci.

12. *The Merchant's Clever Youngest Daughter—Die jüngste, kluge Kaufmannstochter, Nr. 10*

Tale Type AaTh 956 B—The Clever Maiden Alone at Home Kills the Robbers, AaTh 311—Rescue by the Sister, and AaTh 958 E—Deep Sleep Brought on by a Robber. This story is not a fairy tale but more of a popular romance about a young woman who outsmarts and defeats a ruthless robber. There are many different European variants in the works of Zingerle, Schleicher, Nerucci, Pitrè, and Imbriani.

13. *Maruzzedda—Von Maruzzedda, Nr. 3*

Tale Type AaTh709—Snow White, and AaTh 410—Sleeping Beauty. This story is similar to "Maria, the Evil Stepmother, and the Seven Robbers," Nr. 51 and "Beautiful Anna," Nr. 87 in Gonzenbach's collection. Here Maruzedda is persecuted twice—once by her jealous sisters at her home and later by her mother-in-law. Giuseppe Pitrè published a variant, "Suli, Perna e Anna" in *Fiabe, novelle e racconti popolari siciliani* (1875).

14. *Armaiinu—Von Armaiinu, Nr. 59*

Tale Type AaTh 301A—Quest for a Vanished Princess. This story is similar to "The Abbot Who Rescued the Princess," Nr. 35; "The Courageous Prince and His Many Adventures, Nr. 38; "Fata Morgana," Nr. 36; "Bensurdatu," Nr. 52; "The Four Princesses," Nr. 78. See note 35 in *Beautiful Angiola*. What is unique in this tale is Armaiinu's refusal at the end of the tale to keep his youth and to marry a princess. He would prefer to remain the loyal old servant until the end of his days.

15. *The Golden Lion—Vom goldnen Löwen, Nr. 68*

Tale Type 854—The Golden Ram. This story was widespread in Europe, Turkey, and South America. The earliest European literary version is Ser Giovanni Fiorentino's "Arrighetto, figlio dell'Imperadore," *Il Pecorone* (1554). Other versions can be found in Francesco Sansovino's *Cento novelle scelte* (1556), and Lippo Lorenzi and Paolo Minucci's *Malmantile racqvistato* (1688). In most of the tales, the hero, often a prince, conceals himself in the skin of an animal such as a lamb or lion, or transforms himself as a bird (hawk, eagle) to enter the bedroom of a princess to seduce her or to entice her to come with him.

In contrast to Gonzenbach's more pristine version, Giuseppe Pitrè published an interesting Sicilian variant, "L'Acula chi sona" in *Fiabe, novelle e racconti popolari siciliani* (1875), in which a young man arrives as an eagle, and after the princess recovers from her shock, she spends an entertaining evening with him until the early hours of the next morning.

16. *The Twelve Robbers—Die Geschichte von den zwölf Räubern, Nr. 79*
Tale Type AaTh 676—Open Sesame.

This story can be traced back to the Middle Ages in the Orient. Antoine Galland translated it into French as "Ali Baba and the Forty Thieves" and included it in *The Thousand and One Nights* (1704–1713). From this point on, this tale became one of the most popular in the written and oral tradition in Europe and North America. Giuseppe Pitrè published two Sicilian variants, "Li frati scarsi" and "Mastru Juseppi" in *Fiabe, novelle e racconti popolari siciliani* (1875). Gonzenbach included a second dialect version (see N. 93), which more or less places the blame on the greed of Master Antoni's wife rather than on her husband's envy. It is generally the envy or greed of the brother/friend that brings about his death at the hands of the robbers. Other variants can be found in the works of Simrock, Pröhle, the Brothers Grimm, and Otmar, and in English, this tale was made famous through the various nineteenth-century translations of *The Thousand and One Nights* by Edward Lane and Richard Burton.

17. *Three Good Pieces of Advice—Die Geschichte von den drei guten Rathschlägen, Nr. 81*
Tale Type AaTh 910 B—The Servant's Good Counsels,
and AaTh 910—Wise through Experience.

This tale or exemplum was widespread in the medieval and Renaissance periods throughout the Orient and Europe. Versions can be found in *The Forty Vezirs* and in *The Thousand and One Nights*, as well as in many collections of exemplars. There are variants in the Latin epic *Ruodlieb* (c. 1000), in *El Conde Lucanor* by Don Juan Manel (1282–1348), and in the *Gesta Romanurum* (Deeds of the Romans, fourteenth century). In most of the versions, the last piece of advice is always given to prevent the protagonist from murdering his own son and wife. Aside from the good advice, the protagonist generally receives a loaf of bread or a cake, which he is not to cut open until he reaches home, or until he is filled with joy. The bread or a cake always contains some kind of monetary reward or treasure. The motif of murder at the beginning of Gonzenbach's tale is not always the same. The protagonist leaves his pregnant wife at home for different reasons as is the case in Giuseppe Pitrè's version, "Li tri Rigordi," in *Fiabe, novelle e racconti popolari siciliani* (1875).

18. *Tobià and Tobiòla—Die Geschichte von Tobià und Tobiòla, Nr. 89*
Tale Type AaTh 507 B—The Monster in the Bridal Chamber.

This story can be traced to the Old Testament of the Bible and to the apocryphal work, *Tobit* (c. 200). Given the great diffusion of *Tobit*, the tale was spread in many different versions throughout Europe and often used as an exemplar. The emphasis in most of the tales is on charity and the caring of dead souls.

19. *Joseph the Just—Die Geschichte von Joseph dem Gerechten, Nr. 91*
Story of Joseph—There is no classification in Aarne/Thompson.

This story is in Genesis of the Old Testament and was spread widely through word of mouth and print throughout the Orient and Europe. There are many elements of the biblical tale missing in Gonzenbach's text. For instance, there is no dream, and there are three brothers instead of twelve. For the most part, however, the tale emphasizes the traditional message of forgiveness.

20. *The Two Brothers—Von den zwei Brüdern, Nr. 40*
Tale Type AaTh 303—The Twins or Blood-Brothers,
and AaTh 300—The Dragon Slayer.
This story is similar to "The Twins," Nr. 75, and "The Dragon Slayer," Nr. 88 in
Gonzenbach's collection. One of the most widespread tales in Europe, it is similar to
the literary versions by Giovan Francesco Straparola, "Cesarino, the Dragon Slayer"
["Cesarino de' Berni"] in *Le Piacevoli Notti* (1550–1553); Giambattista Basile, "The
Merchant" ["Il Mercante"] in *Lo cunto de li cunti* (1634–1636); Jacob and Wilhelm
Grimm, "The Two Brothers" ["Die zwei Brüder"] in *Kinder-und Hausmärchen* (1857).

Although there are many romances and tales about dragon slayers in the medieval
period, Straparola's tale was the first literary fairy tale to develop this motif along
with the theme of brotherly love. There are, of course, many other motifs that occur
in the fairy-tale and romance tradition: the unintentional injury, the animal helpers,
the rescue of the princess, the cutting out of the dragon's tongues, the woman who
enchants men with her hair, the sword that protects the honor of the brother's wife,
the evil witch, the magic plant or balm that saves one of the brothers, and the
reunion of the brothers. All these motifs are used by Straparola, Basile, and the
Grimms in slightly different ways with the animals providing comic relief. Important
in each of these tales are the notions of faith and honor. Basile's tale, "La cerva fata"
("The Enchanted Doe") is also related to the tales in this group. Other variants can
be found in the collections of Hahn, Campbell, Widter-Wolf, Vernaleken, Simrock,
Strackerjan, and Schneller.

21. *The Seven Brothers with Magic Talents—Von den sieben Brüdern,*
die Zaubergaben hatten, Nr. 45
Tale Type AaTh 653—The Four Skillful Brothers.
This story was popular throughout the Orient and Europe, particularly in Italy. The
important literary versions are: Girolamo Morlini, "Three Brothers Who Become
Wealthy Wandering the World" ["De fratibus qui per orbem pererrando ditati sunt"] in
Novellae, fabulae, comoedia (1520); Giovan Francesco Straparola, "The Three Brothers"
["Tre fratelli poveri andando pel mondo divennero molto ricchi"] in *Le Piacevoli Notti*
(1550–1553); Giambattista Basile, "The Five Brothers" ["I Cinque Figli"] in *Lo cunto de li
cunti* (1634–1636); Jacob and Wilhelm Grimm, and "The Four Skillful Brothers" ["Die
vier kunstreichen Brüder"] in *Kinder-und Hausmärchen* (1857).

Most of the material in these tales can be traced to ancient India, especially the
motif of the extraordinary talents acquired by the sons. In the old Hindu collection
Vetalapanchauinsati [Twenty-five Tales of a Demon] there is a story in which a beautiful
princess named Somaprabha will only marry a man if he has one of the following quali-
ties: courage, wisdom, or magic power. Three suitors arrive and convince three separate
family members that they are suitable for the princess. Each receives a promise that he
can marry her. However, when the suitors seek to claim her, there are major problems
because the family members had not consulted with one another. But suddenly the
princess disappears, and the royal family asks the suitors to help them. The first suitor,
the man of wisdom, informs them that a demon has abducted the princess and taken
her to a forest. The second, the man of magic power, takes them to the forest in a
magic chariot. The third, the man of courage, kills the demon. But the question
remains: who deserves the princess? The answer is the man of courage because the first
two men were created by God to be his instruments and were intended to help him kill
the demon. The first European literary version of this tale type was written in Latin by
Girolamo Morlini, and Straparola translated it into Italian and adapted it. Given the
comic element of the tale and the common problems regarding the education of the
sons, it was popular in both the oral and literary tradition. Basile took delight in the
tale and gave it a special twist at the end by having the father win the princess. The
social conditions of apprenticeship and the father's concern for the future of his sons

served as the social historical background for the humorous adventures. The individual "trades" that the sons learn formed the basis for other types of folk tales. For instance, the son's art of thievery is related to the "art" of other master thieves in the oral and literary tradition of the seventeenth and eighteenth centuries. Other important versions are Eberhard Werner Happel's tale about three peasant sons in his novel, *Der ungarische Kriegs-Roman* [*The Hungarian War Novel*, 1685] and Clemens Brentano's important fairy tale "Das Märchen von dem Schulmeister Klopfstock und seinen fünf Söhnen," ["The Fairy Tale about the Schoolmaster Klopfstock and His Five Sons" c. 1811–1815], which was based on Basile's "The Five Brothers."

22. *The Pious Young Man Who Went to Rome—Von dem frommen Jüngling,*
der nach Rom ging, Nr. 47
Tale Type AaTh 460 A—The Journey to God to Receive Reward.
This story has interesting literary antecedents in Giambattista Basile, "Li sette Palommielle," *Lo cunto de li cunti* (1634–1636) and in Jacob and Wilhelm Grimm "The Devil with the Three Golden Hairs" ["Der Teufel mit den drei goldenen Haaren"] in *Kinder- und Hausmärchen* (1857). Reinhold Köhler traces the tale even further back in history to the Indian *Pantchatantra*. There are also variants in the works of Zingerle and Pitrè.

23. *Sabedda and Her Brother—Von Sabedda und ihrem Brüderchen, Nr. 49*
Tale Type AaTh 450—Little Brother and Little Sister,
and AaTh 327—Hansel and Gretel.
This story has literary sources in Johannes de Alta Silva's "Historia septimi spaientis" in *Dolopathos* (thirteenth century), Giambattista Basile's "Ninnillo e Nennella" in *Lo Cunto de li cunti* (1634–1636), and Jacob and Wilhelm Grimm's "Hansel and Gretel" and "Brüderchen und Schwesterchen" ["Little Brother and Little Sister"]. In versions of this popular tale, the brother, transformed into an animal, generally regains his human form. There are some exceptions, as in Giuseppe Pitrè's Sicilian variant, "La Parrastra," *Fiabe, novelle e racconti popolari siciliani* (1875). Here the brother is transformed into a little golden calf.

24. *The Clever Shoemaker—Von dem listigen Schuster, Nr. 70*
Tale Type AaTh 1539—Cleverness and Gullibility,
and AaTh 1535—The Rich and the Poor Peasant.
This story is similar to "Sciauranciovi," Nr. 41, in Gonzenbach's collection. See note 41 in *Beautiful Angiola* for background information

25. *The Twins—Von den Zwillingsbrüdern, 39*
Tale Type 303—The Twins or Blood Brothers.
This story is similar to "The Two Brothers," Nr. 70, and "The Dragon Slayer," Nr. 88, in Gonzenbach's collection. See note 70 for background information. There are two Sicilian versions in Giuseppe Pitrè's collections, "I due gemelli fatati" in *Fiabe, novelle e racconti popolari siciliani* (1875) and "Li dui frati fidili" in *Fiabe e Leggende popolari siciliani* (1888).

26. *Beautiful Innocenta—Von der schönen Nzentola, Nr. 14*
Tale Type AaTh 408—The Three Oranges,
and AaTh 313—The Forgotten Fiancée.
This story is similar to "The Beautiful Maiden with the Seven Veils," Nr. 11 See note 11 for background information.

27. *The Wicked Schoolmaster and the Wandering Princess—Der böse Schulmeister und*
die wandernde Königstochter, Nr. 11
Tale Type 894—The Ghoulish Schoolmaster and the Stone of Pity,
and AaTh—The False Bride Takes Heroine's Place.
The initial part of this story recalls the frame tale of Giambattista Basile's *Lo cunto de li cunti* (1634–1636). The Princess Zoza must weep three days and fill a jug with her tears in order to wake the enchanted prince Tadeo, who is under a curse. Zoza succeeds, but

on the last day she falls unconscious because she is so exhausted. A slave girl assumes her place and takes credit for saving Tadeo. Eventually Zoza regains her rightful place as is the case in another of Basile's tales, "La schiavotella" ["The Slave Girl"] in *Lo cunto de li cunti* (1634–1636). Jacob and Wilhelm Grimm published a variant, "Das Gänsemädchen" ["The Goose Girl"] in *Kinder- und Hausmärchen* (1857). Another variant can be found in Johann Georg Hahn's *Griechische und albenische Märchen* (1864).

28. *The Four Princesses—Von den vier Königstöchtern, Nr. 58*
Tale Type AaTh 301—A Quest for a Vanished Princess.
This story is similar to "The Abbot Who Rescued the Princess," Nr. 35; "The Courageous Prince and his Many Adventures, Nr. 38; "Fata Morgana," Nr. 36; "Bensurdatu," Nr. 52; and "Armaiinu," Nr. 63. See note 35 in *Beautiful Angiola* for background information. This particular version has an unusual feature to it: the brothers abandon the youngest before he even sends the four princesses back up the cistern. Then he has to fly on an eagle's back with all four sisters.

29. *Zafarana—Zafarana, Nr. 9*
Tale Type AaTh 425—Beauty and the Beast, AaTh 884—A Girl Disguised as a Man is Wooed by the Queen, and AaTh 425 K—Search in Men's Clothing.
This story is similar to "Prince Scursuni" Nr. 19, "The Pig King," Nr. 37, and "King Cardiddu," Nr. 49. For background information, see note 19 in *Beautiful Angiola*. Giuseppe Pitrè published another interesting Sicilian version, "Rusina 'mperatrici," in *Fiabe, novelle e racconti popolari siciliani* (1875).

30. *Peasant Truthful—Bauer Wahrhaft, Nr. 8*
Tale Type AaTh 889—The Faithful Servant.
This story can be traced back to the medieval period in the Orient and in Europe. There are versions in *The Forty Vezirs* (associated with *The Thousand and One Nights*) and in the *Gesta Romanurum* (Deeds of the Romans, fourteenth century). The variant in the *Gesta Romanurum* recalls the myth of Mercury and Argus in Ovid's Metamorphosis. Giovan Franceso Straparola published an interesting version, "Travaglino," in *Le piacevoli notte* (1550–1553), and there are two other important Italian variants, Giuseppe Pitrè, "Lu Zu Viritati" in *Fiabe, novelle e racconti popolari siciliani* (1875), and Vittorio Imbriani, "Giuseppe 'a Veretà" in *XII Conti Pomiglianesi* (1876).

31. *About Joseph, Who Set out to Seek His Fortune—Vom Joseph, der auszog sein Glück zu suchen Nr. 6*
Tale Type AaTh—The Golden Mountain, AaTh 400—The Man on a Quest for His Lost Wife, and AaTh 302—The Ogre's [Devil's] Heart in the Egg.
There are hundreds of similar popular tales in the world in which the male protagonist discovers a beautiful young woman who is an enchanted animal or bird (seal, mermaid, swan, dove). Before she goes bathing, she takes off her skin. The hero steals her skin so that she cannot escape him, and she must live with him as his wife until she finds a way to recover the skin and escape. Quite often, unlike in Gonzenbach's tale, she does not return to her captor. This tale was popular in the Mediterranean region, and there are two versions in *The Thousand and One Nights*. Giuseppe Pitrè included a Sicilian variant, "Dammi lu velu!" in *Fiabe, novelle e racconti popolari siciliani* (1875).

32. *The Wasteful Giovanninu—Vom verschwenderischen Giovanninu, Nr. 60*
Tale Type AaTh 401—The Princess Transformed into Deer, and AaTh—The Man on a Quest for His Lost Wife.
This story is unusual because it inverts the traditional tale of the male transformed into a beast. Here the dissolute hero must prove his merit by completing chores that are difficult for him to fulfill due to his negligence. Versions of this tale can be found in the works of Campbell, Zingerle, Schneller, and Pitrè.

33. *The Banished Queen and Her Two Abandoned Children—Die verstoßene Königin und ihre beiden ausgesetzten Kinder, Nr. 5*
Tale Type AaTh 707—The Three Golden Sons.

This story has many important literary sources: Giovan Francesco Straparola, "Ancilotto, King of Provino" ["Ancilotto, re di Provino"] in *Le Piacevoli Notti* (1550–1553); Marie-Catherine d'Aulnoy, "Princesse Belle-Etoile and Prince Cheri" ["La Princesse Belle-Étoile et le Prince Chéry"] in *Suite des Contes Nouveaux ou des Fées à la mode* (1698); Eustache Le Noble, "The Bird of Truth" ["L'Oiseau de vérité"] in *Le Gage touché, histoires galantes* (1700); Antoine Galland, "The Two Sisters Who Envied their Cadette" ["Histoire de deux soeurs jalouses de leur cadette"] in *Les Milles et une nuit* (1704–1717); and Jacob and Wilhelm Grimm, "The Three Little Birds" ["De drei Vügelkens"] in *Kinder-und Hausmärchen* (1857). In addition, Carlo Gozzi wrote a play, *La 'ngannatrice ingannata* (1765), based on the tale.

Though this fairy tale may have originated in the Orient, the source is not clear. Straparola's version was widely known by the French writers at the end of the seventeenth century, and it is certainly the source of Mme d'Aulnoy's and Le Noble's tales. However, it may have even influenced Galland's version. His tale of "The Two Sisters Who Envied Their Cadette" was told to him in Paris by a Maronite Christian Arab from Aleppo named Youhenna Diab or Hanna Diab. There was no Arabic manuscript for this tale, and Galland created it from memory after listening to Diab and may have introduced elements from the European tales he knew. His tale of "The Two Sisters" in *The Thousand and One Nights* and Mme D'Aulnoy's tale of "Princesse Belle-Étoile" had an influence through the French and German eighteenth-century chapbooks (*Bibliothèque Bleue* and *Blaue Bibliothek*) in Europe and in England. Justus Heinrich Saal published his version entitled "Der wahrredende Vogel" ["The Truth-Speaking Bird"] in his book *Abendstunden in lehrreichen und anmuthungen Erzählungen* (1767), and there was also a Scottish adaptation in *Popular Ballads* (1806). The Grimms' source was a tale told in 1813 by a shepherd in a Westfalian dialect, indicating how widespread the fairy tale had also become in the oral tradition.

There tend to be four crucial components in the plot of this tale 1) the wishes of the sisters 2) the envy of the two older sisters and/or mother-in-law 3) the abandonment of the children and unjust punishment of the mother and 4) the reunion of the family often brought about by a singing bird or some magic gift. A bird that reveals the truth is a common motif in many fairy tales throughout the world, and can be found in the collections of Schneller, Hahn, Pröhle, Zingerele, Vernaleken, Peter, Wolf, Curtze, and Saal. Giuseppe Pitrè published a Sicilian version, "Li figghi di lu cavuliciddaru" in *Fiabe, novelle e racconti popolari siciliani* (1875) and Domenico Comparetti, two Italian variants in *Novelline popolari italiane* (1875).

34. *The Pious Child—Vom frommen Kinde, Nr. 86*
Tale Type AaTh 767—Food for the Crucifix.

This popular story has its origins as a religious exemplar in the thirteenth century and reveals a certain anticonformist spirit because of the boy's simple solidarity with the suffering of Christ, according to Italo Calvino in his collection of *Fiabe italiane* (1956). Giuseppe Pitrè published another Sicilian version, "Lu Puvireddu," in *Fiabe, novelle e racconti popolari siciliani* (1875).

35. *Katerina's Fate—Die Geschichte von Caterina und ihrem Schicksal, Nr. 21*
Tale Type AaTh 938—Misfortunes in Youth.

This story is similar to "The Godchild of Saint Francis of Paula," Nr. 46, in Gonzenbach's collection. See note 46 in *Beautiful Angiola* for background information. In this particular tale, the role of fate/fortune is extremely important. The Sicilians believed in the mythic power of fate, which could never be clearly described and could either bless or destroy a person's life, which was controlled by a fate or fortune.

Everything depended on fate, and a person could not negotiate directly with his or her fate. For more information about the theme of fate, see Elisa Miranda, "Fortuna," in vol. 5, *Enzyklopädie des Märchens* (1987).

36. *Godfather Death—Gevatter Tod, Nr. 19*
Tale Type AaTh 332—Godfather Death.
This religious story has its origins in the Middle Ages, and it almost always ends on a tragic note. It was widespread in Europe, and there are variants in the collections of Schönwerth, Widter-Wolf, Saal, and the Brothers Grimm. Giuseppe Pitrè published a Sicilian version, "La Morti e so figghiozzu," in *Fiabe, novelle e racconti popolari siciliani* (1875). In both the Gonzenbach and the Pitrè versions, there is an important episode missing: death gives a gift to the son that enables him to become a rich and famous doctor, as in the tale "Godfather Death" ["Der Gevatter Tod"] in the Grimms' *Kinder- und Hausmärchen* (1857).

37. *Beautiful Anna—Von der schönen Anna, Nr. 4*
Tale Type AaTh 709—Snow White, and AaTh 410—Sleeping Beauty.
This story is similar to "Maria, the Evil Stepmother, and the Seven Robbers," Nr. 51, and "Maruzzedda, Nr. 60," in Gonzenbach's collection. See notes 6 and 13 for background information.

38. *The Dragon Slayer—Von dem, der den Lindwurm mit sieben Köpfen tötete, Nr. 44*
Tale Type AaTh 300—The Dragon Slayer,
and AaTh—The Ogre's [Devil's] Heart in the Egg.
This story is similar to "The Two Brothers," Nr. 70 and "The Twins," Nr. 75, in Gonzenbach's collection. See notes 20 and 25 for background information.

39. *Saint James of Galicia—Die Geschichte von San Japicu alla Lizia, Nr. 90*
Tale Type AaTh 516 C—St. James of Galicia.
This religious legend began as a tale about friendship in a *chanson de geste* about Amico and Amelio (c. 1050). The basic plot concerns two young men who resemble each other perfectly and swear a vow of brotherhood to each other. Later one of the young men sacrifices his sons to cure the friend of leprosy with their pure blood. The sons are brought back to life after the sacrifice is successful. The religious element linked to the pilgrimage to St. James was added in the fourteenth century. A prominent example is Kunz Kistener's *Die Jacobsbrüder* (1899), written and circulated in the fourteenth century. Many oral and literary versions as exemplar and legend were spread in verse and prose since that time, and "Saint James of Galicia" became one of the more popular tales about undying friendship in Europe.

40. *The Hermit—Die Geschichte vom Einsiedler, Nr. 92*
Tale Type AaTh—759 God's Justice Vindicated (The Angel and the Hermit).
This story is one of the most popular and widespread exempla and legends in Europe and can be traced back to the Middle Ages. The "classical" plot concerns a hermit or saint who doubts divine justice. Therefore, God sends an angel who takes the hermit on a journey, and the hermit is not permitted to ask any questions as he watches the angel commit inexplicable if not unjust actions. However, in the end everything turns out to be just, and the hermit realizes that he should never doubt God's wisdom and justice. The more important literary sources can be found in Jacques de Vitry, *Sermones Vulgares* (thirteenth century), *Gesta Romanurum* (Deeds of the Romans, fourteenth century), Giovanni Gobi, *Scala Coeli* (fourteenth Century), *Fiore di virtù* (fourteenth century), and Michele Somma, *Quello che sembra inguisto agli occhi degli uomini, è giusti agli occhi di Dio* (1822). In addition, Giuseppe Pitrè published a Sicilian version, "S. Petru e lu vacili d'argentu," *Fiabe e Leggende popolari siciliani* (1888).

41. *The Prince's Two Children from Monteleone—Die beiden Fürstenkinder*
von Monteleone, Nr. 7
Tale Type AaTh 882—The Wager on the Wife's Chastity.

This story is notable for the motifs of the wager, the chastity and dignity of the sister, and the proof of her innocence. There are important literary sources in *Le Comte de Poitiers* (French verse romance, thirteenth century), Giovanni Boccaccio's "Bernabò da Genova" in *Decameron* (1349–1350), and William Shakespeare's *Cymbeline* (1609). In Italy the tale was made popular through a fourteenth-century song *Madonna Elena*, and there are two important nineteenth-century variants: Giuseppe Pitrè, "La Stivala," *Fiabe, novelle e racconti popolari siciliani* (1875), and Vittorio Imbriani, "La novella del signor Giovanni," *La Novellaja Fiorentina* (1877).

42. *The Clever Farmer—Von klugen Bauer, Nr. 50*
Tale Type AaTh 921—The Four Coins,
and AaTh 922 B—The King's Face on the Coin.

This story was very popular as exemplum in the Middle Ages in the Orient and Europe and was spread in sermons, stories, novellas, and primers. There is a version that dates back to the fourth century, and aside from the variant in the *Gesta Romanurum* (Deeds of the Romans, fourteenth century), there are many similar tales in collections of sermons and exempla from the fourteenth through the nineteenth century. Giuseppe Pitrè published his Sicilian version, "Lu viddanu e lu Re," in *Fiabe, novelle e racconti popolari siciliani* (1875).

Bibliography

Albrecht, Sophie. *Graumännchen oder die Burg Rabenbühl*. Hamburg: Altona, 1799.

Alfonsi, Petrus. *The Disciplina of Petrus Alfonsi*. Edited by Eberhard Hermes. Berkeley: University of California Press, 1977.

Aprile, Renato. *La fiaba di magia in Sicilia*. Palermo: Sellerio, 1991.

Apuleius, Lucius. *The Golden Ass*. Translated and edited by Jack Lindsay. Bloomington: Indiana University Press, 1962.

Arnason, Jón, *Icelandic Legends*. Edited by Eiríkr Magnússon. Translated by George Powell. London: Bentley, 1864.

———. *Icelandic Folk and Fairy Tales*. Edited by May and Hallberg Hallmundsson. Reykjavik, Iceland: Iceland Review, 1987.

Arnim, Friedmund von. *Hundert neue Mährchen im Gebirge gesammelt*. Charlottenburg: Egbert Bauer, 1844.

———. *Hundert neue Mährchen im Gebirge gesammelt*. Edited by Heinz Röllecke. Cologne: Eugen Diederichs, 1986.

Asbjørnsen, Peter Christen. *Norske huldreeventyr of folkesagn*. Christiania: C. A. Oybwad, 1848.

———. *Round the Yule. Norwegian Folk and Fairy Tales*. Translated by H. L. Braekstad. London: Sampson Low, Marston, Seaarle, and Rivington, 1881.

Asbjørnsen, Peter Christen, and Jorgen Moe. *Norske folke-eventyr*. Christiania: J. Dahl, 1852.

———. *Popular Tales from the Norse*. Introduction by George Dasent. Edinburgh: Edmonstron & Douglas, 1859.

Astemio, Lorenzo. *Fabulae [Esopi] ex Greco in Latinum per Laurentium Vallam*. Venice: Joannes Tacuinus, 1495.

Aulnoy, Marie-Catherine Le Jumel de Barneville, Baronne de. *Les Contes de fées*. 4 vols. Paris: Claude Barbin, 1697.

———. *Contes Nouveaux ou les Fées à la mode*. 2 vols. Paris: Veuve de Théodore Girard, 1698.

———. *Suite des Contes Nouveaux ou des Fées à la mode*. 2 vols. Paris: Veuve de Théodore Girard, 1698.

————. *The Fairy Tales of Madame d'Aulnoy.* Translated by Annie Macdonell. Introduction by Anne Thackeray Ritchie. London: Lawrence and Bullen, 1895.

————. *Contes.* Edited by Philippe Houcade. Introduction by Jacques Barchilon. 2 vols. Paris: Société des Textes Français Modernes, 1997–1998.

Bandello, Mateo. *La prima parte de le novelle del Bandello.* Lucca: Il Bustrago, 1554.

————. *Delle novelle del Bandello.* Venice: Francheschini, 1566.

————. *Twelve Stories.* London: Nimmo, 1895.

Barchilon, Jacques, ed. *Nouveau Cabinet des fées.* 18 vols. Geneva: Slatkine Reprints, 1978. Partial reprint of *Le Cabinet des fées,* edited by Charles-Joseph Mayer.

Baring-Gould, Sabine, ed. *Notes on the Folklore of the Northern Countries of England and the Borders.* By W. Henderson. With an Appendix on Household-Stories by. S. Baring-Gould. London, 1866.

Basile, Giambattista. *Lo cunto de li cunti overo Lo trattenemiento de peccerille.* De Gian Alessio Abbattutis. 5 vols. Naples: Ottavio Beltrano, 1634–36.

————. *The Pentamerone of Giambattista Basile.* Translated and edited by N. M. Penzer. 2 vols. London: John Lane and the Bodley Head, 1932.

————. *Lo cunto de li Cunti.* Edited by Michele Rak. Milan: Garazanti, 1986.

————. *Il racconto dei racconti.* Edited by Alessandra Burani and Ruggero Guarini. Translated by Ruggero Guarini. Milan: Adelphi Edizioni, 1994.

Beauvois, Eugène. *Contes populaires de la Norvège, de la Finlande et de la Bourgogne.* Paris: Dentus, 1862.

Bechstein, Ludwig. *Deutsches Märchenbuch.* Leipzig: Wigand, 1845.

————. *Ludwig Bechsteins Märchenbuch.* Leipzig: Wigand, 1853.

————. *Neues Deutsches Märchenbuch.* Vienna: Hartleben, 1856.

————. *Sämtliche Märchen.* Edited by Walter Scherf. Munich: Winkler, 1968.

Behrnauer, Walter. *Die vierzig Veziere oder weisen Meister. Ein altmorgendländischer Sittenroman zum ersten Male vollständig aus dem Türkischen übertragen.* Annotated by W. Fr. Teubner. Leipzig: 1851.

Bello, Francesco. *Il Mambriano.* Venice: Antonelli, 1840.

Bernard, Catherine. *Inès de Cardoue, nouvelle espagnole.* Paris: Jouvenol, 1696; Geneva: Slatkine Reprints, 1979.

Bierling, Friedrich Immanuel, ed. *Cabinet der Feen.* 9 vols. Nürnberg: Raspe, 1761–66.

Bignon, Abbé Jean-Paul. *Les Aventures d'Abdalla, fils d'Hani, envoyé par le sultan des Indes à la découverte de l'ile de Borico.* Paris: P. Witte, 1710–1714.

Birgliner, Anton. *Volkstümliches aus Schwaben.* 2 vols. Freiburg: Herd'sche Verlagsbuchhandlung, 1861–1862.

Bladé, Jean-François. *Contes et Proverbes recueillis en Armagnac.* Paris: Franck, 1867.

Boccaccio, Giovanni. *Decameron.* Edited by Vittore Branca. Turin: Einaudi, 1984.

Bodenstedt, Friedrich Martin von. *Märchen vom Zaren Saltan.* Berlin: Euphorion, 1921.

Böhm-Korff, Regina. *Deutung und Bedeutung von "Hansel und Gretel."* Frankfurt am Main: Peter Lang, 1991.

Busk, Rachel Henriette. *The Folk-Lore of Rome Collected by Word of Mouth from the People.* London: Longmans, Green and Co., 1874.

Caballero, Fernán. *Cuentos y Poesías populares andaluces.* Leipzig: Brockhaus, 1861.

Calvino, Italo, ed. *Fiabe.* Torino: Einaudi, 1970.

————. *Italian Folktales.* Translated by George Martin. New York: Harcourt Brace Jovanovich, 1980.

Cambell of Islay, John Francis, ed. *Popular Tales of the West Highlands.* 4 vols. Orally collected and translated. Edinburgh: Edmonstron and Douglas, 1860–1862.

Castrén, M. Alexander. *M. Alexander Castrén's Ethnologische Vorlesungen der altaischen Völker nebst samojedischen Märchen und Tatarischen Heldensagen.* St. Petersburg: Kaiserliche Akademie der Wissenschaften, 1857.

Cénac Moncant, Justin. *Contes populaires de la Gascogne.* Paris: Dentu, 1861.

Chaucer, Geoffrey. *The Canturbury Tales*. Edited by Nevill Coghill. Harmondsworth, England: Penguin, 1977.

Chodzko, Alexander. *Contes des paysans et des pâtres slaves*. Paris: Hachette, 1861.

———. *Fairy Tales of the Slavs and Herdsmen*. London: Allen, 1896.

Cirese, Alberto, and Liliana Serafini. *Tradizioni orali non cantate. Primo inventario nazionale per tipi, motivi o argomenti*. Rome: Ministero dei Beni Culturali e Ambientali, 1975.

Clodd, Edward. *Tim Tit Tot: An Essay of Savage Philosophy*. London: Duckworth, 1898.

Colshorn, Carl, and Theodor Colshorn. *Märchen und Sagen aus Hannover*. Hannover: Rümpler, 1854.

Comparetti, Domenico. *Novelline popolari italiene*. Turin: Loescher, 1875.

Coronedi Berti, Carolina. *Favole bolognesi*. Bologna: Forni, 1883.

Corrao, ed. *Le storie di Giufà*. Palermo: Sellerio, 2001.

Crane, Thomas Frederick. *Italian Popular Tales*. Boston: Houghton, Mifflin, 1889.

Croce, Giulio Cesare. *Le piacevoli e ridiculose semplicità di Bertoldino figliuolo dell'astuto ed accorto Bertaldo*. Lucca: Marescandoli, 1600.

———. *Le astuzie di Bertoldo e le semplicità di Bertoldino*. Milan: Garzanti, 1993.

D'Ancona, Alessandro. *Sacre rappresentazioni dei secoli XIV, XV, e XVI*. Vol. 3. Florence: 1872.

———. *La Leggenda di Vergogna*. Bologna: Commissione per i testi di lingua, 1968.

Dasent, George. *Popular Tales from the Norse*. Edinburgh: Edmonstron and Douglas, 1859.

De Simone, Roberto, ed. *Fiabe campane*. 2 vols. Turin: Einaudi, 1994.

Delarue, Paul, and Marie-Louise Tenèze. *Le Conte populaire français. Un catalogue raisonné des versions de France et des pays de langue française et d'Outre-mer*. 4 vols. Paris: Maisonneuve et Larose, 1957–1976.

Delarue, Paul, ed. *French Fairy Tales*. Illustrated by Warren Chappell. New York: Knopf, 1968.

Deulin, Charles. *Les Contes de ma Mère l'Oye avant Perrault*. Paris: Dentu, 1878.

Dundes, Alan, ed. *Cinderella: A Folklore Casebook*. New York: Garland, 1982.

Engelien, August, and Wilhelm Lahn. *Der Volksmund in der Mark Brandenburg*. Berlin: Schultze, 1868.

Ey, Karl August Eduard, ed. *Harzmärchenbuch. Oder Sagen und Märchen aus der Oberharze*. 4th ed. Stade: Steudel, 1862.

Fiorentino, Ser Giovanni. *Il Pecorone*. Milan: Giovanni Antonio, 1554; reprinted and edited by Enzo Esposito, Ravena: Longo, 1974.

France, Marie de. *The Lais of Marie de France*. Edited by Glyn Burgess and Keith Busby. Harmondsworth, England: Penguin, 1986.

Frere, Mary. *Old Deccan Days; or, Hindoo Fairy Legends*. London: Murray, 1868.

Gaal, Georg von. *Ungarische Volksmärchen*. Pesth: Heckenast, 1857.

Galland, Antoine. *Les Milles et une nuit*. 12 vols. Vols. 1–4 Paris: Florentin Delaulne, 1704; Vols. 5–7, Paris: Florentin Delaulne, 1706; Vol. 8, Paris: Florentin Delaulne, 1709; Vols. 9–10, Florentin Delaulne, 1712; Vols. 11–12, Lyon: Briasson, 1717.

Glinski, Antoni Jozef. *Polish Fairy Tales*. Translated by Maude Ashurst Briggs. London: John Lane, 1920. Based on Ginski's collection *Bajarz polski* (Vilna, 1862).

Gobi, Jean. *Scala coeli*. Lübeck: Brandiss, 1476.

Goldberg, Christine. *The Tale of the Three Oranges*. Helsinki: Academia Scientiarum Fennica, 1997.

———. "The Donkey Skin Folktale Cycle (AT 501B)." *Journal of American Folklore* 110 (Winter 1997): 28–46.

Gonzenbach, Laura. *Sicilianische Märchen*. 2 vols. Leipzig: W. Engelmann, 1870.

———. *Fiabe siciliane*. Edited and translated by Luisa Rubini. Rome: Donzelli, 1999.

Gower, John. *Confessio Amantis*. Edited by Terrence Tiller. Baltimore: Penguin, 1963.

Gozzi, Carlo. *Opere ed inedite*. Venice: Zanardi, 1801–1802.

————. *Five Tales for the Theatre*. Edited and translated by Albert Bermel and Ted Emery. Chicago: University of Chicago Press, 1989.

————. *Fiabe teatrali*. Milan: Garzanti, 1994.

Grimm, Albert Ludwig. *Kindermährchen*. Heidelberg: Morhr und Zimmer,1808.

————. *Lina's Mährchenbuch*. Frankfurt am Main: Wilmans, 1816.

Grimm, Jacob, and Wilhelm Grimm. *Kinder- und Hausmärchen. Gesammelt durch die Brüder Grimm*. Berlin: Realschulbuchhandlung, 1812.

————. *Kinder- und Hausmärchen. Gesammelt durch die Brüder Grimm.*Vol. 2. Berlin: Realschulbuchhandlung, 1815.

————. *German Popular Stories, Translated from the Kinder- und Hausmärchen*. Translated by Edgar Taylor. London: C. Baldwin, 1823.

————. *Kinder- und Hausmärchen. Gesammelt durch die Brüder Grimm*. 7th rev. and exp. edition. 2 vols. Göttingen: Dieterich, 1857.

————. *Household Stories from the Collection of the Brothers Grimm*. Translated by Lucy Crane. London: Macmillan, 1882.

————. *The Complete Fairy Tales of the Brothers Grimm*. Edited and translated by Jack Zipes. New York: Bantam, 1987; 3rd rev. ed. New York: Bantam, 2003.

Grimmelshausen, Hans Jakob Christoph von. *Grimmelshausens Simplicissimus Teutsch*. Edited by Jan Scholte. Tübingen: Niemeyer, 1956.

————. *Der abenteuerliche Simplicissimus*. Edited by Alfred Kelletat. Munich: Winkler, 1956.

Grundtvig, Sven. *Gamle danske minder i folkemunde*. Copenhagen: Akademisk Forlag, 1854.

————. *Danish Fairy Tales*. Translated by Jesse Grant Cramer. Boston: Badger, 1912.

Gueullette, Thomas Simon. *Les Mille et Un Quarts d'heure, contes tartares*. Paris: 1715.

Guglielminetti, Marziano. *Novellieri del Cinquecento*. Milan: Ricciardi, 1972.

Hahn, Johann Georg. *Griechische und albenische Märchen*. Leipzig: Engelmann, 1864.

Haltrich, Josef, ed. *Deutsche Volksmärchen aus dem Sachsenlande in Siebenbürgen*. Hermannstadt: Krafft, 1885.

Haupt, Leopold, and Johann Ernst Schmaler. *Volkslieder der Wenden in der Ober- und Nieder-Lausitz*. Grimma: Gebhardt, 1841.

Historia Di Campriano Contadino. Florence: 1579.

Hunt, Robert. *Popular Romances of the West of England*. London: Hotton, 1865.

Imbriani, Vittorio. *La Novellaja fiorentina*. Livorno: F. Vigo, 1871.

Jacobs, Joseph, ed. *English Fairy Tales*. London: Nutt, 1890.

————. *Indian Fairy Tales*. London: Nutt, 1892.

Jamieson, Robert. *Popular Ballads and Songs from Tradition, Manuscripts and Scarce Editions*. Edinburgh, A. Constable, 1806.

Joisten, Charles. *Contes Populaires du Dauphiné*. Vol. 1 Grenoble: Publications du Musée Dauphinois, 1971.

Kistener, Kunz. *Die Jakobsbrüder*. Breslau: M & H. Marcus, 1899.

Knust, Hermann. *Italienische Märchen* in *Jahrbuch für romanische und englische Literatur* VII (1866): 381–401.

Köhler, Reinhold. *Italienische Volksmärchen* in *Jahrbuch für romanische und englische Literatur* VIII (1867): 241–260.

Korn, Johann Friedrich. *Abendstunden in lehrreichen und anmuthigen Erzählungen*. Breslau: 1776.

Kreutzwald, Friedrich. *Ehstnische Märchen*. Halle: Verlag der Buchhandlung Waisenhauses, 1869.

————. *Old Estonian Fairy Tales*. Translated by A. Jogi. Tallinn: Perioodika, 1985.

Kuhn, Adelbert. *Sagen, Gebräuche und Märchen aus Westfalen*. 2 vols. Leipzig: Brockhaus, 1859.

La Fontaine, Jean de. *Les amours de Psyché et de Cupidon*. Edited by Françoise Charpentier. Paris: Flammarion, 1990.

La Force, Charlotte-Rose Caumont de. *Les contes des contes par Mlle ****. Paris: S. Bernard, 1698.

Lane, Edward, ed. and trans. *The Thousand and One Nights*. London: J. Murray, 1859.

Le Noble, Eustache. *Le Gage touché, histoires galantes*. Amsterdam: Jaques Desbordes, 1700.

Le Prince de Beaumont, Marie. *Magasin des enfans, ou Dialogue d'une sage gouvernante avec ses élèves de la première distinction*. Lyon: Reguilliat, 1756.

Lhéritier de Villandon, Marie-Jeanne. *Oeuvres meslées, contenant l'Innocente tromperie, l'Avare puni, les Enchantements de l'éloquence, les Aventures de Finette, nouvelles, et autres ouvrages, en vers et en prose, de Mlle de L'H***—avec le Triomphe de Mme Des-Houlières tel qu'il a été composé par Mlle ****. Paris: J. Guignard, 1696.

———. *La Tour ténébreuse et les jours lumineux, contes anglois, accompagnés d'historiettes et tirés d'une ancienne chronique composée par Richard, surnommé Coeur de Lion, roi d'Angleterre, avec le récit des diverse aventures de ce roi*. Paris: Veuve de Claude Barbin, 1705.

Lippi, Lorenzo, and Paolo Minucci. *Malmantile racquistato*. Florence: Taglini, 1688.

Lo Nigro, Sedbastiano. *Racconti popolari siciliani: Classificazione e bibliografia*. Florence: Olschki, 1957.

Lütolf, Alois. *Sagen, Bräuche und Legenden aus den fünf Orten Lucern, Uri, Schwyz, Unterwalden und Zug*. Lucerne: Schiffmann, 1865.

Malespini, Celio. *Ducento novelle del signor Celio Malespini*. Venice: Al segno dell'Italia, 1609.

Maurer, Konrad von. *Isländische Volkssagen der Gegenwart*. Leipzig: J. C. Hinrichs, 1860.

Mayer, Charles-Joseph, ed. *Le cabinet des fées; ou Collection choisie des contes des fées, et autres contes merveilleux*. 41 vols. Amsterdam: s.n., 1785.

Meier, Hermann. *Ostfriesland in Bildern und Skizzen*. Leer: H. Securus, 1868.

Milá y Fontanals, Manuel. *Observaciones sobre la poesía popular*. Barcelona: Ramirez, 1853.

Morlini, Girolamo. *Hieronymi Morlini Parthenopei novellae, fabulae, comoedia*. Lutetiae Parisiorium: Jannet, 1855.

———. *Novelle e favole*. Edited by Giovanni Villani. Rome: Salerno, 1983.

Müllenhoff, Karl. *Sagen, Märchen und Lieder der herzogrhümer Schleswig, Holstein und Lauenburg*. Kiel: Schwerssche Buch, 1845.

Murat, Henriette Julie de Castelnau. *Contes de fées*. Paris: Claude Barbin, 1698.

———. *Les nouveaux contes de fées*. Paris: Claude Barbin, 1698.

Musäus, Johann Karl August. *Volksmährchen der Deutschen*. 5 vols. Gotha: Ettinger, 1782–1787.

Nerucci, Gherardo. *Sessanta novelle popolari montalesi*. Florence: Le Monnier, 1880.

Perrault, Charles. *Griseldis, nouvelle. Avec le conte de Peau d'Ane, et celui des Souhaits ridicules*. Paris: Jean Baptiste Coignard, 1694.

———. *Histoires ou Contes du temps passé*. Paris: Claude Barbin, 1697.

Peter, Anton. *Volksthümliches aus Oesterreichisch-Schlesien*. Troppau: Sebstverlag, 1867.

Philippson, Ernst. *Der Märchen Typus von König Drosselbart*. F. F. Commnications No. 50. Greifswald: Suomalainen Tiedeakatemia, 1923.

Pitrè, Giuseppe. *Fiabe e Leggende Popolari Siciliane*. Palermo: L. Pedone Lauriel, 1870.

———. *Fiabe, novelle e racconti popolari siciliani*. 4 vols. Palermo: L. Pedone Lauriel, 1875.

———. *Fiabe e Leggende popolari siciliane*. Palermo: Pedone Lauriel, 1888.

Praetorius, Johannes. *Der abentheuerliche Glücks-Topf*. 1669.

Pröhle, Heinrich. *Kinder und Volksmärchen*. Leipzig: Avenarius and Mendelssohn, 1853.

———. *Harzsagen*. Leipzig: Mendelssohn, 1886.

Rak, Michele, ed. *Fiabe campane*. Milan: Mondadori, 1984.

Rehfues, Philipp Joseph. *Italienische Miszellen*. 2 vols. Tübingen: J. G. Cotta'sche Buchhandlung, 1805.

Roussel, Claude, ed. *La Belle Hélène de Constantinople: chanson de geste du XIVe siècle*. Geneva: Droz, 1995.

Rubini, Luisa. *Fiabe e mercanti in Sicilia. La raccolta di Laura Gonzenbach e la comunità tedesca a Messina nell'Ottocento*. Florence: Olschki, 1998.

Sachetti, Franco. *Novelle di Franco Sacchetti, cittadino fiorentino*. Florence: Borghi, 1833.

————. *Il trecentonovelle*. Edited by Antonio Lanza. Florence: Sansoni, 1984.

Sarnelli, Pompeo. *Posilecheata di Pompeo Sarnelli*. Edited by Vittorio Imbriani. Naples: Morano, 1885.

Schambach, George and Wilhelm Müller. *Niedersächsiche Sagen und Märchen*. Göttingen: Vandenhoeck & Ruprecht, 1855.

Scheidegger, Jean, ed. *Le Roman de Renart*. Geneva: Droz, 1989.

Schenda, Rudolf. *Folklore e Letteratura Popolare: Italia—Germania—Francia*. Rome: Istituto della Enciclopedia Italiana, 1986.

Schleicher, August. *Litauischer Märchen, Sprichwortem Rätsel und Lieder*. Weimar: Wagner, 1857.

Schneller, Christian. *Märchen und Sagen aus Wälschtirol*. Innsbruck: Wagner, 1867.

Schönwerth, Franz Xaver von. *Aus der Oberpfalz*. Augsburg: Rieger, 1857–1859.

Schott, Arthur, and Albert Schott, eds. *Walachische Märchen*. Stuttgart: J. G. Cotta, 1845.

————. *Rumänische Volkserzählungen aus dem Banat*. Edited by Rolf Brednich and Ion Talos. Bucharest: Kriterion, 1973.

Schulz, Friedrich. *Kleine Romane*. 5 vols. Leipzig: Göschen, 1788–1790.

Sercambi, Giovanni. *Novelle*. 2 vols. Florence: Casa Editrice Le Lettere, 1995.

Simrock, Karl Joseph. *Deutsche Märchen*. Stuttgart, 1864.

Stahl, Karoline. *Fabeln und Erzählungen für Kinder*. Nuremberg, 1818.

Strackerjan, Ludwig. *Aberglaube und Sagen aus dem Herzogthum Oldenburg*. Olenburg: Stalling, 1867.

Straparola, Giovan Francesco. *Le piacevoli notti*. 2 vols. Venice: Comin da Trino, 1550/1553.

————. *Le piacevoli notti*. Edited by Pastore Stocchi. Rome-Bari: Laterza, 1979.

————. *Le piacevoli notti*. Edited by Donato Pirovano. 2 vols. Rome: Salerno, 2000.

————. *The Facetious Nights of Straparola*. Translated by William G. Waters. Illustrated by Jules Garnier and E. R. Hughes. 4 vols. London: Lawrence and Bullen, 1894.

Suttermeister, Otto. *Kinder- und Hausmärchen aus der Schweiz*. Aarau: Sauerländer, 1869.

Tendlau, Abraham. *Das Buch der Sagen und Legenden jüdischer Vorzeit*. Stuttgart: J. Cast, 1842.

Töppen, Max. *Aberglauben aus Masuren*. Danzig: Bertling, 1867.

Troyes, Nicolas de. *Le grand parangon des nouvelles nouvelles* (1510). Edited by Krystyna Kasprzyk. Paris: Didier, 1970.

Uther, Hans-Jörg, ed. *Märchen vor Grimm*. Munich: Eugen Diederichs Verlag, 1990.

Vernaleken, Theodor. *Alpenmärchen*. Munich: Borowsky, 1863.

————. *Kinder- und Hausmärchen dem Volk treunacherzählt*. Vienna: Braumüller, 1900.

Vonbun, Franz Josef. *Volkssagen aus Vorarlberg*. Innsbruck: Witting, 1850.

————. *Alpenmärchen*. Stuttgart: Canstatt, 1910.

Villeneuve, Gabrielle-Suzanne Barbot de. *La jeune Amériquaine et Les Contes marins*. La Haye aux dépens de la Compagnie, 1740.

Vitry, Jacques de. *The exempla or Illustrative Stories from the Sermons Vulgares of Jacques de Vitry*. Edited by Thomas Frederick Crane. London: Nutt, 1890.

Waldau, Alfred. *Bohmisches Märchenbuch*. Prague: Gerzabek, 1860.

Wenzig, Josef. *Westslawischer Märchenschatz*. Leipzig: Lorck, 1857.

Wesseleski, Albert, ed. *Deutsche Märchen vor Grimm*. Brünn: Rudolf M. Rohrer, 1938.

Widter-Wolf, Georg, and Adam Wolf. *Volksmärchen aus Venetien* in *Jahrbuch für romantische und englische Literatur* VII (1866): 1–36; 121–154; 249–290.

Wolf, Johann Wilhelm, ed. *Deutsche Märchen und Sagen*. Leipzig: F. A. Brockhaus, 1845.

————. *Deutsche Hausmärchen*. Göttingen: Dieterich, 1851.

Zingerele, Ignanz Vinzenz, and Joseph Zingerele. *Tirols Volksdichtungen und Volksbräuche*. Innsbruck: Wagner, 1852.